Street Food

Table of Contents

Acarajé	1	
Aloo Chaat	2	
Arancini	2	
Arepa	3	
Bagel	5	
Banana cue	8	
Banh canh	9	
Bánh hỏi	9	
Bánh xèo	10	
Beondegi	10	
Bhelpuri	11	
Brochette	11	
Bun cha	12	
Burrito	12	
Calzone	15	
Camote cue	16	
Chaat	16	
Chi'Lantro BBQ	17	
Chimichanga	18	
Cockle (bivalve)	18	
Coxinha	20	
Crêpe	21	
Dahi puri	23	
Dim sum	24	
Doner kebab	28	
Enchilada	36	
Esquites	37	
Falafel	38	
Farinata	40	
Fish ball	41	
Focaccia	44	
French fries	45	
Fried chicken	50	
Ginanggang	52	
Hamburger	53	
Hot dog	59	
Hot dog cart	63	
Isaw	64	
Jiaozi	64	
Kaassoufflé	67	
Kapsalon	67	
Kebab	68	
Knish	74	
Korean taco	74	
Laksa	75	
List of street food	77	
Malatang	91	
Maruya (food)	92	
Meat pie (Australia and New Zealand)	92	
Pad Thai	94	
Panipuri	94	
Pani ca meusa	97	
Panzarotti	97	
Papri chaat	98	
Pasty	98	
Pav Bhaji	101	
Pho	102	
Picarones	104	
Pilgrim (sandwich)	104	
Pizza al taglio	105	
Pojangmacha	105	
Poutine	105	
Pretzel	108	
Proben	112	
Quail eggs	113	
Quesadilla	113	
Sabich	115	
Sandwich	115	
Sardenara	117	
Satay	118	
Sausage roll	123	
Sevpuri	124	
Sfenj	124	
Shawarma	124	
Sicilian pizza	125	
Smoke's Poutinerie	126	
Souvlaki	126	
Spizzico	128	
Street food	128	
Street food of Mumbai	130	
Taco	131	
Takoyaki	133	
Tamale	134	
Tang bao	137	
Taquito	137	
Tokneneng	138	
Turon (food)	138	
Vada (food)	139	
Vada pav	141	
Vastedda	142	
Vietnamese noodles	142	
Würstelstand	143	
Yakitori	143	
Yatai (retail)	144	

Preface

Each chapter in this book ends with a URL to a hyperlinked online version. Use the online version to access related pages, websites, footnotes, tables, color photos, updates, or to see the chapter's contributors. Click the edit link to suggest changes. Please type the URL exactly as it appears. If you change the URL's capitalization, for example, it may not work.

Purchase of this book entitles you to a free trial membership in the publisher's book club at www.booksllc.net. (Time limited offer.) Simply enter the barcode number from the back cover onto the membership form on our home page. The book club entitles you to select from millions of books at no additional charge, including a PDF copy of this and related books to read on the go. Simply enter the title or subject onto the search form to find them.

If you have any questions, could you please be so kind as to consult our Frequently Asked Questions page at www.booksllc.net/faqs.cfm? You are also welcome to contact us there.

Publisher: Books LLC, Wiki Series, Memphis, TN, USA, 2013.

Acarajé

Acarajé [ekɛrɛˈʒɛ] (listen) is a dish made from peeled black-eyed peas formed into a ball and then deep-fried in *dendê* (palm oil). It is found in the Nigerian and Brazilian cuisines. The dish is traditionally encountered in Brazil's northeastern state of Bahia, especially in the city of Salvador, often as street food, and is also found in most parts of Nigeria, Ghana and the Republic of Benin.

It is served split in half and then stuffed with *vatapá* and *caruru* – spicy pastes made from shrimp, ground

Acarajé.

cashews, palm oil and other ingredients. The most common way of eating acarajé is splitting it in half, pouring *vatapá* and/or *caruru*, a salad made out of green and red tomatoes, fried shrimps and homemade hot pepper sauce. A vegetarian version is typically served with hot peppers and green tomatoes.

Akara (as it is known in southwest and southeast Nigeria) was a recipe taken to Brazil by the slaves from the West African coast. It is called "akara" by the Igbo people of south-eastern Nigeria and in the Yorubaland of south-western Nigeria, "kosai" by the Hausa people of Nigeria or "koose" in Ghana and is a popular breakfast dish, eaten with millet or corn porridge.

Today in Bahia, Brazil, most street vendors who serve acaraje are women, easily recognizable by their all-white cotton dresses and headscarves and caps. The image of these women, often simply called *baianas*, frequently appears in artwork from the region of Bahia. Acarajé, however, is typically available outside of the state of Bahia as well, including the streets of its neighbor state Sergipe, and the markets of Rio de Janeiro.

In Candomblé

Acarajé is a fixture in the Afro-Brazilian religious traditions of *Candomblé*. Although it is the ritual food of the goddess Iansã, the first acarajé in a candomblé ritual is offered to Exu.

A street vender selling Afro-Brazilian acarajé in Salvador, Brazil.

Source http://en.wikipedia.org/wiki/Acarajé

Aloo Chaat

Aloo Chaat Vendor, Connaught Place, New Delhi

Aloo Chaat (Hindi: 'आलू चाट') is the name of a street food item made in North India. It is prepared by frying Potatoes in oil and adding spices and chutney.

It is a snack which can be served as a potato salad or a light meal. It is made from boiled and fried cubed potatoes served with chat masala. It is a versatile dish that is prepared in many different ways by different people in different regions across the country. The word "Aloo" means potatoes in Hindi and the word "Chaat" is derived from Hindi word *Chatna* which means tasting. Thus, Aloo Chaat means a savory potato snack. It is also spelled as Alu Chaat.

Source http://en.wikipedia.org/wiki/Aloo_Chaat

Arancini

Arancine from Palermo

Arancine from Palermo, Italy (North Sicily)

Arancini or **arancine** are fried rice balls coated with breadcrumbs, said to have originated in Sicily in the 10th century. Arancini are usually filled with ragù (meat sauce), tomato sauce, mozzarella, and/or peas.

There are a number of local variants that differ in fillings and shape. The name derives from the food's shape and color, which is reminiscent of an orange (the Italian word for *orange* is *arancia*, and *arancina* means "little orange").

The main type of arancino sold in Sicilian cafes are *arancini con ragù*, which typically consist of meat in a tomato sauce, rice, and mozzarella. Many cafes also offer *arancini con burro* (béchamel sauce), or specialty arancini, such as *arancini con funghi* (mushrooms), *con pistacchi* (pistachios), or *con melanzane* (aubergine (eggplant)).

The arancini are considered a typical dish of the city of Messina, where they may have been invented and usually have a conical form.

In Roman cuisine, *supplì* are similar, but commonly filled with cheese. In Naples, rice balls are called *pall'e riso*(rice balls).

In popular culture

In Italian literature, Inspector Montalbano, the main character of Andrea Camilleri's novels, is a well-known lover of arancini and he has contributed to making this dish known outside of Italy.

Source http://en.wikipedia.org/wiki/Arancini

Arepa

Cheese-filled *arepa*
Origin
Region or state Northern South America
Details
Main ingredient(s) Tortillas (maize meal or flour)

An **arepa** (Spanish pronunciation: [aˈrepa]) is a dish made of ground corn dough or cooked flour, very prominent in the cuisine of Colombia and Venezuela. It is similar in shape to the Mexican *gordita* and the Salvadoran *pupusa*. Arepas can also be found in Panama, Puerto Rico, the Dominican Republic, and the Canary Islands.

Characteristics

The *arepa* is a flat, round, unleavened patty made of maizemeal or flour which can be grilled, baked, boiled, fried, steamed, etc. The characteristics vary by color, flavor, size, and the food with which it may be stuffed, depending on the region. *Arepa* is a native sort of bread made of ground maize (or flour), water, and salt which is fried into a thick bread. It can be topped or filled with meat, eggs, tomatoes, salad, cheese, shrimp, or fish depending on the meal. Breakfast egg or cheese are the most common arepa fillings. There are several recipes for fillings.

Making *arepas*

The dough can be prepared two ways. The traditional, labor-intensive method requires the maize grains to be soaked, then peeled and ground in a large mortar known as a *pilón*. The pounding removes the pericarp and the seed germ, as only the endosperm of the maize seed is used to make the dough. The resulting mixture, known as mortared maize, or *maíz pilado*, was normally sold as dry grain to be boiled and ground into dough.

The most popular method today is to buy cooked *arepa* cornmeal or flour. The flour is mixed with water and salt, and occasionally oil, butter, eggs, and/or milk. Because the flour is already cooked, the blend forms into patties easily. After being kneaded and formed, the patties are fried, grilled, or baked. This production of corn is unusual for not using the nixtamalization, or alkali cooking process, to remove the pericarp of the corn kernels. *Arepa* flour is lower in nutritive value than nixtamal, with its niacin value reduced by half.

Arepa flour

Arepa flour is specially prepared (cooked in water, then dried) for making *arepas* and other maize dough-based dishes, such as *hallacas*, *bollos*, *tamales*, *empanadas* and *chicha*. The most popular brand names of maize flour are Harina PAN in Venezuela and Areparina in Colombia. Since the rise of the Chavez administration, Harina PAN has since expanded into Colombia and set up parallel production. The *arepa* flour is usually made from white maize, but yellow maize varieties are available. This *arepa* flour was first developed and produced by Empresas Polar, of Venezuela, which owns the PAN brand and is the primary distributor in the country.

Electric *arepa* makers

Tostyarepa

In Venezuela, various kitchen appliance companies sell appliances such as the Tostyarepa and Miallegro's MiArepa, similar to a waffle iron, which cook *arepas* using two hot metallic surfaces clamped with the raw dough inside. In Venezuela, the *arepa* is traditionally grilled on a *budare*, which is a flat, originally nonmetallic surface which may or may not have a handle. Nowadays, it is common to follow the grilling process that forms a crust, known as a *concha*, with 20 to 25 minutes of cooking at high heat in an oven. Electric *arepa* makers reduce cooking time from 15 to 25 minutes per side to seven minutes or less.

History

The predecessor of the *arepa* was a staple of the Timoto-cuicas, an Amerindian group that lived in the northern Andes of Venezuela. Other Amerindian tribes in the region, such as the Arawaks and the Caribs, widely consumed a form known as *casabe* made from cassava (yuca). With the colonization by the Spanish, the food that would become the *arepa* was diffused into the rest of the region, known then as Viceroyalty of New Granada and later became La Gran Colombia (Colombia, Venezuela, Ecuador, Panama) at the time of Independence.

Venezuelans view the *arepa* as a traditional national food with diverse local recipes.

Venezuelan *arepas*

Varieties of native maize or corn

In eastern Venezuela, the most common variety is usually about three to eight inches (7.5 to 20 cm) in diameter and about 3/4 inch (2 cm) thick. Larger *arepas* can be found, made with either white or yellow corn. In the western Andes they are flatter, are typically quarter of an inch (0.6 cm) or less in thickness and three to four inches in diameter, and are made of wheat flour. An *arepa* can be eaten with a filling or with a topping. A filled *arepa* is called an *arepa rellena* or a Venezuelan *tostada*, although the latter term is not commonly used today. Also, there are plenty of sauces to season them while eating them, such as *guasacaca* and *picante* (hot sauce).

Venezuelans prepare *arepas* depending on personal taste or preference and the region in which they are made. Venezuelan varieties include:

Traditional corn (maize)
Corn flour (*arepa blanca* or *viuda*)
Wheat flour (*preñaditas* in Venezuelan slang)
Sweet (*arepa dulce*)
Cheese (*arepa de queso*)
Coconut (*arepa de coco*)
Andean (*arepa andina*)
Manioc (*arepa de yuca*)
Reina pepiada - filled with avocado, chicken, and mayonnaise
Baked (*arepas horneadas*)
Fried (*arepa frita*)
Arepa pelúa - with yellow cheese and pulled beef
Arepa con queso guayanés - with soft Guayanés cheese, similar to mozzarella
Arepa con queso de mano - with firm white cheese from eastern Venezuela
Arepa catira - with yellow cheese and shredded chicken
Arepa de chicharrón - with crisped pork skin
Arepa de dominó - white cheese and black beans
Arepa de Perico - made with perico, a Caribbean type of scrambled eggs
Arepa viuda ("widow" arepa) - an empty arepa usually eaten with soup
Arepa rumbera ("party" arepa) - with pork meat
Arepa llanera - with cuts of beef (parrilla or barbecue), tomato slices, avocado slices and fresh white cheese
Arepa con cazón - with school shark
Arepa Cabimera - from the city of Cabimas in Zulia state. They are fried arepas cut into squares covered with cheese, jam, grained carrots, chicken, and boiled eggs.
Other fillings include *guacuco* (a shellfish), ham, quail eggs with pink sauce, and octopus. Specialized *areperas* can be found across Venezuela, serving a wide array of fillings.

Colombia

In Colombia, the *arepa* has deep roots in the colonial farms and the cuisine of the indigenous people. While its preparation was once a tedious process of processing and cooking raw corn, today, they are usually bought already prepared or made from "instant" flours.

Arepas are usually eaten for breakfast

Colombian arepas: *choclo* (front) and *quesito* (back)

or as an afternoon snack. Common toppings include butter, cheese, scrambled eggs, condensed milk, Colombian *chorizo*, and *hogao*.

Egg (*arepa de huevo* or, colloquially, *arepa 'e huevo*) - this variety originated from the Caribbean coast, but is popular in most major cities. This arepa is deep fried with a single raw egg inside that is cooked by the frying process. Egg *arepas* are made with yellow corn dough and fried in the same manner as Colombian *empanadas*, and are often sold alongside other traditional Colombian foodstuffs at food stands. One variety of egg *arepa* has shredded beef added as well.

Cheese (*arepa de queso, arepa de quesillo*) - is either made with cheese mixed into the ingredients or filled with grated cheese before it is cooked (grilled or fried, in this case).

Arepa Boyacense - these come from the department of Boyacá. They are very hard and dense, and are typically about three to four inches across and filled with a sweet cheese.

Arepa Valluna - is the variety unique to Cali and the rest of the Cauca valley. It is made only with cornmeal, water and salt, and it is buttered before eating, much like toast.

Arepa rellena
Arepa cariseca

Arepa de laja
Arepa de maiz pelado
Arepa de peto
Arepa de choclo (or *chocolo*) - is made with sweet corn and farmer's white cheese.
Arepa antioqueña - a small, spherical arepa, without salt, served to accompany soups, especially *mondongo* is common in the department of Antioquia.
Arepa paisa - a very large, flat *arepa* made of white maize without salt, but accompanied by meat or butter on top is common in the coffee-producing region, often served with *hogao*.
Arepa de arroz - is made with cooked, mashed rice instead of corn dough.
Arepa santandereana - originates from the area around Bucaramanga. It is also called *arepa de maiz pelado*. It is made with yellow corn and has a distinct flavor due to the pork fat added during the preparation. It is usually dry, but soft.
Baked - is variously called *arepa de maiz* or *arepa de queso* at bakeries. Bakeries in Bogotá rarely sell the typical fried or grilled *arepas*, but instead sell a large, baked version, made with yellow corn flour and often with a single cube of cheese on top. It has a similar taste and texture to a North American corn muffin.
In the western part of Colombia, especially around Bogotá, Cali and Medellín, a traditional breakfast includes an *arepa* with hot chocolate.

Companies, such as Don Maíz, have started to market new, less traditional varieties in Colombian grocery stores that are growing in popularity. These include cassava-flavored *arepas* (based on the more traditional *pan de yuca*) and whole-grain arepas made of brown rice, wheat germ and sesame seeds.

Similar dishes

Colombia - The *arepuela* is similar to the traditional *arepa*. It is made with wheat flour and sometimes anise, and when fried, the layers expand and the *arepuela* inflates, similar to miniature tortillas or pancakes. This is very common in the interior of Colombia. In the north, *bollos* are popular for breakfast, which are made with the same dough as an *arepa*, but are boiled rather than fried, which gives them a texture similar to matzo balls or Czech bread dumplings.

Costa Rica - *Arepas* can be made from batter, and may be similar to pancakes. There are at least two sorts, the "pancake" *arepa*, which is made with baking powder, and the "big flat" *arepa*, which is made without baking powder. These big flat *arepas* are, in size, not unlike the big tortillas one finds in Guanacaste (northern Costa Rica), (i.e. some twelve inches in diameter) and are made of white flour and are sugary. Once perfectly cooked, they should resemble a "giraffe skin", or a "jaguar skin" (i.e., white/yellowish with brown spots).

Mexico - Gorditas are similar fried dish, but are different from tortillas.

Puerto Rico - In Puerto Rico, *arepas* are made with coconut milk, lard, or butter, flour, and baking powder. Preparation and cooking varies according to city and family tradition.

El Salvador - Pupusas are similar flat cakes, but the most important difference is the traditional dough is made from nixtamal. It is also filled before it is cooked, usually some pork, white cheese or black beans. Other stypes of *pupusas* are now made from rice dough, particularly in the town called Olocuilta in the department of La Paz. There are also some newer versions of the dish based on plantain dough.

Source http://en.wikipedia.org/wiki/Arepa

Bagel

A plain commercially produced bagel (as evidenced by grate marks used in steaming, rather than boiling)
Origin
Place of origin   Poland
Region or state   Eastern Europe
Details

Type   bread
Main ingredient(s) wheat dough
Variations   multiple

A **bagel** (*also spelled* **beigel**) is a bread product, traditionally shaped by hand into the form of a ring from yeasted wheat dough, roughly hand-sized, which is first boiled for a short time in water and then baked. The result is a dense, chewy, doughy interior with a browned and sometimes crisp exterior. Bagels are often topped with seeds baked on the outer crust, with the traditional ones being poppy or sesame seeds. Some also may have salt sprinkled on their surface, and there are also a number of different dough types such as whole-grain or rye.

Bagels have become a popular bread

Bagels with cream cheese and lox (cured salmon) are considered a traditional part of American Jewish cuisine (colloquially known as lox and a *schmear*).

product in the United States, Canada and the United Kingdom, especially in cities with large Jewish populations, many with different ways of making bagels. Like other bakery products, bagels are available (either fresh or frozen, and often in many flavor varieties) in many major supermarkets in those countries.

The basic roll-with-a-hole design is hundreds of years old and has other practical advantages besides providing for a more even cooking and baking of the dough: the hole could be used to thread string or dowels through groups of bagels, allowing for easier handling and transportation and more appealing seller displays.

History

Contrary to some beliefs, the bagel was *not* created in the shape of a stirrup to commemorate the victory of Poland's King Jan III Sobieski over the Ottoman Turks in the Battle of Vienna in 1683. It was actually invented much earlier in Kraków, Poland, as a competitor to the *obwarzanek*, a lean bread of wheat flour designed for Lent. Leo Rosten wrote in "The Joys of Yiddish" about the first known mention of the word *bajgiel* in the "Community Regulations" of the city of Kraków in 1610, which stated that the item was given as a gift to women in childbirth.

In the 16th and first half of the 17th centuries, the *bajgiel* became a staple of the Polish national diet, and a staple of the Slavic diet generally. That the name originated from *beugal* (old spelling of Bügel, meaning bail/bow or bale) is considered plausible by many, both from the similarities of the word and because traditional handmade bagels are not perfectly circular but rather slightly stirrup-shaped. (This, however, may be due to the way the boiled bagels are pressed together on the baking sheet before baking.)

Additionally, variants of the word *beugal* are used in Yiddish and Austrian German to refer to a somewhat similar form of sweet filled pastry (*Mohnbeugel* (with poppy seeds) and *Nussbeugel* (with ground nuts)), or in southern German dialects (where *beuge* refers to a pile, e.g., *holzbeuge*, or

A sbitenshchik (left) selling *bubliks* and *baranki* (19th century)

woodpile). According to the Merriam-Webster's dictionary, 'bagel' derives from the transliteration of the Yiddish *'beygl'*, which came from the Middle High German *'böugel'* or ring, which itself came from *'bouc'* (ring) in Old High German, similar to the Old English *'bēag'* (ring), and *'būgan'* (to bend or bow). Similarly another etymology in the Webster's New World College Dictionary says that the Middle High German form was derived from the Austrian German *'beugel'*, a kind of croissant, and was similar to the German *'bügel'*, a stirrup or ring.

In the Brick Lane district and surrounding area of London, England, bagels, or as locally spelled *"beigels"* have been sold since the middle of the 19th century. They were often displayed in the windows of bakeries on vertical wooden dowels, up to a metre in length, on racks.

Bagels were brought to the United States by immigrant Polish-Jews, with a thriving business developing in New York City that was controlled for decades by Bagel Bakers Local 338, which had contracts with nearly all bagel bakeries in and around the city for its workers, who prepared all their bagels by hand. The bagel came into more general use throughout North America in the last quarter of the 20th century, which was due at least partly to

the efforts of bagel baker Harry Lender, his son, Murray Lender, and Florence Sender, who pioneered automated production and distribution of frozen bagels in the 1960s. Murray also invented pre-slicing the bagel.

In modern times, Canadian-born astronaut Gregory Chamitoff is the first person known to have taken a batch of bagels into space on his 2008 Space Shuttle mission to the International Space Station. His shipment consisted of 18 sesame seed bagels.

Three Montreal-style bagels: one poppy and two sesame bagels

Preparation and preservation

At its most basic, traditional bagel dough contains wheat flour (without germ or bran), salt, water, and yeast leavening. Bread flour or other high gluten flours are preferred to create the firm and dense but spongy bagel shape and chewy texture. Most bagel recipes call for the addition of a sweetener to the dough, often barley malt (syrup or crystals), honey, sugar, with or without eggs, milk or butter. Leavening can be accomplished using either a sourdough technique or using commercially produced yeast.

Bagels are traditionally made by:
mixing and kneading the ingredients to form the dough
shaping the dough into the traditional bagel shape, round with a hole in the middle, from a long thin piece of dough
proofing the bagels for at least 12 hours at low temperature (40–50 °F = 4.5–10 °C)
boiling each bagel in water that may or may not contain additives such as lye, baking soda, barley malt syrup, or hon-

ey baking at between 175 °C and 315 °C (about 350–600 °F)

It is this unusual production method which is said to give bagels their distinctive taste, chewy texture, and shiny appearance. In recent years, a variant of this process has emerged, producing what is sometimes called the steam bagel. To make a steam bagel, the process of boiling is skipped, and the bagels are instead baked in an oven equipped with a steam injection system. In commercial bagel production, the steam bagel process requires less labor, since bagels need only be directly handled once, at the shaping stage. Thereafter, the bagels need never be removed from their pans as they are refrigerated and then steam-baked. The steam-bagel is not considered to be a genuine bagel by purists, as it results in a fluffier, softer, less chewy product more akin to a finger roll that happens to be shaped like a bagel. Steam bagels are also considered lower quality by purists as the dough used is intentionally more basic. The increase in pH is to aid browning since the steam injection process uses neutral water steam instead of a basic solution bath.

If not consumed immediately, there are certain storing techniques that can help to keep the bagel moist and fresh. First, cool bagels in a paper bag, then wrap the paper bag in a plastic bag (attempting to rid the bags of as much air as possible without squishing the bagels), then freeze for up to six months.

Varieties

Saturday morning bagel queue at St-Viateur Bagel, Montreal, Quebec (Courtesy: M. Rehemtulla)

The two most prominent styles of traditional bagel in North America are the Montreal-style bagel and the New York-style bagel. The Montreal bagel contains malt and sugar with no salt; it is boiled in honey-sweetened water before baking in a wood-fired oven; and it is predominantly either of the poppy "black" or sesame "white" seeds variety. The New York bagel contains salt and malt and is boiled in water prior to baking in a standard oven. The resulting New York bagel is puffy with a moist crust, while the Montreal bagel is smaller (though with a larger hole), crunchier, and sweeter.

Chicago-style bagels are baked or baked with steam.

Poppy seeds are sometimes called by their Yiddish name, spelled either *mun* or *mon* (written מאָן) which is very similar to the German word for poppy, *Mohn*, as used in *Mohnbrötchen*. The traditional London bagel (or beigel as it is spelled) is harder and has a coarser texture with air bubbles.

American chef John Mitzewich suggests a recipe for what he calls "San Francisco-Style Bagels". His recipe yields bagels flatter than New York-style bagels and characterized by a rough-textured crust.

Bagels around the world

"Vesirinkeli" from Finland.

Pretzels, especially the large soft ones, are similar to bagels, the main exceptions being the shape and the alkaline water bath that makes the surface dark and glossy.

In Russia, Belarus and Ukraine, the *bublik* is essentially a much larger bagel, but have a wider hole, and are drier and chewier Other ring-shaped breads known among East Slavs are *baranki* (smaller and drier) and *sushki* (even smaller and drier).

In Lithuania, bagels are called *riestainiai*, and sometimes by their Slavic name *baronkos*.

In Finland, *vesirinkeli* are small rings of yeast-leavened wheat bread. They are placed in salted boiling water before being baked. They are often eaten for breakfast toasted and buttered. They are available in several different varieties (sweet or savoury) in supermarkets.

The Uyghurs of Xinjiang, China, enjoy a form of bagel known as *girdeh nan* (from Persian, meaning round bread), which is one of several types of nan, the bread eaten in Xinjiang.

In Turkey, a salty and fattier form is called *açma*. However, the ring-shaped simit, is sometimes marketed as Turkish bagel. Archival sources show that the *simit* has been produced in Istanbul since 1525. Based on Üsküdar court records (Şer'iyye Sicili) dated 1593, the weight and price of simit was standardized for the first time. Famous 17th century traveler Evliya Çelebi wrote that there were 70 simit bakeries in Istanbul during 1630s Jean Brindesi's early 19th century oil-paintings about Istanbul daily life show simit sellers on the streets. Warwick Goble made an illustration of these simit sellers of Istanbul in 1906. Surprisingly, simit is very similar to the twisted sesame-sprinkled bagels pictured being sold in early 20th century Poland. *Simit* are also sold on the street in baskets or carts, like bagels were then.

A "girdeh" (the hole does not go all the way through) from a Muslim restaurant in Guangzhou, China

In some parts of Austria, ring-shaped pastries called *Beugel* are sold in the weeks before Easter. Like a bagel, the yeasted wheat dough, usually flavored with caraway, is boiled before baking. However, the *Beugel* is crispy and can be stored for weeks. Traditionally it has to be torn apart by two individuals before eating.

In Poland, bagels are sold in the bakery in Kielce's Market Square and are well known in the city. Polish bagels are usually sold with sesame and poppy seeds.

In Romania, bagels are popular topped with poppy, sesame seeds or large salt grains, especially in the central area of the country, and the recipe does not contain any added sweetener. They are named *covrigi*.

In Japan, the first kosher bagels were brought by BagelK (ベーグルK) from New York in 1989. BagelK created green tea, chocolate, maple-nut, and banana-nut flavors for the market in Japan. There are three million bagels exported from the U.S. annually, and it has a 4%-of-duty classification of Japan in 2000. Some Japanese bagels are sweet; the orthodox kosher bagels are the same as in the U.S.

"Bagel" is also a Yeshivish term for sleeping 12 hours straight, e.g., "I slept a bagel last night." There are various opinions as to the origins of this term. It may be a reference to the fact that bagel dough has to "rest" for at least 12 hours between mixing and baking, or simply to the fact that the hour hand on a clock traces a bagel shape over the course of twelve hours.

Non-traditional doughs and types

While normally and traditionally made of yeasted wheat, in the late 20th century many variations on the bagel flourished. Nontraditional versions which change the dough recipe include pumpernickel, rye, sourdough, bran, whole wheat, and multigrain. Other variations change the flavor of the dough, often using blueberry, salt, onion, garlic, egg, cinnamon, raisin, chocolate chip, cheese, or some combination of the above. Green bagels are sometimes created for St. Patrick's Day.

Many corporate chains now offer bagels in such flavors as chocolate chip and French toast. Sandwich bagels have been popularized since the late 1990s by bagel specialty shops such as Bruegger's and Einstein Brothers, and fast food restaurants such as McDonald's. Breakfast bagels, a softer, sweeter variety usually sold in fruity or sweet flavors (e.g., cherry, strawberry, cheese, blueberry, cinnamon-raisin, chocolate chip, maple syrup, banana and nuts) are commonly sold by large supermarket chains. These are usually sold sliced and are intended to be prepared in a toaster.

A flat bagel, known as a 'Flagel', can be found in a few locations in and around New York City and Toronto. According to a review attributed to New York's Village Voice food critic Robert Seitsema, the Flagel was first created by Brooklyn's *Tasty Bagels* deli in the early 1990s.

Though the original bagel has a fairly well defined recipe and method of production, there is no legal standard of identity for bagels in the United States. Bakers are thus free to call any bread torus a bagel, even those that deviate wildly from the original formulation.

Large scale commercial sales

United States supermarket sales

According to the American Institute of Baking (AIB), Year 2008 supermarket sales (52 week period ending January 27, 2009) of the top eight leading commercial fresh (not frozen) bagel brands in the United States:
totalled to US$430,185,378 based on 142,669,901 package unit sales.
the top eight leading brand names for the above were (by order of sales): Thomas', Sara Lee, (private label brands) Pepperidge Farm, Thomas Mini Squares, Lender's Bagels (Pinnacle Foods), Weight Watchers and The Alternative Bagel (Western Bagel).
Further, AIB-provided statistics for the 52 week period ending May 18, 2008, for refrigerated/frozen supermarket bagel sales for the top 10 brand names totalled US$50,737,860, based on 36,719,977 unit package sales.

Source http://en.wikipedia.org/wiki/Bagel

Banana cue

Banana cue is usually served on bamboo skewers

Banana cue being cooked

A **Banana cue** or **Banana Q** (Tagalog: *Banana kyu*) is a popular snack food in the Philippines of deep fried bananas coated in caramelized brown sugar. Banana cue is made from *Saba* bananas. It is usually skewered on a bamboo stick, and is sold on the streets. The skewer stick is just for ease of serving and eating. It is not cooked on the skewer (as opposed to *ginanggang*). The term is a portmanteau of banana and barbecue (which in Philippine English refers to meat cooked in a style similar to kebabs).

Source http://en.wikipedia.org/wiki/

Banh canh

Bánh canh with pork, fish balls, prawn cakes and fried tofu

Origin

Place of origin	Vietnam

Details

Type	Soup
Main ingredient(s)	Tapioca flour, optionally rice flour

Bánh canh (literally "soup cake") is a thick Vietnamese noodle that can be made from tapioca flour or a mixture of rice and tapioca flour.

Bánh canh cua - a rich, thick crab soup
Bánh canh bột lọc - a more translucent version of the noodle
Bánh canh chả cá - the dish includes fish sausage and is popular in the South Central, Vietnam.
Bánh canh giò heo tôm thịt - includes pork knuckle and shrimp
Bánh canh Trảng Bàng - *bánh canh* made in the southeastern Vietnamese town of Trang Bang, served with boiled pork, rice paper, and local herbs
Bánh canh tôm - a shrimp-flavoured broth that is also mixed with coconut milk

The Vietnamese word *bánh* refers to items such as noodles or cakes that are made from flour, and *canh* means "soup."

Commercial variants of bánh canh with soup

There are many variations of the bánh canh with soup. For example, in Tan Lac Vien Restaurant, Melbourne, Australia, its most popular dish is the **Bánh canh cua**, a thick crab soup is served with mud crab. At My Hanh Restaurant, South El Monte, Canada, it's specialty is the **Bánh canh giò heo** with a clear soup.

Source http://en.wikipedia.org/wiki/Banh_canh

Bánh hỏi

A dish of bánh hỏi

Bánh hỏi is a Vietnamese dish consisting of rice vermicelli woven into intricate bundles and often topped with chopped scallions or garlic chives sauteed in oil, served with a complementary meat dish. The strings of noodles are usually only as thin as a toothpick; the texture is firm enough so the noodles do not fall apart, but is not at all sticky to keep the dish light and suitable for a breakfast treat.

Origin

Bánh hỏi originated from the Bình Định Province of Vietnam's south central coast. People in Bình Định eat *bánh hỏi* for almost any meal during the day, instead of rice or noodle soups.

Production

Making *bánh hỏi* is a multistep process. First, good rice is soaked in water overnight, then washed with water again three or four times until the water comes out clear. Then the rice is either ground with water into a mixture, or ground without water, but mixed into water three or four times afterward to leaven it without using any additional agent. The flour mixture is then either steamed and kneaded, or cooked in a pan, stirred continuously until it starts to coagulate, but no flour gets stuck on the stirring tool. This step is crucial in making *bánh hỏi* soft, light, and not sticky, but the strings of noodles will still have a firm texture. When the experienced *bánh hỏi* maker feels the dough is done, it is ready for pressing.

Special copper or aluminum cylinders, with several small holes (the size of a needle eye), shape the cooked dough into noodle form. Pressing the dough requires great strength, as the dough is hard and the holes are small, so it is usually done with leverage. When one person presses the dough, another "catches" the noodles coming out on the other side, presses them together and cuts them off every 10 cm or so, creating a kind of mesh of noodle, which is then laid onto a flat surface, but not in layers. Finally, the sheets are steamed one last time for about five minutes.

Serving

Like *bún* (rice vermicelli) dishes, *bánh hỏi* is served cold. Traditionally *bánh hỏi* in Bình Định is rolled into bundles and always served with chopped garlic chives. The garlic chives are quickly stir-fried with oil, its aroma and taste goes well with *bánh hỏi*, which makes the dish enjoyable by itself and without any other kinds of herbs.

In central Vietnam, such as Huế, *bánh hỏi* is eaten with dried prawns and *nước chấm*. In southern Vietnam, *bánh hỏi* is eaten with a variety of meats, especially roast pork or duck. There are also *bánh hỏi chả giò*, *bánh hỏi* with shrimp paste on sugar cane stick, and *bánh hỏi* with grilled pork, chicken, or beef. At the Gò Duối market in Xuân Lộc commune, Sông Cầu district, Phu Yen Province, one also finds *bánh hỏi lòng heo Gò Duối*, which is *bánh hỏi* with boiled pig offal.

Since making *bánh hỏi* is a skillful process, the dish is highly regarded, and is served at ceremonial parties, such as wedding and ancestor memorial days.

Covering *bánh hỏi* tightly reduces surface drying, which can make it sour, so market sellers put fresh *bánh hỏi* in bamboo baskets with banana leaves, and usually leave it open to air. For convenience or sanitary reasons, there are dried, packaged *bánh hỏi*, similar to dried, packaged rice vermicelli, for people who want to cook it themselves instead of buying fresh *bánh hỏi* from the markets.

Source http://en.wikipedia.org/wiki/Bánh_hỏi

Bánh xèo

Vietnamese-style *bánh xèo* (Top), Cambodian-style *banh chao* (Bottom)
Origin
Place of origin Vietnam
Details
Main ingredient(s) rice flour, water, turmeric powder

Bánh xèo [ɓǎɲ sêw], literally "sizzling cake" is named for the loud sizzling sound it makes when the rice batter is poured into the hot skillet (Khmer: បាញ់ឆែវ: Khmer pronunciation: [baɲ cʰaeʋ]) are Vietnamese savoury fried pancakes made of rice flour, water, turmeric powder, stuffed with slivers of fatty pork, shrimp, diced green onion, and bean sprouts. Southern-style *bánh xèo* contains coconut milk and certain Central region skips the turmeric powder altogether. They are served wrapped in mustard leaf, lettuce leaves or banh trang wrappers, and stuffed with mint leaves, basil, fish leaf and/or other herbs, and dipped in a sweet and sour diluted fish sauce. In the Central region, the pancake is also dipped in a special sauce which consists of fermented soy bean and sticky rice sauce, ground pork liver, ground and toasted peanut and seasonings.

Southern style *bánh xèo* are larger and thinner compared to the small pan-fried versions in the central and northern regions. In Huế, the former imperial capital, it is called *bánh khoái* (literally "delicious cake") and is served open faced instead of being folded in half. *Bánh khoái* is always served with the fermented soy bean sauce mentioned above. In the central region, it is considered cold weather food because of its greasiness. Therefore, most families make them from scratch only during the winter.

The dish is also popular in Cambodian cuisine, where the dish is called បាញ់ឆែវ (most often transliterated as *banh chao*). It has also been introduced into Thailand where it known by two names: ขนมเบื้องญวน (*khanom beuang yuan*), where *yuan* is the Thai word for "Vietnamese", and บันแส่ว (*Ban sao*).

Source http://en.wikipedia.org/wiki/Bánh_xèo

Beondegi

Beondegi

Beondegi for sale by a street vendor in South Korea

Korean name
Hangul 번데기
Hanja n/a
Revised Romanization beondegi
McCune–Reischauer pŏnteki

Beondegi (Korean: 번데기) are a popular snack food in Korean cuisine. Literally meaning "chrysalis" or "pupa" in Korean, Beondegi are steamed or boiled silkworm pupae which are seasoned and eaten as a snack. Beondegi are often served by street vendors, as well as in restaurants and drinking establishments. They are also sold in cans in grocery stores and convenience stores, but they must be boiled in water before serving. Beondegi is not always sold in the market and is usually sold from street vendors, although it is possible to buy the live variant for personal preparation.

Source http://en.wikipedia.org/wiki/Beondegi

Bhelpuri

Bhelpuri	
Origin	
Alternative names(s)	Bhelpuri (Mumbai), Bhela, Churu Muri (Bangalore), Jha Muri (Kolkata), Jhāla Mudhi (Orissa)
Place of origin	India
Details	
Type	Snack, chaat
Main ingredient(s)	Puffed rice, sev
Variations	Sevpuri, Dahi puri, Sev papd chaat

Bhelpuri (Hindi भेलपूरी, Marathi भेळ) is a savoury Indian snack, and is also a type of chaat. It is made out of puffed rice, vegetables and a tangy tamarind sauce.

Bhelpuri is often identified with the beaches of Mumbai (Bombay), such as Chowpatty. Bhelpuri is thought to have originated within the Gujarati cafes and street food stalls of Bombay, and the recipe has spread to most parts of India where it has been modified to suit local food availability. The Kolkata variant of Bhelpuri is called *Jhaal Muri* (meaning "hot puffed rice"). A native Mysore variant of Bhelpuri is known as *Churumuri* in Bangalore. A dry variant of Bhelpuri popularly known as *Bhadang* is consumed after garnishing with onions, coriander and lemon juice.

History

There is no clear mention of when and where bhelpuri was first prepared, but it likely originated in Gujarati cafes and street food stalls of Mumbai (formerly Bombay). Bhelpuri belongs to the food family of chaats, which are salty and spicy snacks sold on carts throughout India.

Commonly used ingredients

Bhelpuri is made from puffed rice and Sev (a fried snack shaped like thin noodles made from besan flour) mixed with potatoes, onions, Chat masala and chutney and mixture (a mix of different types of fried snacks), as the base of the snack. Bhelpuri has a typically Gujarati balance of sweet, salty, tart and spicy flavors, with different textures as well, including crispy and crunchy from the puffed rice and fried sev. Other commonly used ingredients include tomatoes, onions and chilis added to the base; In northern India recipes also made by adding boiled potatoes cut into small pieces.

Different chutneys impart a sweet, tangy or spicy flavour. There are two popular chutneys used: a dark brown sweet one made mainly from dates and tamarind (*saunth chutney*) and a green spicy chutney made from coriander leaves and green chillies.

Variations

Bhelpuri is also made by sprinkling the puffed rice mixture with chunks of diced raw-sweet mango. The finished snack is often garnished with a combination of diced onions, coriander leaves and chopped green chilies. It is sometimes served with papri puris, a deep fried small round and crispy wheat bread.

The other variants of Bhelpuri:
Sevpuri - a mixture of bhelpuri, chutney, papdi and sev.

A street-side vendor preparing Bhelpuri

Dahi puri - a mixture of bhelpuri, chutney, papdi and savoured with lot of yogurt.
Sev papdi chaat - a lot like sevpuri but with 2-3 types of chutney, potatoes, chana masala.
Churmuri - In this finely cut pieces of onion, tomato, coriander leaves along with chilli powder are mixed adding few drops of coconut oil. Sometimes fried or roasted groundnuts may be added.

Serving

Bhel puri can be served in many ways, but it is usually served in a paper folded in the form of a cone and is consumed using a paper spoon or by the 'papdi' which is itself an edible component of the 'Bhel Puri'.

Source http://en.wikipedia.org/wiki/Bhelpuri

Brochette

In cooking, *en brochette* refers to food cooked, and sometimes served, on *brochettes*, or skewers. The French term generally applies to French cuisine, while other terms like shish kebab, satay, or souvlaki describe the same technique in other cuisines. Food served *en brochette* is generally grilled.

Brochettes made of wood in a *pincho americano* from Venezuela.

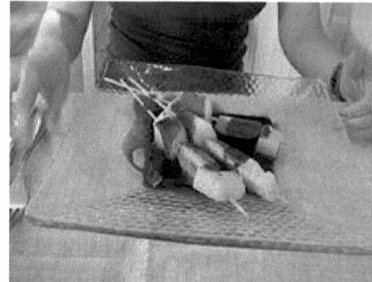

Brochettes as *dessert*.

Brochettes made of metal.

"Pinchos Morunos" ready to eat.

Description

The skewer itself, the *brochette* can also be used to dip pieces of food in a fondue. In those cases it normally takes a slightly different form and is sold as a *brochette de fondue* or as a set along with the *fondue* pot.

Typically, meats and vegetables are put on a brochette, but small pieces of bread can also be skewered along with the other ingredients as well.

In Louisiana barbecue, brochette is sometimes cooked at the barbecue in addition to ribs, sausage, steak, and chicken. This is due to the influence of Cajun cuisine, which is in turn influenced by French cuisine.

In Portuguese cuisine, they are known as Espetada.

Latin American and Spanish barbecued pinchos

Mixed grill, barbecued meat and vegetables on sticks, are known as *espetinhos*, *pinchos*, *pinchos americanos* or *anticuchos* in Central & South America. These barbecued pinchos may include pieces of beef, pork, chicken, fish/shark, Mexican chorizo (or sausage), kidney, or liver, among others.

In Puerto Rico, a barbecued type of pincho is served by street vendors. Unlike the Basque pincho, usually only one or two slices of bread are in the pincho, while the rest is barbecued chicken, pork, shark, or other meat. The meats and the bread are skewered on a wooden stick, rather than served on a plate; the stick is grabbed from the bottom and the contents are eaten.

In Spain, barbecued meat pinchos previously marinated in a spicy garlic and red pepper mixture are known as *Pinchos morunos* (Moorish skewers). They are similar (but not identical) to Middle Eastern kebabs. When they are small they are also known as *pinchitos*.

Source http://en.wikipedia.org/wiki/Brochette

Bun cha

Origin	
Alternative	Grilled pork noodle
name(s)	soup
Place of origin	Vietnam
Region or state	Hanoi
Type	Soup

Bún chả is a Vietnamese dish, a grilled pork noodle soup, which is thought to have originated from Hanoi, the capital of Vietnam. Bun cha is served with a plate of white rice noodle (*bún*) grilled fatty pork (*chả*), and herbs in a steamy broth of nước mắm (fish sauce). The dish was described in 1959 by Vietnamese food writer Vu Bang (1913–1984) who described Hanoi as a town "transfixed by bún chả." Hanoi's first bún chả restaurant was on Gia Ngư, Hoàn Kiếm District, in Hanoi's Old Quarter.

Bún chả is popular in the Northern region of Vietnam. In the South, a similar dish of rice vermicelli and grilled meat is called bún thịt nướng.

Source http://en.wikipedia.org/wiki/Bun_cha

Burrito

Origin	
Alternative name(s)	Taco de harina
Place of origin	Mexico
Details	
Main ingredient(s)	Flour tortillas, meat and refried beans

A **burrito** (US English /bəˈritoʊ/, Spanish: [buˈrito]), or **taco de harina** [ˈtako ðe aˈrina], is a type of Mexican food. It consists of a wheat flour tortilla wrapped or folded into a cylindrical shape to completely enclose a filling. (In contrast, a taco is generally formed by simply folding a tortilla in half around a filling, leaving the semicircular perimeter open.) The flour tortilla is usually lightly grilled or steamed, to soften it and make it more pliable. In Mexico, meat and refried beans are sometimes the only fillings.

In the United States, burrito fillings generally include a combination of ingredients such as Mexican-style rice or plain rice, refried beans or beans, lettuce, salsa, meat, guacamole, cheese, and sour cream, and the size varies. Typically, American-style burritos are stuffed with more ingredients than the primary meat and/or vegetable filling.

Etymology

The word *burrito* means "little donkey" in Spanish, as a diminutive form of *burro*, or "donkey". The name *burrito* as applied to the food item possibly derives from the appearance of a rolled up wheat tortilla, which vaguely resembles the ear of its namesake animal, or from bedrolls and packs that donkeys carried.

History

Hand-held take-out foods like the burrito have a long history. Before the Spanish colonization of the Americas, indigenous peoples were eating hand-held snack foods like corn on the cob, popcorn and pemmican. In Mexico, the Spanish observed Aztecs selling take-out foods like tamales, tortillas, and sauces in open marketplaces. The Pueblo people of the desert Southwest also made tortillas with beans and meat sauce fillings prepared much like the modern burrito we know today.

Cuisine preceding the development of the modern taco, burrito, and enchilada was created by the Pre-Columbian Mesoamerican Aztec peoples of Mexico, who used tortillas to wrap foods, with fillings of chili peppers, tomatoes, mushrooms, squash, and avocados. Spanish missionaries like Bernardino de Sahagún wrote about Aztec cuisine, describing the variety of tortillas and their preparation, noting that the Aztecs not only used corn in their tortillas, but also squash and amaranth, and that some varieties used turkey, eggs, or honey as a flavoring.

The precise origin of the modern burrito is not known. It may have originated with farmworkers in the fields of California's Central Valley, in Fresno and Stockton or with northern Sonoran miners of the 19th century. In the 1895 *Diccionario de Mexicanismos*, the burrito was identified as a regional item from Guanajuato and defined as "Tortilla arrollada, con carne u otra cosa dentro, que en Yucatán llaman *coçito*, y en Cuernavaca y en Mexico, *taco*" (A rolled tortilla with meat or other ingredients inside, called 'coçito' in Yucatán and 'taco' in the city of Cuernavaca and in Mexico City).

An often-repeated folk history is that of a man named Juan Mendez who sold tacos in a street stand in the Bella Vista neighborhood of Ciudad Juárez, using a donkey as a transport for himself and the food, during the Mexican Revolution period (1910–1921). To keep the food warm, Mendez wrapped it in large homemade flour tortillas inside individual napkins. As the "food of the *burrito*" (i.e., "food of the little donkey") grew in popularity, "burrito" was eventually adopted as the name for these large tacos.

In 1923, Alejandro Borquez opened the Sonora cafe in Los Angeles, which later changed its name to the El Cholo Spanish Cafe. Burritos first appeared on American restaurant menus at the El Cholo Spanish Cafe during the 1930s. Burritos were mentioned in the U.S. media for the first time in 1934, appearing in the *Mexican Cookbook*, a collection of regional recipes from New Mexico authored by historian Erna Fergusson.

Development of regional varieties

Mexico

Burritos are a traditional food of Ciudad Juárez, a city in the northern Mexican state of Chihuahua, where people buy them at restaurants and roadside stands. Northern Mexican border towns like Villa Ahumada have an established reputation for serving burritos. Authentic Mexican burritos are usually small and thin, with flour tortillas containing only one or two ingredients: some form of meat or fish, potatoes, rice, beans, asadero cheese, *chile rajas*, or *chile relleno*. Other types of ingredients may include *barbacoa*, *mole*, refried beans and cheese, and *deshebrada* (shredded slow-cooked flank steak). The *deshebrada* burrito also has a variation with *chile colorado* (mild to moderately hot) and *salsa verde* (very hot). The Mexican burrito may be a northern variation of the traditional *taco de Canasta*, which is eaten for breakfast, lunch, and dinner.

Although burritos are one of the most popular examples of Mexican cuisine outside of Mexico, in Mexico they are only popular in the northern part of the country. However, they are beginning to appear in some nontraditional venues in other parts of Mexico. Wheat flour tortillas used in burritos are now often seen throughout much of Mexico (possibly due to these areas being less than optimal for growing maize), despite at one time being peculiar to northwestern Mexico, the Southwestern US Mexican American community, and Pueblo Indian tribes.

Burritos are commonly called *tacos de harina* (wheat flour tacos) in central and southern Mexico and **burritas** (feminine variation, with 'a') in northern-style restaurants outside of northern Mexico proper. A long and thin fried burrito similar to a chimichanga is prepared in the state of Sonora and vicinity, and is called a *chivichanga*.

San Francisco

The origins of the Mission burrito can be traced back to Mission District taquerias of the 1960s and 1970s. This type of burrito is produced on a steam table assembly line, characterized by a large stuffed tortilla, wrapped in aluminum foil, which may include fillings such as carne asada (beef), Mexican style rice, whole beans (non refried), sour cream and light onion.

Febronio Ontiveros claims to have offered the first retail burrito in San Francisco at El Faro (The Lighthouse) in 1961, a corner grocery store on Folsom Street. Ontiveros claims credit for inventing the "super burrito" style leading to the early development of the "San Francisco style". This innovation involved adding rice, sour cream and guacamole to the standard meat, bean and cheese burrito. The Mission burrito emerged as a regional culinary movement during the 1970s and 1980s. The popularity of San Francisco-style burritos has grown locally, with Mission Street taquerias like El Farolito, and nationally with chains such as *Chipotle Mexican Grill*, *Illegal Pete's*, *Freebirds World Burrito*, *Qdoba*, and *Barberitos*. In 1995, *World Wrapps* opened in San Francisco's Marina District, bringing a burrito-inspired sandwich wrap style to the restaurant industry.

San Diego

San Diego-style burritos include California and carne asada burritos. The style has been described as an "austere meal of meat, cheese and salsa", in contrast to the Mission-style burrito, which is typically larger and contains more ingredients. A significant subgenre of Mexican restaurants in San Diego serves burritos described as "no-frills"; in contrast to Mission-style burritos, the assembly-line is not used. In the early 1960s, Roberto Robledo opened a *tortilleria* in San Diego and learned the restaurant business. Robledo began selling small bean burritos at "La Lomita" in the late 1960s, and by 1970, he had established the first "Roberto's" taco shop. By 1999, Roberto's had expanded to a chain of 60 taco shops offering fresh burritos known for their distinctive quality. Hoping to draw on the prestige of Roberto's, new taco shops in San Diego began using the "-bertos" suffix, with names such as Alberto's, Filiberto's, Hilberto's, among others.

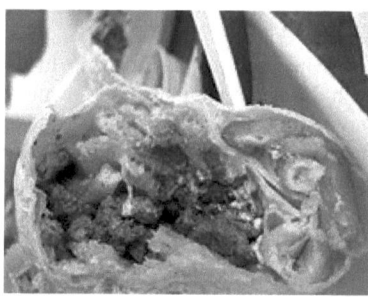
Contents of a California burrito.

The California burrito originated at an unknown -berto's named restaurant in San Diego in the 1980s. The earliest-known published mention was in a 1995 article in the Albuquerque Tribune. The California burrito typically consists of chunks of carne asada meat, French fries, cheese, and either cilantro, pico de gallo, sour cream, onion, or guacamole (or some combination of these five). The ingredients are similar to those used in the carne asada fries dish, and it is considered a staple of the local cuisine of San Diego. With its merging of French fries with more traditional burrito fillings, the California burrito is an example of fusion border food. Variants of this burrito add shrimp (surf and turf), or substitute carnitas or chicken for carne asada.

The carne asada burrito is considered a regional food of San Diego. It is served with chunks of carne asada, guacamole, and pico de gallo salsa.

Los Angeles

While not as recognizable as the San Diego- or Mission-style burrito, Los Angeles does possess a uniquely local burrito variety, exemplified by the versions at Mexican-American restaurants such as Al & Bea's, Lupe's #2, and Tonia's. These restaurants have often been in existence for decades and offer a distinctly Americanized menu compared with the typical taqueria. The burrito itself can take multiple forms, but is almost always dominated by some combination of refried beans, meat (often stewed beef or chili), and cheese (usually cheddar), with rice and other typical Mission burrito ingredients offered as add-ons if at all.

The most basic variant consists of only beans and cheese; beyond this there are the "green chile" and "red chile" burritos, which may simply mean the addition of chiles or a meatless chile sauce to the plain beans (as at Al & Bea's), or meat and/or cheese as well. Rice, again, is rarely included, which along with the choice of chiles is one of the style's most defining traits. The menu will then usually go on to list multiple other combinations, such as beef and bean, all-beef, a "special" with further ingredients, etc. If the restaurant also offers hamburgers and sandwiches it may sell a burrito version of one or more of these, such as a hot dog burrito.

Other varieties

Breakfast burrito

The breakfast burrito, a variety of American breakfast, is composed of breakfast items wrapped inside a flour tortilla. This style was invented and popularized in several different regional American cuisines, most notably New Mexican cuisine, Southwestern cuisine, and Tex-Mex. Southwestern breakfast burritos may include scrambled eggs, potatoes, onions, chorizo, or bacon. *Tia Sophia's*, a Mexican café in Santa Fe, New Mexico, claims to have invented the original breakfast burrito in 1975, filling a rolled tortilla with bacon and potatoes, served wet with chili and cheese. Fast food giant McDonald's introduced their version in the late 1980s, and by the 1990s, more fast food restaurants caught on to the style, with Sonic Drive-In, Taco Bell, and Carl's Jr. offering breakfast burritos on their menus.

Smothered burrito

Wet burrito style

A smothered (often called "wet" or enchilada style) burrito is smothered with a red chili sauce similar to enchilada sauce with melted shredded cheese on top. It is usually eaten off a plate with a fork and knife, rather than hand held. When served in a Mexican restaurant in the U.S., a melted cheese covered burrito is sometimes called a *burrito suizo* [bu.'ri.to su.'i.so] (*suizo* meaning Swiss, an adjective used in Spanish to indicate dishes topped with cheese or cream).

Related foods

Steak burrito bowl

A **burrito bowl** is not technically a burrito, as it consists of burrito fillings served without the tortilla, with the fillings placed in a bowl, and a layer of rice at the bottom. It is not to be confused with a taco salad, which has a foundation of lettuce inside a fried tortilla. The burrito bowl is found in some form at many national Mexican food chain restaurants.

A **chimichanga** is a deep-fried burrito popular in Southwestern and Tex-Mex cuisines, and in the Mexican states of Sinaloa and Sonora.

There is a dish with similar apperiance in Turkey called Dürüm Döner. This has similar filling and taste as the **Doner kebab / Gyro (food)**(Greek) or **Shawarma** Arab, but is rolled in **Lavash** bread. This kind of food can be found all around Europe, the Balkan, Middle East Asia.

Research

Taco Bell research chef Anne Albertine experimented with grilling burritos to enhance portability. This grilling technique allowed large burritos to remain sealed without spilling their contents. This is a well known cooking technique used by some San Francisco taquerias and Northern Mexico burrito stands. Traditionally, grilled burritos are cooked on a comal (griddle).

Bean burritos, which are high in protein and low in saturated fat, have been touted for their health benefits. Black bean burritos are also a good source of dietary fiber and phytochemicals.

Source http://en.wikipedia.org/wiki/Burrito

Calzone

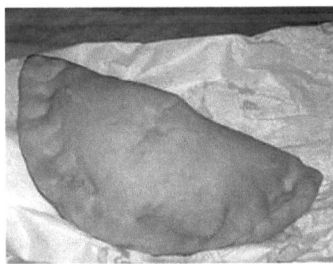

Apulian fried calzone
Origin
Place of origin Italy
Details
Type Turnover
Main ingredient(s) Tomato, mozzarella

A **calzone** (pron.: /kæl'zoʊni/, US /kæl'zoʊneɪ/, or /kæl'zoʊn/, UK /kæl'tsoʊni/; Italian: [kal'tso:ne], "stocking" or "trouser") is a turnover commonly mistaken as a folded pizza. It is shaped like a half-moon and made of salted bread dough. The calzone is folded over and filled with ingredients common to pizza. The typical calzone is stuffed with tomato, mozzarella, and

Calzone topped with tomato sauce, cheese, pine nuts and pesto, as served at PIizza-Braises in Theix, France

sauce, and may include other ingredients that are normally associated with pizza toppings.

Regional variations

Sandwich-sized calzones are often sold at Italian lunch counters or by street vendors because they are easy to eat while standing or walking. Fried versions typically filled with tomato and mozzarella, are made in Puglia and are called *Panzerotti*.

Somewhat related is the Sicilian *cuddiruni* or *cudduruni* pizza. This is stuffed with onions (or sometimes other vegetables such as potatoes or broccoli), anchovies, olives, cheese, mortadella: the rolled pizza dough is folded in two over the stuffing and the edge is braided, prior to frying.

In the United States

In the United States, calzones are characteristically made from pizza dough and stuffed with meats, cheeses, and vegetables. Traditional calzone dough consists of flour, yeast, olive oil, water, and salt. Calzones are similar to stromboli, but traditionally the two are distinct dishes.

As a rule, calzones are usually stuffed with cheeses such as ricotta, mozzarella, Parmesan, Provolone or a type of regional cheese. The dough is folded into a half-moon shape then sealed with an egg wash mixture, or formed into a spherical shape and baked or fried. After cooking, calzones are typically served smothered in marinara sauce or topped with a combination of garlic, olive oil, and parsley.

Scacciata is similar to a calzone but is filled with either broccoli, spinach, potatoes or onions, and sometimes sausage.

Source http://en.wikipedia.org/wiki/Calzone

Camote cue

Camote cue being sold in a stall along with Banana cue (left).

A **Camote cue** or **Camote fritter** (Tagalog: *Kamote kyu*) is a popular snack food in the Philippines made from *camote*, the local sweet potato. Slices of camote are coated with brown sugar and then fried to cook the potatoes and to caramelize the sugar. It is one of the most common street foods in the Philippines, along with banana cue and turon.

The term is a portmanteau of 'Camote' and 'Barbecue', (which in Philippine English refers to meat cooked in a style similar to kebabs). Though served skewered on bamboo sticks, it is not cooked on the stick. The skewer is purely for easier handling as it is usually sold on the streets to passers by.

Source http://en.wikipedia.org/wiki/Camote_cue

Chaat

Bhala Papri chaat in dahi with Saunth chutney

Origin

| Place of origin | India |
| Type | Snack |

Chaat (Hindi: चाट,Urdu: چاٹ) is a term describing savoury snacks, typically served at road-side tracks from stalls or food carts in India and some parts of Pakistan. With its origins in Uttar Pradesh, chaat has become immensely popular in the rest of South Asia. The word derives from Hindi *cāṭ* चाट (tasting, a delicacy), from *cāṭnā* चाटना (to lick), from Prakrit *caṭṭei* चट्टेइ (to devour with relish, eat noisily).

Overview

Aloo tikki served with *hari* (Mint and cilantro chutney), Saunth chutneys, and dahi

The chaat variants are all based on fried dough, with various other ingredients. The original chaat is a mixture of potato pieces, crispy fried bread Dahi vada or Dahi Bhalla ("Bhalla" in Hindi), gram

A young man at his chaat stand in Mussoorie, India. The main text on the front says "bhel puri" and "sev puri" in Hindi. In the plastic bag are puris for panipuri; the yellow substance is sev; the fried crackers are papdi; the white substance is puffed rice; and the other things are chopped onions, limes and tomatoes.

or chickpeas and tangy-salty spices,

with sour home-made Indian chilli and Saunth (dried ginger and tamarind sauce), fresh green coriander leaves and yogurt for garnish, but other popular variants included Aloo tikkis (garnished with onion, coriander, hot spices and a dash of curd), bhel puri, dahi puri, panipuri, dahi vada, papri chaat, and sev puri.

There are common elements among these variants including dahi, or yogurt; chopped onions and coriander; sev (small dried yellow salty noodles); and chaat masala. This is a masala, or spice mix, typically consisting of amchoor (dried mango powder), cumin, Kala Namak (rock salt), coriander, dried ginger, salt, black pepper, and red pepper. The ingredients are combined and served on a small metal plate or a banana leaf, dried and formed into a bowl.

History

Most chaats originated in some parts of Uttar Pradesh in India, but they are now eaten all across the Indian Sub-continent. Some are results of cultural syncretism - for instance, pav bhaji (Bread/bun with cooked and mashed vegetables) reflects a Portuguese influence, in the form of a bun, and bhel puri & Sevpuri, were created by a Gujarati migrant to Mumbai.

Regions

In cities where chaat is popular, there are popular chaathouses or *dhabas*, such as Mumbai's Chowpatty Beach. The chaat specialities vary from city to city. Chaat from Agra and Mathura are famous throughout India. In Hyderabad, chaat is mostly prepared by vendors hailing from Bihar, and is different in taste.

Types of chaat

Delhi Chaat with saunth chutney

Aloo Chaat - Aloo (potatoes) are cut into small pieces and then fried till crisp and served with chutney
Aloo tikki
Bedai - Puri stuffed with dal and fried till crisp. Typically served with aloo sabji and eaten for breakfast
Bhala/Aloo Tikki

Aloo chaat vendor, Connaught Place, New Delhi

Bhelpuri
Chila - Besan pancakes served with chutney and sooth (sweet chutney)
Dahi puri
Dahi vada
Mangode - Similar to pakora, but besan paste is replaced with yellow moong paste
Pakora - Different things such as paneer, vegetable dipped in besan (Chickpea/gram flour) paste and fried.
Panipuri/Gol gappa
Papri chaat
Samosa Chaat - Samosa is broken into pieces with green and sweet chutney added to it.
Sevpuri
Source http://en.wikipedia.org/wiki/Chaat

Chi'Lantro BBQ

Chi'Lantro BBQ is a Korean and Mexican fusion mobile truck and catering service. Chi'Lantro serves in the Austin and Fort Hood, Texas areas. In 2012, Chi'lantro expanded beyond the Austin market and opened a truck in Houston. The name "Chi'Lantro" is a portmanteau of "kimchi" and "cilantro", two distinct cultural staples, reinventing traditional Korean and Mexican cuisine. They are locally known as the originator of a dish known as Kimchi Fries.

Menu

The menu for Chi'Lantro features hybrid cuisine inspired by Korean and Mexican food traditions. Items include Kimchi Fries, Seoul Burritos, Spicy Fries, Tacos, Quesadillas and bulgogi Burgers. Ingredients include combinations of bulgogi, Korean vinaigrette salad, eggs, Monterey Jack Cheese, lime-juice, a proprietary "magic sauce" and sesame seeds. Its signature food, Kimchi Fries, are covered in caramelized bulgogi, shredded cheddar cheese, chile mayonnaise, yellow onion, chopped fresh cilantro, Thai chile sauce, and sesame seeds.

Style of Operation

Chi'Lantro functions primarily as a mobile kitchen or food truck. The trucks make scheduled stops throughout Austin and Ft. Hood, Texas in the mornings, afternoons and evenings in highly commercial areas. The scheduled routes of the Austin trucks reflects an appeal to consumers in the white-collar workforce in addition to manual laborers, the stereotypical customers for such establishments. Example stops include tech-industry hubs like the Austin offices of Google, NCSoft, and BioWare. They also offer catering services for parties, corporate events, promotions, weddings, festivals, conventions, and various large social events in the area.

Use of Internet and Social Media

Chi'Lantro has made extensive use of social media applications such as Twitter, Foursquare, Yelp, and Facebook to connect with its tech savvy customer base in the Austin area. They rely on publishing of tweets to keep their customers informed about where each truck is going to be located. Chi'Lantro is also one of the many food trucks in the Austin area and nationwide to pioneer the use of Android and Apple mobile devices for credit card transactions and the organization of finances. Chi'Lantro is popular on YouTube for its series of commercials targeted to its fans: It's That Good, Fries Like a G6 and Chi'Lantrofied!

Participation in Special Events and Promotions

Nocturnal Festival: September 6, 2010
21st place in Food Network's *The Great Food Truck Race*: August 10, 2010
Gypsy Picnic Trailer Food Festival, Austin, TX: November 2010
Charity promotion for Japanese Earthquake Relief: March 2011
SXSW Promotion with Intuit GoPayment and Loopt
Texas Craft Brewers Festival: September 24, 2011
Fun Fun Fun Festival: November 2011
Source http://en.wikipedia.org/wiki/Chi'Lantro_BBQ

Chimichanga

A chimichanga with rice

Origin

Alternative name(s)	Chivichanga, chimmy chonga
Place of origin	Mexico / United States
Region or state	Northern Mexico/ Southwestern United States

Details

Type	Burrito
Main ingredient(s)	Tortillas, rice, cheese, machaca, carne adobada or shredded chicken

Chimichanga (pron.: /tʃɪmiˈtʃæŋɡə/; Spanish: [tʃimiˈtʃaŋɡa]), also known as **chivichanga** or **chimmy chonga** is a deep-fried burrito that is popular in Southwestern U.S. cuisine, Tex-Mex cuisine, and the Mexican states of Sinaloa and Sonora. The dish is typically prepared by filling a flour tortilla with a wide range of ingredients, most commonly rice, cheese, machaca, carne adobada, or shredded chicken, and folding it into a rectangular package. It is then deep-fried and can be accompanied with salsa, guacamole, sour cream and/or cheese.

Origins

Debate over the origins of the chimichanga is ongoing:
According to one source, the founder of the Tucson, Arizona, restaurant El Charro, Monica Flin, accidentally dropped a pastry into the deep fat fryer in 1922. She immediately began to utter a Spanish curse-word beginning "chi..." (chingada), but quickly stopped herself and instead exclaimed *chimichanga*, a Spanish equivalent of *thingamajig*.

A Chimichanga with refried beans and rice served at an Illinois restaurant.

Woody Johnson, founder of Macayo's Mexican Kitchen, claims he invented the Chimichanga (chim-ee-ch-anga) in 1946 when he put some burritos into a deep fryer as an experiment at his original restaurant Woody's El Nido. These "fried burritos" became so popular that by 1952 when Woody's El Nido became Macayo's the chimichanga was one of the restaurant's main menu items.Johnson opened Macayo's in 1952.

Although no official records indicate when the dish first appeared, retired University of Arizona folklorist Jim Griffith recalls seeing chimichangas at the Yaqui Old Pascua Village in Tucson in the mid-1950s.

Given the variant *chivichanga*, mainly employed in Mexico, another derivation would have it that immigrants to the United States brought the dish with them, mainly through Nogales into Arizona. A third, and perhaps most likely possibility, is that the chimichanga, or chivichanga, has long been a part of local cuisine of the Pimería Alta of Arizona and Sonora, with its early range extending southward into Sinaloa. In Sinaloa the chimichangas are small. In any case, it is all but uncontroversial that within the United States, knowledge and appreciation of the dish spread slowly outward from the Tucson area, with popularity elsewhere accelerating in recent decades. Though the chimichanga is now found as part of the Tex-Mex repertoire, its roots within the U.S. seem to be in Pima County, Arizona.
Source http://en.wikipedia.org/wiki/Chimichanga

Cockle (bivalve)

Cockle

Cockle (bivalve)

Live specimens of *Cerastoderma edule* from France

Scientific classification

Kingdom:	Animalia
Phylum:	Mollusca
Class:	Bivalvia
Order:	Veneroida
Superfamily:	Cardioidea
Family:	**Cardiidae**

Lamarck, 1809

Genera
Numerous, see text

Synonyms
Lymnocardiidae

Cockle is the common name for a group of (mostly) small, edible, saltwater clams, marine bivalve molluscs in the family **Cardiidae**.

Various species of cockles live in sandy, sheltered beaches throughout the world.

The distinctive rounded shells of cockles are symmetrical, and are heart-shaped when viewed from the end. Numerous radial ribs occur in most but not all genera. For an exception, see the genus *Laevicardium*, the egg cockles, which have very smooth shells.

The mantle has three apertures (inhalant, exhalant, and pedal) for siphoning water and for the foot to protrude. Cockles typically burrow using the foot, and feed by filtering plankton from the surrounding water.

Cockles are capable of "jumping" by bending and straightening the foot.

Like many bivalves, cockles display gonochorism (the sex of an individual varies according to conditions), and some species reach maturity quickly. Confusingly, the common name "cockle" is also given (by seafood sellers) to a number of other small, edible bivalves which have a somewhat similar shape, but these bivalves are in other families such as the Veneridae (Venus clams) and the Arcidae (ark clams). Cockles in the family Cardiidae are sometimes known as "true cockles" to distinguish them from these other species.

Species

There are more than 200 living species of cockles, with many more fossil forms.

The common cockle, *Cerastoderma edule*, is widely distributed around the coastlines of Northern Europe, with a range extending west to Ireland, the Barents Sea in the north, Norway in the east, and as far south as Senegal.

The dog cockle, *Glycymeris glycymeris*, has a similar range and habitat to the common cockle, but is unrelated. It is inedible due to its toughness when cooked, although a process is being developed to solve this.

The blood cockle, *Anadara granosa* (not related to the true cockles, instead in the family Arcidae) is extensively cultured from southern Korea to Malaysia.

An example group of true cockles that have shells which are completely smooth, without ribs, is the genus *Laevicardium*. These are often known as egg cockles.

Genera

Genera within the family Cardiidae include:
Acanthocardia
Acrosterigma Dall, 1900
Americardia
Cardium
Cerastoderma
Clinocardium
Corculum
Ctenocardia
Dinocardium
Discors
Fragum
Fulvia
Hypanis Pander in Menetries, 1832
Laevicardium
Lophocardiium
Lunulicardia
Lyrocardium
Microcardium
Nemocardium
Papyridea
Parvicardium
Plagiocardium
Pratulum
Ringicardium
Serripes
Trachycardium
Tridacna, the 'giant clams'
Trigoniocardia

Acrosterigma cignorum

Ctenocardia fornicata

Ctenocardia virgo

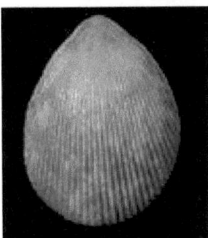

Trachycardium maculosum

In cuisine and culture

Cockles are a popular type of edible

shellfish in both Eastern and Western cooking. They are collected by raking them from the sands at low tide. However, collecting cockles is hard work and, as seen from the Morecambe Bay disaster, in which 23 illegal immigrants died, can be dangerous if local tidal conditions are not carefully watched. In England and Wales, the Magna Carta grants every citizen the right to collect up to eight pounds of cockles from the foreshore. However, pickers wishing to collect more than eight pounds are deemed to be engaging in commercial fishing and are required to obtain a permit from the Inshore Fisheries and Conservation Authority.

Cockles are sold freshly cooked as a snack in the United Kingdom, particularly in those parts of the British coastline where cockles are abundant. Boiled, then seasoned with malt vinegar and white pepper, they can be bought from seafood stalls, which also often have for sale mussels, whelks, jellied eels, crabs and shrimps. Cockles are also available pickled in jars, and more recently, have been sold in sealed packets (with vinegar) containing a plastic two-pronged fork. A meal of cockles fried with bacon, served with laver bread, is known as a traditional Welsh breakfast.

Boiled cockles (sometimes grilled) are sold at many hawker centers in Southeast Asia, and are used in *laksa*, *char kway teow* and steamboat. They are called *kerang* in Malay and *see hum* in Hokkien.

A study conducted in England in the early 1980's showed a correlation between the consumption of cockles, presumed to be incorrectly processed, and an elevated local occurrence of hepatitis.

Cockles are an effective bait for a wide variety of sea fishes.

The folk song "Molly Malone" is also known as "Cockles and Mussels" because the title character's sale of the two foods is referenced in the song's refrain.

They are also mentioned in the English nursery rhyme "Mary, Mary, Quite Contrary".

They are also eaten by the indigenous peoples of North America.

Empty cockle shell on the beach
Bags of cockles picked from Morecambe Bay
Boiled "cockles" served in Tanjong Pagar, Singapore are actually ark clams in the family Arcidae

Alternate meanings

The common English phrase "it warms

the cockles of my heart", is used to mean that a feeling of deep-seated contentment has been generated.

Differing derivations of this phrase have been proposed, either directly from the perceived heart-shape of a cockleshell, or indirectly (the scientific name for the type genus of the family is *Cardium*, from the Latin for heart), or from the Latin diminutive of the word heart, corculum. Another proposed derivation is from the Latin for the ventricles of the heart, *cochleae cordis*, where the second word is an inflected form of *cor*, heart, while *cochlea* is the Latin for snail.

Source http://en.wikipedia.org/wiki/Cockle_(bivalve)

Coxinha

Medium-sized *coxinha*.

Medium-sized *coxinha* before frying.

The **Coxinha** (Portuguese: [koˈʃiɲɐ], *little chicken thigh*) is a popular food in many countries in South America. The drumstick is a snack Brazilian origin in São Paulo, also common in Portugal, based dough made with wheat flour and chicken broth, which involves a filling made with spiced meat chicken. It includes chicken, spices generally including tomato sauce, onion, parsley and scallions (with occasional catupiry cheese), enclosed in wheat flour – variants including potato or manioc are also commonly sold – batter, and deep fried. It is shaped to roughly resemble a chicken leg.

Coxinhas were originally made with a chicken thigh, thus the origin of its traditional shape. The batter used to make the dough is often prepared with the broth of the chicken, enhancing the flavor of the dough.

Coxinha literally means "little thigh", and it is how deep fried chicken legs are informally named in Brazil (*coxa frita* means a deep fried chicken leg, while *sobrecoxa frita* stands for a deep fried upper drumstick; there, it is not uncommon for people possessing a strong preference for certain poultry cuts in detriment of others). Battered and deep fried chicken breast, for example, are generally called by a name of English influence, nugget.

Different variations of the original are becoming more prevalent today – for example, the *coxinha mineira*, where the filling include maize, named so because maize is deemed as a culinary tradition in the state of Minas Gerais, as well areas where the caipira and sertanejo dialects are spoken. Cheese coxinhas are also very common on snack bars. They usually put a toothpick where the bone would be in order to separate chicken coxinhas to cheese coxinhas.

Other unconventional ingredients, generally used for home-made *coxinhas* made by aficionados, include peas, chopped button mushrooms, palmheart, carrot, as well whole-wheat flour batter or even a vegetarian version of either textured vegetable protein (soy meat) or falafel with appropriate seasonings that can make its taste resemble more closely a traditional *coxinha*. Nevertheless, these variants are extremely uncommon to be sold in snack bars.

In the book Stories & Recipes, Nadir Cavazin says that the son of Princess Isabel of Brazil and the Count D'Eu, a child who lived in seclusion for having mental problems had a favorite dish, chicken, but only ate the thigh. One day, not having enough thigh, the cook decided to turn a whole chicken into thighs, shredding it and making the filling for a flour dough shaped into a drumstick. The child endorsed the results and Empress Teresa Cristina when she was visiting him, could not resist the tasty delicacy, she liked it so much she requested that the master of the imperial kitchen learn how to prepare the snack. So coxinha won the nobility and became history.

Source http://en.wikipedia.org/wiki/Coxinha

Crêpe

A stack of crêpes

Origin	
Alternative name(s)	Crepe
Place of origin	France
Region or state	Brittany
Details	
Type	Pancake
Main ingredient(s)	Wheat flour or buckwheat flour, milk, eggs

A **crêpe** or **crepe** (/kreɪp/ or /krɛp/ French: [kʁɛp] (listen), Quebec French: [kʁaɛp] (listen)) is a type of very thin pancake, usually made from wheat flour (*crêpes de Froment*) or buckwheat flour (galettes). The word is of French origin, deriving from the Latin *crispa*, meaning "curled". While crêpes originate from Brittany, a region in the northwest of France, their consumption is widespread in France and Quebec. In Brit-

A sweet crêpe opened up, with whipped cream and strawberry sauce on it. This variation of crêpes – especially when they are curled up to form a tube, and finished with a topping of powdered sugar, whipped cream, or both – is called *French pancakes*.

tany, crêpes are traditionally served with cider. Crêpes are served with a variety of fillings, from the most simple with only sugar to flambéed crêpes Suzette or elaborate savoury.

Preparation

Crêpes are made by pouring a thin liquid batter onto a hot frying pan or flat circular hot plate, often with a trace of butter on the pan's surface. The batter is spread evenly over the cooking surface of the pan or plate either by tilting the pan or by distributing the batter with an offset spatula. There are also specially designed crêpe makers with a heatable circular surface that can be dipped in the batter and quickly pulled out to produce an ideal thickness and evenness of cooking.

Common savoury fillings for crêpes served for lunch or dinner are cheese, ham, and eggs, ratatouille, mushrooms, artichoke (in certain regions), and various meat products.

When sweet, they can be eaten as part of breakfast or as a dessert. They can be filled and topped with various sweet toppings, often including Nutella spread, preserves, sugar (granulated or powdered), maple syrup, lemon juice, whipped cream, fruit spreads, custard, and sliced soft fruits or confiture.

Types and special crêpes

Crêpes are especially popular throughout France. The common ingredients include flour, eggs, milk, butter, and a pinch of salt. Crêpes are usually of two types: *sweet crêpes* (*crêpes sucrées*) made with wheat flour and slightly sweetened; and *savoury galettes* (*crêpes salées*) made with buckwheat flour and unsweetened. The name "galette" came from the French word *galet* ("pebble"),

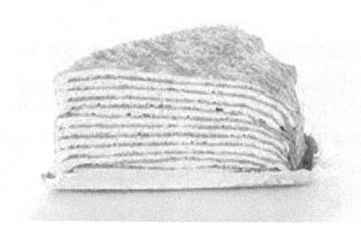

Mille crêpe

since the first gallettes were made on a large pebble heated in a fire. Batter made from buckwheat flour is gluten-free, which makes it possible for people who have a gluten allergy or intolerance to eat this type of crêpe. *Mille crêpe* is a French cake made of many crêpe layers. The word *mille* means "a thousand", implying the many layers of crêpe. Another standard French and Belgian crêpe is the *crêpe Suzette*, a crêpe with lightly grated orange peel and liqueur (usually Grand Marnier) which is subsequently lit upon presentation.

Swedish pancakes, also called Nordic pancakes, are similar to the French crêpes. In some of the Nordic countries they are served with jam or fruit, especially lingonberries (or the butter from that fruit) as a dessert with a variety of savory fillings. Traditional Swedish variations can be exotic. Beside the usual thin pancakes, called pannkakor, which resembles the French crêpes and, often served with whipped cream and jam, are traditionally eaten for lunch on Thursdays with pea soup, the Swedish cuisine has plättar which resemble tiny English pancakes, and are fried several at a time in a special pan. Others resemble German pancakes but include fried pork in the batter (fläskpannkaka); these are baked in the oven. Potato pancakes called raggmunk contain shredded raw potato, and may contain other vegetables (sometimes the pancake batter is omitted, producing rårakor). Raggmunk and rårakor are traditionally eaten with pork rinds and lingonberry jam. A special Swedish pancake is saffron pancake from Gotland, made with saffron and rice, baked in the oven. It is common to add lemon juice to the sugar for extra taste. The pancakes are often served after a soup. Another special "Swedish pancake" is the äggakaka (eggcake), also called skånsk äggakaka (scanian eggcake), it is almost like an ordinary Swedish pancake but it is a lot thicker and also a lot more difficult to make due to the risk of burning it. It is made in a frying pan and is about 1½ to 2 inches thick and is served with lingonberries and bacon. The Norwegian variety is commonly eaten for dinner, traditionally with bacon, jam (typically bilberry jam) or sugar.

A plate of 49er flapjacks

The 49er flapjack is a sourdough crepe which is popular in the United States, getting it's name from the popularity of this style of pancake during the gold rush. During the Klondike gold rush of 1898, it was said that a real "Alaskan Sourdough" would just as soon spend a year in the hills without his rifle, as to tough it through without his bubbling sourdough pot. Since food was scare, food provisions were more valuable than gold. In extreme cold, miners would put the dough ball under their clothes, next to their skin, or tuck it into their bedroll with them at night, anything to keep the yeast in it alive. The 49er is a signature menu item at The Original Pancake House, Walker Bros., and Good Day Cafe among other establishments. OHP advertises the crepe as "ooey, gooey, and chewy." Because it is similar to a Swedish pancake the 49er is sometimes served with lingonberry sauce, although most often it is rolled up with butter and powdered sugar, or served open faced and topped with maple syrup.

Cherry Kijafa Crêpes are also often common and are made with a traditional crêpe base, but filled with cherries simmered in a Kijafa wine sauce.

Crêpe dentelle is a crispy biscuit made with a very thin layer of crêpe folded in a cigar shape and then baked. It is usually enjoyed with a hot drink during the *Goûter*, or Afternoon Tea, in France.

Crêperies

A small crêperie

A **crêperie** may be a takeaway restaurant or stall, serving crêpes as a form of fast food or street food, or may be a more formal sit-down restaurant or café.

Crêperies are typical of Brittany in France; however, crêperies can be found throughout France and in many other countries.

Because a crêpe may be served as both a main meal or a dessert, crêperies may be quite diverse in their selection and may offer other baked goods such as baguettes. They may also serve coffee, tea, buttermilk and cider (a popular drink to accompany crêpes).

In other countries

A sweet crêpe served with strawberries and whipped cream

In Norwegian, it's called *Pannekake*, in most German regions it's *Pfannkuchen*, and in Dutch it's *pannenkoeken*. In

Swedish, a crêpe is called *pannkaka*, and in Danish, *pandekager* ("pancake"); in Dutch it is a *pannenkoek* or *flensje*, and in Afrikaans a *pannekoek*, which is usually served with cinnamon sugar. In the Spanish regions of Galicia and Asturias they are traditionally served at carnivals. In Galicia they're called *filloas*, and may also be made with pork blood instead of milk. In Asturias they are called *fayueles* or *frixuelos*, and in Turkey, "Akıtma".

In areas of Eastern Europe formerly belonging to the Austro-Hungarian empire, there is a thin pancake comparable to a crêpe that in Austro-Bavarian is called *Palatschinken* or *Omletten*; in Hungarian: *palacsinta*; and in Bosnian, Serbian, Bulgarian, Macedonian, Montenegrin, Czech, Croatian and Slovene: *palačinka*; in Slovak: *palacinka*. In the Balkan region such as the countries of Albania, Bosnia, Croatia, Macedonia, Montenegro, and Serbia, *palačinka* or *palaçinka* may be eaten with fruit jam, quark cheese, sugar, honey, or the hazelnut-chocolate cream Nutella. In Ashkenazi Jewish cuisine, there is a similar dish known as the blintz. The *Oxford English Dictionary* derives the German and Slavic words from the Hungarians *palacsinta*, which it derives from the Romanian *plăcintă* ("pie, pancake"), which comes in turn from classical Latin *placenta* ("small flat cake").

Crêpes have also become popular in Japan, with sweet and savoury varieties being sold at many small stands, usually called crêperies. In Argentina they are called *panqueques* and are often eaten with dulce de leche. They have also become popular in North America with several crêpe franchises opening. Typically, these franchises stick to the traditional French method of making crêpes but they have also put their own spin on the crêpe with new types such as the hamburger and pizza crêpe.

In addition to crêperies and crêpe franchises, there are crêpe manufacturers that use modern equipment to produce crêpes in bulk.

Chocolate-Coconut Crêpe served in crêperie near the Patheon in Paris, France

Dishes with similar appearance, taste and preparation methods exist in other parts of the world as well. In South India, a crêpe made of fermented rice batter is called a dosa, which often has savoury fillings. In Western India, a crepe made of gram flour is called Pudlaa/Poodla, with the batter consisting of vegetables and spices. Another variety is called Patibola and is sweet in taste due to milk, jaggery or sugar. The injera of Ethiopian/Eritrean/Somali/Yemeni cuisine is often described as a thick crêpe. Also in Somalia, malawax is very similar to a crêpe. It is mostly eaten at breakfast.

The names for thin crêpes in other parts of Europe are:
Estonian: *pannkook, ülepannikook*
Faroese: *pannukaka*
Finnish: *ohukainen, lätty or räiskäle*
Greek: κρέπα (*krépa*)
Icelandic: *pönnukaka*
Kazakh: құймақ (*quymaq*)
Latvian: *pankūka*
Lithuanian: *Lietiniai blynai*
Bulgarian: палачинка
Polish: *naleśniki*
Portuguese: *crepe*
Romanian: *clătită*
Russian: блины (*bliny*)
Spanish: *tortitas*
Ukrainian: млинці (*mlyntsi, nalysnyky*)

Crêpes in culture

In France, crêpes are traditionally served on Candlemas (*La Chandeleur*), February 2. This day was originally Virgin Mary's Blessing Day, but became known in France as "Le Jour des Crêpes" (literally translated "The Day of the Crêpes", but sometimes given colloquially as "Avec Crêpe Day" or "National Crêpe Day"), referring to the tradition of offering crêpes. The belief was that if you could catch the crêpe with a frying pan after tossing it in the air with your right hand and holding a gold coin in your left hand, you would become rich that year.

Source http://en.wikipedia.org/wiki/Crêpe

Dahi puri

Dahi puri

Origin

Place of origin	India
Region or state	Maharashtra
Details	
Main ingredient(s)	Sev, moong dal and coriander leaves
Variations	Sev-Dahi-Batata-Puri, Sev-Potato-Dahi-Puri

Dahipuri, or **Dahi puri**, is an Indian snack which is especially popular in the state of Maharashtra. The dish is a form of chaat and originates from the city of Mumbai. It is served with mini-puri shells (*golgappa*), which are more popularly recognized from the dish pani puri. Dahi puri and pani puri chaats are often sold from the same vendor.

Preparation

The round, hard, puffy puri shell is first broken on top and partially filled with the main stuffing of mashed potatoes or chickpeas. A small amount of haldi powder or chilli powder, or both, may be added for taste, as well as a pinch of salt. Sweet tamarind chutney and spicy green chutney are then poured into the shell, on top of the stuffing. Finally, sweetened beaten yoghurt is generously poured over the shell, and the finished product is garnished with sprinklings of crushed sev, *moong* dal and finely chopped coriander leaves.

Dahi puri typically comes as 5 or 6 dahi puris per plate. While pani puri is typically served one piece at a time, a plate of many dahi puri is often served together. Each dahi puri is intended to be eaten whole, like pani puri, so that the spectrum of flavors and textures within may all be tasted together.

Source http://en.wikipedia.org/wiki/Dahi_puri

Dim sum

Dim sum

Typical dim sum breakfast in Hong Kong.

From left to right and top to bottom:

har gau, jasmine tea, chicken and vegetable congee, steamed dumpling, rice noodle roll (on plate), cha siu baau

Traditional Chinese	點心
Simplified Chinese	点心
Hanyu Pinyin	diǎn xin
Cantonese Jyutping	dim2 sam1

Dim sum (/ˈdɪmˈsʌm/) refers to a style of Cantonese food prepared as small bite-sized or individual portions of food traditionally served in small steamer baskets or on small plates. Dim sum is also well known for the unique way it is served in some restaurants, wherein fully cooked and ready-to-serve dim sum dishes are carted around the restaurant for customers to choose their orders while seated at their tables.

Eating dim sum at a restaurant is usually known in Cantonese as going to "*drink tea*" (yum cha, 飲茶), as tea is typically served with dim sum.

History

Dim sum is usually linked with the older tradition from *yum cha* (tea tasting), which has its roots in travelers on the ancient Silk Road needing a place to rest. Thus teahouses were established along the roadside. Rural farmers, exhausted after working hard in the fields, would go to teahouses for a relaxing afternoon of tea. At first, it was considered inappropriate to combine tea with food, because people believed it would lead to excessive weight gain. People later discovered that tea can aid in digestion, so teahouse owners began adding various snacks.

The unique culinary art of dim sum originated with the Cantonese in southern China, who over the centuries transformed yum cha from a relaxing respite to a loud and happy dining experience. In Hong Kong, and in most cities and towns in Guangdong province, many restaurants start serving dim sum as early as five in the morning. It is a tradition for the elderly to gather to eat dim sum after morning exercises. For many in southern China, *yum cha* is treated as a weekend family day. More traditional dim sum restaurants typically serve dim sum until mid-afternoon. However, in modern society it has become commonplace for restaurants to serve dim sum at dinner time, various dim sum items are even sold as take-out for students and office workers on the go.

While dim sum (literally meaning: touch the heart) was originally not a main meal, only a snack, and therefore only meant to touch the heart, it is now a staple of Cantonese dining culture, especially in Hong Kong. Health officials have recently criticized the high amount of saturated fat and sodium in some dim sum dishes, warning that steamed dim sum should not automatically be assumed to be healthy. Health officials recommend balancing fatty dishes with boiled vegetables without sauce.

Cuisine

Serving dim sum in a restaurant in Hong Kong

A traditional dim sum brunch includes various types of steamed buns such as *cha siu baau*, dumplings and rice noodle rolls (cheong fun), which contain a range of ingredients, including beef, chicken, pork, prawns and vegetarian options. Many dim sum restaurants also offer plates of steamed green vegetables, roasted meats, congee porridge and other soups. Dessert dim sum is also available and many places offer the customary egg tart.

Dim sum can be cooked by steaming and frying, among other methods. The serving sizes are usually small and normally served as three or four pieces in one dish. It is customary to order family style, sharing dishes among all members of the dining party. Because of the small portions, people can try a wide variety of food.

Dishes

Cha siu sou as served in a dim sum restaurant in Singapore

Dim sum brunch restaurants have a wide variety of dishes, usually several dozen. Among the standard fare of dim sum are the following:

Dim-sum dumpling in Chicago

Lo mai gai wrapped in lotus leaf

Main

Gao, or ***Dumpling*** (Chinese: 餃; 餃子; Cantonese Yale: gaau2; gaau2 ji2): Jiao zi is a standard in most teahouses. They are made of ingredients wrapped in a translucent rice flour or wheat starch skin, and are different from *jiaozi* found in other parts of China. Though common, steamed rice-flour skins are quite difficult to make. Thus, it is a good demonstration of the chef's artistry to make these translucent dumplings. There are also dumplings with vegetarian ingredients, such as tofu and pickled cabbage.

Har gow (shrimp dumplings) (蝦餃 *haa1 gaau2*): A delicate steamed dumpling with whole or chopped-up shrimp filling and thin wheat starch skin.

Chiu-chao style dumplings (潮州粉果 *ciu4 zau1 fan2 gwo2*): A dumpling said to have originated from the Chaozhou prefecture of eastern Guangdong province, it contains peanuts, garlic, chives, pork, dried shrimp, and Chinese mushrooms in a thick dumpling wrapper made from glutinous rice flour or Tang flour. It is usually served with a small dish of chili oil.

Guotie (pot stickers) (鍋貼, *wo1 tip3*): Northern Chinese style of dumpling (steamed and then pan-fried jiaozi), usually with meat and cabbage filling. Note that although potstickers are sometimes served in dim sum restaurants, they are not considered traditional Cantonese dim sum.

Shaomai (燒賣 *siu1 maai6*): Small steamed dumplings with either pork, prawns or both inside a thin wheat flour wrapper. Usually topped off with crab roe and mushroom.

Haam Seoi Gaau (鹹水餃 *haam4 seoi2 gaau2*, salt-water (i.e. savoury) stuffed-dumpling, alternatively 鹹水角 *haam4 seoi2 gok3*): deep fried oval-shaped dumpling made with rice-flour and filled with pork and chopped vegetables. The rice-flour surrounding is sweet and sticky, while the inside is slightly salty.

Dumpling soup (灌湯餃 *gun3 tong1 gaau2*): soup with one or two big dumplings.

Bau (包 *baau1* or 包子 *baau1 zi2*): Baked or steamed, these fluffy buns made from wheat flour are filled with food items ranging from meat to vegetables to sweet bean pastes.

Char siu baau (叉燒包 *caa1 siu1 baau1*): the most popular bun with a Cantonese barbecued pork filling. It can be either steamed to be fluffy and white or baked with a light sugar glaze to produce a smooth golden-brown crust.

Shanghai steamed buns (上海小籠包 *seong6 hoi2 siu2 lung4 baau1*): These dumplings are filled with meat or seafood and are famous for their flavor and rich broth inside. These dumplings are originally Shanghainese so they are not considered traditional Cantonese dim sum. They are typically sold with pork as a filling.

Mantou (饅頭 *maan4 tau4*): plain steamed bun like *cha siu baau* without filling stuff.

Phoenix claws (鳳爪 *fung6 zaau2*): These are chicken feet, deep fried, boiled, marinated in a black bean sauce and then steamed. This results in a texture that is light and fluffy (due to the frying), while moist and tender. Fung zau are typically dark red in color. One may also sometimes find plain steamed chicken feet served with a vinegar dipping sauce. This version is known as "White Cloud Phoenix Claws" (白雲鳳爪 *baak6 wan4 fung6 jaau2*).

Steamed meatball (牛肉球 *ngau4 juk6 kau4*): Finely ground beef is shaped into balls and then steamed with preserved orange peel and served on top of a thin bean-curd skin.

Spare ribs: In the west, it is mostly known as spare ribs collectively. In the east, it is Char siu when roasted red, or (排骨 *paai4 gwat1*) when roasted black. It is typically steamed with douchi or fermented black beans and sometimes sliced chilli.

Lotus leaf rice (糯米雞 *lo6 mai5 gai1*): Glutinous rice is wrapped in a lotus leaf into a triangular or rectangular shape. It contains egg yolk, dried scallop, mushroom, water chestnut and meat (usually pork and chicken). These ingredients are steamed with the rice and although the leaf is not eaten, its flavour is infused during the steaming. *Lo mai gai* is a kind of rice dumpling. A similar but lighter variant is known as "Pearl Chicken" (珍珠雞 *zan1 zyu1 gai1*).

Congee (粥 *zuk1*): Thick, sticky rice porridge served with different savory items. The porridge one will see most often is "Duck Egg and Pork Porridge" (皮蛋瘦肉粥 "*pei4 daan6 sau3 juk6 zuk1*")

Sou (酥 *sou1*): A type of flaky pastry. Char siu is one of the most common ingredient used in dim sum style sou. Another common pastry seen in restaurants are called "Salty Pastry" (鹹水角 "*haam4 seoi2 gok3*") which is made with flour and seasoned pork.

Taro dumpling (芋角 *wu6 gok3*): This is made with mashed taro, stuffed with diced shiitake mushrooms, shrimp and pork, deep-fried in crispy batter.

Crispy fried squid (魷魚鬚 *jau4 jyu4 sou1*): Similar to fried calamari, the battered squid is deep-fried. A variation of this dish may be prepared with a salt and pepper mix. In some dim sum restaurants, octopus is used instead of squid.

Rolls (捲 *gyun2*)

Egg roll (春捲 *ceon1 gyun2*): a roll consisting of various types of vegetables — such as sliced carrot, cabbage, mushroom and wood ear fungus — and sometimes meat are rolled inside a thin flour skin and deep fried.

Rice noodle rolls or ***coeng fan*** (腸粉 *coeng4 fan2*): These are wide rice noodles that are steamed and then rolled. They are often filled with different types of meats or vegetables inside but can be served without any filling. Rice noodle rolls are fried after they are steamed and then sprinkled with sesame seeds. Popular fillings include beef, dough fritter, shrimp, and barbecued pork. Often topped with a sweetened soy sauce.

Tofu skin roll (腐皮捲 *fu6 pei4 gyun2*): a roll made of Tofu skin

Cakes (糕 *gou1*)

Turnip cake (蘿蔔糕 *lo4 baak6 gou1*): cakes are made from mashed daikon radish mixed with bits of dried shrimp and pork sausage that are steamed and then cut into slices and pan-fried.

Taro cake (芋頭糕 *wu6 tao4 gou1*): cakes made of taro.

Water chestnut cake (馬蹄糕 *maa5 tai2 gou1*): cakes made of water chestnut. It is mostly see-through and clear. Some restaurants also serve a variation of water chestnut cake made with bamboo juice.

Sweets

Chien chang go (千層糕 *cin cang gou*): "Thousand-layer cake", a dim sum dessert made up of many layers of sweet egg dough.

Egg tart (蛋撻 *daan taat*): composed of a base made from either a flaky puff pastry type dough or a type of non-flaky cookie dough with an egg custard filling, which is then baked. Some high class restaurants put bird's nest on top of the custard. In other places egg tarts can be made of a crust and a filling of egg whites and some where it is a crust with egg yolks. Some egg tarts now have flavors such as taro, coffee, and other flavors. There are also different kinds of crust. There is also a flaky crisp outer crust with many layers of crunchy crumbs.

Jin deui or ***Matuan*** (煎堆 or 麻糰): Especially popular at Chinese New Year, a chewy dough filled with red bean paste, rolled in sesame seeds, and deep fried.

Dou fu fa (豆腐花): A dessert consisting of silky tofu served with a sweet ginger or jasmine flavored syrup.

Mango pudding (芒果布甸 *mong guo bou din*): A sweet, rich mango-flavoured pudding usually with large chunks of fresh mango; often served with a topping of evaporated milk.

Sweet cream buns (奶皇包 *naai5 wong4 baau1*): Steamed buns with milk custard filling.

Malay Steamed Sponge Cake (馬拉糕 *ma5 laai1 gou1*): A very soft steamed sponge cake flavoured with molasses.

Longan Tofu: almond-flavoured tofu served with longans, usually cold.

Tea service

The drinking of tea is as important to dim sum as the food. The type of tea to serve on the table would typically be one of the first things the server would ask dining customers. Several types of tea are served during dim sum :

Chrysanthemum tea – Chrysanthemum tea does not actually contain any tea leaves. Instead it is a flower-based tisane made from chrysanthemum flowers of the species *Chrysanthemum morifolium* or *Chrysanthemum indicum*, which are most popular in East Asia. To prepare the tea, chrysanthemum flowers (usually dried) are steeped in hot water (usually 90 to 95 °C (194 to 203 °F) after cooling from a boil) in either a teapot, cup, or glass. However, Chrysanthemum flowers are often paired with Pu-erh tea, and this is often referred to as guk pou or guk bou (菊普; pinyin: jú pǔ).

Green tea – Freshly picked leaves only go through heating and drying processes, but do not undergo fermentation. This enables the leaves to keep their original green color and retain most natural substances like polyphenols and chlorophyll contained within the leaves. This kind of tea is produced all over China and is the most popular category of tea. Representative varieties include Dragon Well (Long Jing) and Biluochun from Zhejiang and Jiangsu Provinces respectively.

Oolong tea – The tea leaves are partially fermented, imparting to them the characteristics of both green and black teas. Its taste is more similar to green tea than black tea, but has a less "grassy" flavor than green tea. The three major oolong-tea producing areas are on the southeast coast of China e.g. Fujian, Guangdong and Taiwan.

Bo-Lei tea (Cantonese) or Pu-erh tea (Mandarin) – The tea has undergone years of fermentation, giving them a unique earthy flavor. This variety of tea is usually compressed into different shapes like bricks, discs and bowls.

Scented teas – There can be various mixtures of flowers with green tea, black tea or oolong tea. Flowers used include jasmine, gardenia, magnolia, grapefruit flower, sweet-scented osmanthus and rose. There are strict rules about the proportion of flowers to tea. Jasmine tea is the most popular type of scented tea, and is often the most popular type of tea served at yum cha establishments.

The above teas are produced in most of China. Chinese tea bushes (*Camellia sinensis*) are cultivated in the mountain areas of tropical and subtropical regions or wherever there is a proper climate, sufficient humidity, adequate sunshine and fertile soil. Chinese tea is classified in many ways, e.g., quality, method of preparation or place of production. The main processing methods include fermentation (oxidation), heating, drying and addition of other ingredients like flowers, herbs or fruits. These help to develop the special flavor of the raw tea leaves.

Various preparation methods mean that different teas contain different bioactive substances. For example, green tea undergoes limited processing so it retains a relatively high content of natural ingredients, meaning that green tea has stronger anti-aging, anti-cancer and anti-bacterial properties. Oolong tea, which is partially fermented, is quite potent at breaking down protein and fat, which aids weight loss. Red tea that has undergone the full fermentation process has lost 90% of its polyphenols but retains its high caffeine content.

Restaurants and pricing

One aspect unique to dim sum is its method of serving in specialized dim sum brunch restaurants or teahouses. Here dishes are pushed around the restaurant on steam carts, with servers offering the dishes to customers. Pricing of dishes at these types of restaurants may vary, but traditionally the dishes are classified as "small", "medium", "large", or "special" (a menu item not typically considered dim sum fare, such as a plate of chow mein). For example, a basket of dumplings may be considered a small dish, while a bowl of congee or plate of *Lo mai gai* may be considered a large dish. Dishes are then priced accordingly by size, with orders typically recorded with a rubber stamp onto a bill that remains on the table. Servers in some restaurants use distinct stamps, so that sales statistics for each server can be recorded. Another way of pricing the food consumed is to use the color of the dishes left on the patron's table as a guide, similar to what is used in some sushi restaurants.

Other Chinese restaurants may not offer dim sum on the steam push carts and instead offer it a la carte. Prices of each dim sum dish may then vary depending on the actual dish ordered.

Etiquette

There are common tea-drinking and eating practices or etiquette that Chinese people commonly recognize and use. These are practiced not only during dim sum meals but during other types of Chinese meals as well.

It is customary to pour tea for others during dim sum before filling one's own cup. When pouring tea for people on one's left side, the right hand should be used to hold the teapot and vice versa. A custom unique to the Cantonese is to

A typical set of eating utensils for yum cha

thank the person pouring the tea by tapping the bent index finger if you are single, or by tapping both the index and middle finger if you are married, which symbolizes 'bowing' to them.

This is said to be analogous to the ritual of bowing to someone in appreciation. The origin of this gesture is described anecdotally: an unidentified Emperor went to yum cha with his friends, outside the palace; not wanting to attract attention to himself, the Emperor was disguised. While at yum cha, the Emperor poured his companion some tea, which was a great honor. The companion, not wanting to give away the Emperor's identity in public by bowing, instead tapped his index and middle finger on the table as a sign of appreciation.

Given the number of times tea is poured in a meal, the tapping is a timesaver in loud restaurants or lively company, as an individual being served might be speaking to someone else or have food in their mouth.

Leaving the lid balanced on the side of the tea pot is a common way of attracting a server's attention, and indicates a request for more hot water in the tea pot.

Fast food

Certain kinds of instant dim sum have come onto the market in Hong Kong, Mainland China, Taiwan and Singapore. People can enjoy snacks after a 3-minute defrosting and reheating of the instant dim sum in a microwave oven.

Some stalls serve "street dim sum" which usually consists of dumplings or meatballs steamed in a large container,

Two women picking microwave ready dim sum from the freezer in Circle K, Hong Kong.

but served on a bamboo skewer. The customer can dip the whole skewer into a sauce bowl and eat while standing or walking.

Dim sum can be purchased from major grocery stores in most countries with a Chinese population. These dim sum can be easily cooked by steaming or microwaving. Major grocery stores in Hong Kong, Philippines, Singapore, Taiwan, Mainland China, Malaysia, Brunei, Thailand, Australia, United States and Canada have a variety of dim sum stocked at the shelves. These include dumplings, *siu maai, bau, cheong fun, lo bak go* and steamed spare ribs. In Singapore, as well as other countries, dim sum can also be purchased from convenience stores, coffee shops and other eateries. There is also halal certified dim sum available, with chicken taking the place of pork which in addition to Singapore is very popular in Malaysia, Indonesia and Brunei.

Source http://en.wikipedia.org/wiki/Dim_sum

Doner kebab

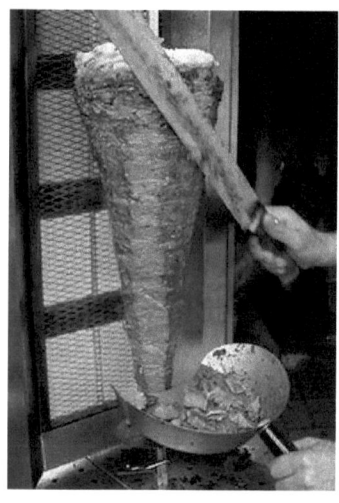

Döner meat being sliced from a rotating spit. The iron heating-plate behind the spit is used to cook the meat.

Origin	
Place of origin	Turkey
Region or state	Bursa, Erzurum, Erzincan and Kastamonu
Creator(s)	dates to 18th century
Details	
Course	Snack or main course
Serving temperature	Hot
Main ingredient(s)	Beef and Lamb
Variations	İskender, Chicken döner

Doner kebab (Turkish: *döner, döner kebap or döner kebabı*) is a Turkish

Doner kebab

dish made of meat cooked on a vertical spit, normally veal or beef but also a mixture of these with lamb; a cheaper version of chicken is also found. The dish is also widely known by its Arabic name, shawarma, or in Greek as gyro.

The sliced meat of a Doner kebab may be served wrapped in a flatbread such as lavash or pita or as a sandwich instead of being served on a plate. It is a common fast food item in the Balkans, Middle East, Europe, Australia, and New Zealand. Seasoned meat in the shape of an inverted cone is turned slowly against a vertical rotisserie, then sliced vertically into thin, crisp shavings. Toppings include tomato, onion, lettuce, pickled cucumber and chili.

History

Cağ kebabı, a related dish. Note that the meat is horizontally stacked.

Döner being carved in Bursa to prepare "Iskender"

Before taking its modern form, as mentioned in Ottoman travel books of the 18th century, the doner used to be a horizontal stack of meat rather than vertical, probably sharing common ancestors with the Cağ Kebabı of the Eastern Turkish province of Erzurum.

In his own family biography, İskender Efendi of 19th century Bursa writes that "he and his grandfather had the idea of roasting the lamb vertically rather than horizontally, and invented for that purpose a vertical mangal". Since then Hacı İskender is known as the inventor of Turkish Döner Kebap. With time, the meat took a different marinade, got leaner, and eventually took its modern shape. The Greek gyro, along with the similar Arab Shawarma and Mexican Tacos al Pastor, are derived from this dish.

Names

A doner kebab is sometimes spelled *döner kebap* (the Turkish spelling), lit. 'rotating roast', or can be shortened to doner (Turkish: *döner*), lit. 'turn around', also spelled "doener", "donar", "donair", "doner", or sometimes "donner".

The name gyro comes from Greek γύρος ('turn'), a calque of the Turkish *döner*, a name which was used in Ecuador as well as ντονέρ [doˈner] The Greek pronunciation is [ˈʝiros], but the pronunciation in English is often /ˈdʒaɪroʊ/ or, occasionally /ˈɡɪəroʊ/ or /ˈjɪəroʊ/. The final 's' of the Greek form is often reinterpreted as a plural in English.

The word *shawarma* (pron.: /ʃəˈwɑːrmə/) is believed to have evolved from the Turkish word *çevirme* [tʃeviɾˈme], a synonym of döner (turning, spinning, rotating) and is used in most Arab countries as well as those Latin American countries where there are Arab colonies who have emigrated from the Ottoman Empire. Shawarma is, almost always, made of lamb though. In Turkey the dish is usually called simply *döner*" rather than "döner kebap or "döner kebabı", the latter of those being the most correct form in Turkish. In Greek, it was formerly called ντονέρ /doˈner/, and now called gyros 'turned'; in Armenian, it is "tarna", literally meaning "to turn".

Tacos al pastor ("shepherd style tacos") is a dish developed in Central Mexico, likely as a result of the adoption of the shawarma spit-grilled meat brought by Lebanese immigrants to Mexico. Having derived from the shawarma, it is also similar to the Turkish döner kebap and the Greek gyro]. While döner kebaps are almost all made from lamb and beef as are gyros, *tacos al pastor* in Mexico are made of pork. In Chile there are "döner", "shawarma" and "gyro" stands. The last one is made of pork.

Döner in Turkey

There are many variations of *döner* in Turkey:

Porsiyon ("the Portion", döner on a slightly heated plate, sometimes with a few grilled peppers or broiled tomatoes on the side)

Pilavüstü ("Ricetop", döner served on a base of pilaf rice that gets tastier as the fat in the meat drips into the rice)

İskender (specialty of Bursa, served in an oblong plate, atop a base of thin pita, complete with a dash of pepper or tomato sauce and boiling fresh butter)

Dürüm, wrapped in a thin lavaş that is sometimes also grilled after being rolled, to make it crispier. It has two main variants in mainland Turkey:

Soslu dürüm or *SSK* (sos, soğan, kaşar; in English: sauce, onion, cheese) (speciality of Ankara, contains İskender kebap sauce, making it juicier)

Kaşarlı dürüm döner (speciality of Istanbul, grated kaşar cheese is put in the wrap which is then toasted to melt the cheese and crisp up the Lavash)

Tombik or *gobit* (literally "the Fatty", doner in a bun-shaped pita, with crispy crust and soft inside, and generally less meat than a dürüm)

Ekmekarası ("in a bread", generally the most filling version, consisting of a whole (or a half) regular Turkish bread filled with doner)

İskender or "Bursa kebabı"
Döner served in a "*tombik pide*" ("fatty" pita) also called in (Turkish: *gobit*).

Regional variations

Caucasus, Middle East and Asia

Afghanistan

In Afghanistan, it is called shawarma. Döner is popular in Afghanistan and it is sometimes referred to as "Turkish kebab" or ("kababe Torki", Persian/Pashto: کباب ترکی), usually served with a variety of vegetables and a special yogurt sauce called "mast."

Armenia

In Armenia *Ġarsi khorovats*, *šaurma* or in the Armenian diaspora, "Tarna" (literally, "it turns"); it is usually lamb, pork or chicken on a vertical rotisserie, sliced and wrapped in Lavash, served with tahini, yogurt or garlic sauce and with a side dish of pickled vegetables or *tourshi*.

Azerbaijan

In Azerbaijan, doner is called Shaurma (Aze: Şaurma) or Döner (Aze: Dönər). *Şaurma* is made with chicken and always include garlic sauce, whereas *döner* can be made with either chicken or beef, and does not include garlic sauce. Both can be served in bread, lavash or in plate. Döner also can be served in tandoor bread. The most popular variety is Turkish döner.

Bangladesh

In Bangladesh *shawarma* along with

döner kebab is becoming more popular mainly as a fast-food item in Dhaka and to a lesser extent in Chittagong. Initially, fast food shops like Shawarma House and Arabian Fast Food added shawarma in their menu. These days, however, they are becoming more common in many fast food shops and restaurants.

China
Doner is widespread in Western China, especially among Uyghurs, owing to the common Turkish culture.

Georgia
Doner is a popular fast food in Georgia.

Iran
Doner is popular in Iran and it is known as "Turkish kebab" or ("kabab Torki", Persian: کباب ترکی), Some times it is called "kabob Estanboli" (Kebab from Istanbul).

Kazakhstan
In Kazakhstan, doner has become popular since declaration of independence when Turkish business in Kazakhstan started to develop rapidly. Now doner is one of the most favorite types of fastfood in Kazakhstan, especially in Almaty.

Japan

A döner location in Ueno, Tokyo.

In Japan, doner kebabs are starting to appear, mostly in Tokyo, where they are predominantly sold from parked vans. Doner kebabs have been adjusted to suit Japanese tastes; the salad is usually omitted in favour of shredded cabbage, and the sauce is composed primarily of mayonnaise.

Mongolia
Doner kebab is only available in the capital Ulaanbaatar through a fast food chain "Cola and Kebab".

Pakistan
In Pakistan, the doner kebab is referred to by its Arabic name, shawarma. Locals usually prefer to eat Shawarma with fizzy drinks. It is available in all major cities like Karachi, Lahore, Faisalabad, Islamabad, Peshawar, Multan and Quetta.

South Korea
Doner kebab is available throughout much of Seoul, particularly in the foreigner-dominated neighborhood of Itaewon. There are two main varieties: the first, sold from street carts, is modified to suit Korean tastes, with chicken rather than lamb, shredded white cabbage, and honey mustard; the second is offered at permanent takeaways such as Ankara Picnic, Mr. Kebab and Sultan Kebab, and features a lamb option along with more traditional sauces.

Taiwan
Doner kebab is known as Shawarma(沙威瑪) in Taiwan. It is popular among night markets and streets throughout Taiwan and usually made from chicken and is served on leavened buns with julienned cabbage, slice of tomato, sliced onions, ketchup, and mayonnaise.

Thailand
There is at least one doner kebab shop on the island of Koh Samui. There are many kebab shops around the Nana area on Sukhumvit Road in Bangkok, and in Pattaya on Walking Street.

Vietnam
Doner kebab is increasingly becoming popular in Vietnam among the locals. Throughout Hanoi and Ho Chi Minh City many doner kebab stalls can be found, contributing to the local street food variety. Bánh mi doner kebab, the Vietnamese version of the doner kebab, has some fundamental differences with the original doner kebab. First of all, pork is used instead of beef and lamb. Second, the meat is served in a Vietnamese baguette, which is widely available in Vietnam. Thirdly, the meat is topped with sour vegetables and chili sauce. On contrary with many other countries in Asia, the doner kebab in Vietnam has been localized and is primarily consumed by the locals, while in other countries in the Far East kebabs are primarily sold to expats, tourists and the middle class, and the original recipe is used.

Europe

Albania
In Albania, doner kebabs are usually called "sufllaqe" and sold at fast food stores. In southern parts of the country, they are called "gjiro". They are made with either pork or chicken, lettuce, tomatoes, mayonnaise, French fries, ketchup, and/or mustard, etc. In general, a normal gjiro in Southern Albania is made with tomatoes, onions, French fries, ketchup, mustard and "salce kosi" (yogurt sauce). In the capital (Tirana) they are made with meat wrapped in freshly made pitta with thick yoghurt and cucumber sauce. Another variant includes a Russian Salad dressing versus salc kosi or mayonnaise.

Austria

A kebab stand in Wien, Austria

Doner kebab shops can be found in all cities across Austria. Kebabs (rarely referred to as "Döner") outsell burgers or the traditional Würstel (sausage) stands. The range of doner is similar to other German speaking countries, but one is more likely to find a chicken kebab in central Vienna than lamb or beef kebab.

Belgium
Doner kebab restaurants and food stands can be found in almost all cities and smaller towns in Belgium. The va-

riety served is similar to that of Germany and the Netherlands. However, it is not uncommon to see doner served with French fries in Belgium, often stuffed into the bread itself (similar to the German "Kebab mit Pommes"). This is probably done to suit local taste, as fries are still the most common Belgian fast food. Many different sauces are typically offered, including plain mayonnaise, aioli, cocktail sauce, sambal oelek or harissa paste, andalouse sauce, "américaine" sauce and tomato ketchup or curry ketchup. Belgians are renowned for mixing two sauces for maximizing taste effects (e.g., garlic and sambal). Another basic ingredient of the typical Belgian doner kebab is two or three green, spicy, Turkish peppers.

Bulgaria

Doner kebab stands are a common sight in Bulgaria. The Doner kebap or Dyuner (Дюнер) is widely made of chicken meat, and it's wrapped in a flatbread or Turkish wrap. It consist a wide variety of salad choices most commonly used are tomatoes, chopped lettuce, onions, hot peppers, cabbage and cucumbers. Rice and bean salads are offered along the coastline. In recent years the use of French fries has become a popular ingredient. It is served with yoghurt-mayonnaise based garlic sauce, with ketchup or mayonnaise on demand, and hot spices. It's a widely adopted fast food choice, and there are a number of venues that specialize in the Greek, German and Turkish styles of Doner kebabs in the whole country.

Croatia

In growing number of cities in Croatia doners are becoming extremely popular. Called simply, *kebab* (*kebabi* plu.) got a lot of attention over the past few years with number of consumers constantly rising. In bigger cities such as Zagreb, Split, Osijek and Rijeka doner stands can be easily found. Cost of a usual doner kebab in Croatia varies from town to town, although average price is around *20 kuna* (2.75€) with special and extra ingredients such as ketchup, mayonnaise, pepper, salt or different sorts of salad coming free of charge. Common ingredients are: Beef or chicken meat, salad, cabbage, tomatoes, cucumbers, onions, yogurt sauce.

Denmark

In Denmark, doner kebabs are sold under a variety of names depending on the doner salesman's ethnic background. In Copenhagen, doners are usually sold as shawarma, or simply kebab, whereas it is sold as guss in other parts of the country. Doner kebab was first introduced to Denmark in 1981 by Turkish migrant workers, and has since become a staple. The meat would typically be beef, rather than lamb. Doner is typically served with lettuce, tomatoes, sour cream dressing and chili oil either in a pita bread, or as a dürüm. Kebab is also served on pizza along with lettuce and créme fraiche or garlic dressing.

Finland

A plate of doner kebab in Kamppi, Helsinki

In Finland, kebabs have gained a lot of popularity since Turkish immigrants opened restaurants and imported their own traditional food. This popularity is apparent when perusing choices of cuisine, especially in larger cities. Kebabs are generally regarded as fast food, often served in late-night restaurants also serving pizza. However, recently kebab restaurants have begun to appear in shopping malls and in the form of proper high street restaurants as well. There are at least 1122 currently active restaurants that serve kebab foods in Finland. Furthermore, there is on average one kebab restaurant for every 5222 people in mainland Finland. Beef is predominantly used, which also means that it is cheaper and more readily available. Some doners can be a mix of lamb and beef. Unlike in Central Europe, where kebabs are made from whole cuts of meat, practically all available kebab in Finland is made from ground meat. Often restaurants do not prepare the meat themselves, but use processed ready-made pieces instead.

France

Most kebab shops (themselves known simply as kebabs) are generally run by Turkish or North African immigrants in France. The basic kebab consists of either *"pain de maison"* (Turkish soft bread) or *"pain arabe"* (unleavened flatbread) stuffed with grilled lamb shavings, onions and lettuce, with a choice of sauce from sauce blanche (yogurt sauce with garlic and herbs), harissa (spicy red sauce originally from North Africa), ketchup, or several others. Kebabs are usually served with chips, often stuffed into the bread itself. This variation is called *Doner grec* ("Greek kebab"). Other variations include turkey, chicken, veal, beef, and replacing the Turkish bread with pita bread or baguette.

Germany

A version developed to suit German tastes by Turkish immigrants in Berlin has become one of Germany's most popular fast food dishes. Annual sales in Germany amount to 2.5 billion euros. Veal and chicken are widely used instead of lamb, particularly by vendors with large ethnic German customer bases, for whom lamb is traditionally less preferred.

Typically, along with the meat, a salad consisting of chopped lettuce, cabbage, onions, cucumber, and tomatoes is offered, as well as a choice of sauces like hot sauce, herb sauce, garlic sauce, or yogurt sauce. The filling is served in a thick flatbread that is usually toasted or warmed. A German variety of döner presentation is achieved by placing the döner meat and the add-ons on a lahmacun and then rolling the ingredients inside the dough into a tube that is eaten out of a wrapping of usually aluminum foil, sometimes called "*Türkische Pizza*". When plain dough is used instead

Döner, common German style (Berlin)

Döner kebab in a dürüm

of *lahmacun* the rolled fast food is called "dürüm döner" or "döner yufka."

Tarkan Taşyumruk, president of the Association of Turkish Döner Producers in Europe (ATDID), provided information in 2010 that, every day, more than 400 tonnes of döner kebab meat is produced in Germany by around 350 firms. At the same ATDID fair, Taşyumruk stated that 'Annual sales in Germany amount to 2.5 billion euros. That shows we are one of the biggest fast-foods in Germany'. In many cities throughout Germany, "Döner" is at least as popular as hamburgers or sausages, especially with young people.

Germany's large Turkish community is probably the biggest reason for the widespread sale of döner kebap sales there: from the late 60s on, large numbers of Turks were invited to come to Germany as guest workers, to fill a then acute labour shortage caused by the Wirtschaftswunder after the war. Many of these Turkish workers eventually stayed in Germany, some opening small food shops and takeaways which was an excellent option in terms of progressing from some of the more menial jobs.

Greece

In Greece, Doner Kebab is called gyros. The most common form of gyros is prepared with pork, due to its broad availability and low price in Greece. The name comes from Greek γύρος ("turn"), a calque of the Turkish name döner kebap; the dish was formerly called ντονέρ [do'ner] in Greece as well. Today, ντονέρ refers to gyros prepared with lamb or beef and is not common.

Hungary

Doner kebabs are very popular in Hungary since the 1990s but are usually referred to as gyros- even some Turkish restaurants use the Greek term. It is served in two main forms: in a sandwich or on a plate. French fries or pasta are only part of the plate version. The meat is beef, chicken or lamb (the latter is a rarity), and the more popular sandwich version is usually served with lettuce, tomatoes, sliced onion and with some kind of a yoghurt sauce and a mildly hot sauce made of red paprika.

Ireland

In Dublin, increasing numbers of Turkish immigrants have led to growth in the number of late-night kebab eateries, popular with party-goers and evening revellers in the city centre. Doner and other kebabs are often eaten as takeaway food after a night out. Owing to demand for late night food in the city centre, large businesses, such as Abrakebabra, remain open very late. Some businesses apply a surcharge to food purchased later at night.

Italy

Doner is very popular in Italy, especially among Moroccan immigrants and young people, including students and bargoers in many major cities. The most common toppings are cabbage, lettuce, tomato, onions, hot pepper relish, spiced yogurt, tzatziki, and harissa sauce; a kebab with all the said toppings is referred to as a *kebab completo*. Other common toppings include mayonnaise, ketchup, and French fries. It is also possible to get the kebabs without bread in a small foil bowl with all of the toppings over rice. It is referred to as "kebab".

Latvia

Turkebab Restaurant in Riga, Latvia.

Doner kebabs have started to gain popularity in Latvia as well. Turkebab restaurant chain, owned by Turkish immigrants, successfully opened their second restaurant in Riga. Other private kebab restaurants are run by locals, Egyptians, and Turks.

Lithuania

Introduced by Muslim immigrants in the 2000s, doner kebabs exploded in popularity. They are usually sold from small kiosks and carts. Most popular are ones served in lavash bread (Dürüm), though pita bread is also used. The cabbage is the most often used vegetable, along with salad, tomato, bell pepper and cucumber, with a variety of sauces.

Netherlands

Doner kebab is very popular and widely available in the Netherlands. As a snack, it is usually served in or with a pita as a "broodje döner" (doner sandwich) with lettuce, onion, tomato slices and sauces, mainly garlic and sambal.

In the last few years a new form of serving is increasing in popularity. The 'kapsalon', from Rotterdam, is a metal tray filled with French fries with a layer

A Dönerschotel at a snack bar in the Netherlands: sliced "döner-style" grilled veal, French fries, and a simple salad.

of doner (sometimes a layer of sauce) over them, topped by a layer of young cheese. This goes into the oven until the cheese melts. Then a freshly sliced salad is put on top of that. The kapsalon is finished with a large amount of garlic sauce and a bit of sambal. The name kapsalon is the Dutch word for a hairdresser's salon. A hairdresser from Rotterdam working next to a doner stand snack bar wanted to combine the best of both worlds and came up with the idea of the kapsalon. Kapsalon is typically a food mostly served in the Randstad metropolitan area.

The Dutch television programme, Keuringsdienst van Waarde, analyzed doner kebab sandwiches and found out that only one of the analyzed kebabs contained 100% lamb meat, while most consisted of mixes of lamb and beef. Others consisted of 100% beef, chicken, turkey or pork.

Poland
In Poland the kebab bars are spread mostly in major cities, but it is still considered one of the most, if not the most popular fast foods for young people. A very Polish specialty is a fresh cabbage salad with cucumbers, tomatoes and other vegetables, added to the meat in a sandwich. A basic version costs 7–8 zł (€2–€2.5) and includes pita or thick bread, meat with onion, the aforementioned salad and a choice of sauces. It can be super-sized and/or served with extra cheese. Sandwiches are available with hot, medium or mild sauces made of house special ingredients. Kebab shops also serve complete meals, vegetarian dishes and ayran. Undoubtedly Warsaw is the capital of Polish kebab, with shops run by Turkish emigrants, and serving Arab specialties and hookah pipes apart from the sandwiches. As they run 23 hours a day, every day of the week, they are often visited by partying youth and policemen.

Kebabs were rarely seen in Poland before the downfall of the Iron Curtain in 1989. A similar Greek-fashioned dish gyros could have been occasionally encountered in that era. One possible origin of the recent popularity of kebab in Poland is post-communist Berlin, with local Turkish immigrants inspired by their fellow natives in the other country.

Portugal
In Portugal kebabs are fairly recent. The most common kebab in Portugal is served in thick pita bread. Common ingredients are salad, onion, tomato, fresh cheese and sauce.

Romania

A kebab restaurant in Bucharest

In Romania, doner kebab and its locally widespread variant, the shaworma, have gained much popularity since 1990, so much so that shaworma has become a fast food staple.

Russia
In Russia doner kebab is usually called shaurma (Central Russia) or shawerma (North-West). It is widespread and is usually made in booths or small cafes. There are two basic types: in pitah (a type of bun) or in lavash (thin round cake, in which it is packed). Types of meat from which it is usually made are chicken and pork. Other meat is seldom used for doner. Typical recipe includes meat, cabbage and/or carrot salad, cucumbers and/or tomatoes and two types of sauces: ketchup and a type of spicy youghurt. Doner production in Russia is usually subject of a small business, which is most usual owned by Caucasus or Middle Asia migrants. There is especially large number of such booths near railway stations and markets. Shaurma is a very popular meal for students and people who have to eat "on the go" due to its relatively low price. It depends on the region, in big cities it is usually a little higher, but in average one portion costs 2-3 Euro in booths and some higher in cafes. Shaurma can be served also in a plate apart from the bun and can be accompanied with French fries and vegetable salad. Most often it is consumed with light beer.

Slovenia
In Slovenian cities you can find many doner kebab stands that were spread across the country by immigrants from Kosovo and Bosnia. Some places also serve so called jufka kebab (dürüm). Common ingredients are: Beef or chicken meat (and mixed), salad, cabbage, tomatoes, cucumbers, onions, yogurt sauce.

Spain

Doner kebab with cheese and french fries in Madrid, Spain

In Spain, doner kebabs are common, especially in Andalucía. It is often called chawarma, and kebab restaurants can be found in Granada every 100 metres, with one very famous one in Cordoba being found near the old Mosque. The kebabs are served with chicken or veal and with salad, tomatoes, onions, olives, peppers, white sauce, ketchup, or salsa picante (hot sauce). Falafel, French fries, and fried eggs are typical additions to a kebab. The average price in Andalucía for a kebab is €3.40 to €4.

The kebab came to Spain in the mid-2000s. Since then, kebab restaurants have become common throughout the entire country.

Sweden

In Sweden, *Kebab med bröd* (Kebab with bread) can be found in the local pizzeria or specialised kebab/falafel shop. The word "kebab" is normally associated with doner kebab made from pork or beef, more uncommonly chicken. It is a popular fast-food alternative to the more traditional hot dogs and hamburgers, and is a common late-night post-drinking meal, with kebab/falafel restaurants often being open late into the night. Other commonly occurring kebab variants are *kebabrulle* ("kebab roll", a roll of flat bread filled with kebab meat, salad, tomatoes, kebab sauce and sometimes pepperoni or sliced pickles), and *kebabtallrik* ("kebab platter", a plate of doner meat and salad with either French fries, rice, or mashed potatoes). The most common sauce options are "hot", "mild", "garlic" or "mixed", the latter being a mixture of all three. Most pizzerias sell Kebab Pizza, a pizza with doner meat and the aforementioned sauces as a topping, now the most popular pizza in Sweden.

Switzerland

Doner can be found in cities across Switzerland. The doner vendors have popularised the grammatically incorrect way of asking if the customer wants the doner "mit scharf" (i.e. "with hot"). This ubiquitous error originates from a literal translation of the Turkish expression "acılı" and has entered the general usage of German in Austria, Switzerland, and Germany.

United Kingdom

Introduced by Turkish immigrants, the

Döner kebab served in a partitioned tray.

doner kebab with salad and sauce is a very popular dish in the United Kingdom, especially after a night out. The typical kebab shop in the UK will offer hot chilli sauce and garlic yoghurt-style sauce, and in different regions may also offer lemon juice, mayonnaise, or a mint sauce similar to raita. Doner kebabs are most commonly served in a pitta bread in the UK, but are sometimes also wrapped in other types of bread - naan bread or roti, for example. Doner meat is also sometimes served as a pizza topping. The UK doner kebab often uses a different mixture of spices. More UK influenced variation of the dish exist like eating the doner kebab meat with a side of chips. In most kebab shops a chicken doner kebab is served as well, being cooked in the same fashion next to the lamb doner. Lamb doner is most popular and chicken doner tends to be slightly more expensive.

The kebab has become an icon of urban food culture in the United Kingdom, with doner kebabs often purchased and consumed following a night of heavy drinking, and rarely eaten earlier in the day.

The Americas

Brazil

Doner kebab is one of the most popular fast-food dishes on São Paulo streets. It is usually served as a sandwich, and it is called "Churrasco Grego", which means "Greek Barbecue", or much less frequently *Churrasco Turco* (Turkish Steak). It is not associated with the kebab/gyro in fashion districts. It is served in Porto Alegre, Foz do Iguaçu where it is sold as Arabic fast-food.

Canada

A variation known as "donair" was introduced in Halifax, Nova Scotia, Canada in the early 1970s. Peter Gamoulakos immigrated to Canada in 1959. When he failed in his attempt to sell traditional döner, Gamoulakos adapted the dish to local tastes. He substituted beef for lamb and created a sweet sauce. He claimed to invent the donair in 1972 and it debuted at King of Donair's Quinpool Road location in 1973, however this cannot be confirmed.

A King of Donair outlet in Halifax at Pizza Corner.

Donair has gained popularity throughout the Atlantic provinces of Canada, and is also available in some other areas of the country. Halifax donair meat is sliced from a loaf cooked on a vertical spit, made from a combination of ground beef, flour or bread crumbs, and various spices. The sauce is distinctively sweet compared to doner kebabs, being made from evaporated milk, sugar, vinegar, and garlic. The meat and sauce are served rolled in a flatbread with diced tomato and diced onion. While not included on "original" donairs, some restaurants add lettuce and/or cheese as well.

Many Atlantic Canadian restaurants offer a donair pizza featuring all of the donair ingredients served on a pizza crust. In Atlantic Canada one can also find donair meat used in offerings such as donair sausage, donair egg rolls (an egg roll casing stuffed with donair meat), donair pogos (donair meat on a stick, battered and deep-fried, similar to a corn dog), donair calzones/panzerottis, and in donair poutine.

In the summer of 2008, after numerous cases of E. coli related food poisoning due to the consumption of undercooked donair meat in Alberta, the federal government came out with a set of guidelines for the preparation of donairs. The principal guideline is that the meat should be cooked at least twice: once on the spit, and then grilled as the donair is being prepared.

Cayman Islands

Doner kebab is available in Georgetown, Grand Cayman with a Caribbean flair. The meat is cooked on the traditional vertical spit, and the kebab is served on flat bread with a variety of sauces, including garlic and mango pepper sauce.

Mexico

Tacos al pastor being cut from the spit

A similar dish is served in Mexico known as tacos al pastor or "tacos de trompo". The cooking is different from that of the kebab. The meat is cooked and then sliced into a corn tortilla. They can be found all over Mexico, especially in street corners. In Puebla, this was introduced by the numerous Middle-Eastern immigrants, mostly from Lebanon and Syria, but also Turkey and Iraq, in the early 1920s.

A similar dish is called *Tacos Árabes*, which originated in Puebla in the 1930s from Lebanese-Mexican cuisine. Tacos Árabes use shawarma-style meat carved from a spit, but are served in a pita bread called *pan arabe*.

United States

In the United States, doner kebab is not widely known, except in some larger cities with a strong Mideastern immigrant community, e.g., Boston, St. Louis, Detroit, New York, Chicago, Seattle, San Diego, and Los Angeles. In contrast, gyros, considered Greek food, are popular across the U.S., and frequently are found at mobile stands as fair food as well as at Greek- and Italian-style pizza and sandwich shops.

Oceania

Australia

A kebab snack-pack in Sydney, Australia

In Australia, doner and other kebabs are very popular due to immigration from Greece, Turkey, the former Yugoslavia and Lebanon. Many consider them to be a healthier alternative to traditional fast food. In Australian shops or stalls, beef, lamb and chicken doners can be found in all major cities where many suburbs have take-away shops that offer them. They are optionally served with cheese and a salad consisting of lettuce, tomato, onion, and tabouli on either pita (also known in some areas as Lebanese bread) or using thicker but still quite flat Turkish breads. These are sliced in half with the filling placed in between the slices, rather than wrapped, as is common with pita/pide breads.

The most commonly used sauces are tomato sauce, barbecue sauce, hummus (made with chickpeas), yoghurt and garlic sauce, and chili or sweet chilli sauce. Doner kebabs in Sydney and Melbourne can be served with all the ingredients placed onto or next to the pita bread on a plate, or more commonly, with the ingredients rolled into the pita bread in the form of a "wrap". The wrapped version can be toasted in a sandwich press, which has the effect of melting any cheese, heating the meat and baking the bread so that it becomes crisp.

In Canberra, the bread with filling is passed underneath a grill for a minute. The sandwich is then wrapped in paper to stop the filling from falling out and usually placed in a foil/paper sleeve. This variety is also available in New Zealand. In Brisbane, kebabs are influenced by the Turkish variation. They are invariably served in a pita wrap and toasted in a sandwich press for about a minute before being inserted into a foil or paper sleeve. The main meats available are chicken or lamb. Shops or vans selling kebabs are colloquially referred to as "Kebaberies" and "Kebabavans" in some parts of Australia. Kebab meat can also be found as a pizza topping in the western suburbs of Sydney and Melbourne, as a "beef pizza" or "Turkish pizza".

The "late night kebab" has become an icon of urban food culture in Australia, with kebabs often purchased and consumed following a night of drinking. Kebabs are considered suitable following consumption of alcohol due their high content of lipids (fats) which aids in metabolism of alcohol. Another variation found commonly in the western suburbs of Sydney and Melbourne is the "snack pack" or "meat box". This is a take-away box with a layer of chips, kebab meat and sauce on top. It is also common to add lettuce, onion, tomato or cheese on top.

The "dodgy kebab", often blamed for food poisoning has become more rare. Since NSW food safety best practice recommended a second cooking of kebab meat. Most stores have adopted this measure and it is now common practice in Australia. Second cooking requires that meat sliced from the doner is cooked on the hotplate/grill to 60 °C just before serving. Previously, "Dodgy kebab" meat was often sliced from the doner, including some not yet fully heated/cooked meat, at the time of ordering or meat that had been sliced and sat waiting at the bottom of the doner for indiscernible length of time.

Health concerns

Doner kebab is popular in many countries in the form of fast food, often as an end to a night out when preceded by the consumption of an excess of alcohol. Health concerns surrounding doner kebab in the UK and Western Europe, including the hygiene involved in overnight storage and re-heating of partially cooked meat, unacceptable salt and fat levels, and improper labeling of meat used (e.g., illicit addition of pork), are repeatedly reported in the European media. However, Simon Langley-Evans, a professor of human nutrition at Nottingham University states that doner could be a healthier choice of fast food, as it brings together meat, wholemeal bread and vegetables.

Source http://en.wikipedia.org/wiki/Doner_kebab

Enchilada

Enchiladas with mole sauce, served with refried beans and Spanish rice

Origin

| Place of origin | Mexico |

Details

| Main ingredient(s) | Tortillas, chili pepper sauce, meat |

An **enchilada** (pron.: /ˌɛntʃɪˈlɑːdə/, Spanish: [entʃiˈlaða]) is a corn tortilla rolled around a filling and covered with a chili pepper sauce. Enchiladas can be filled with a variety of ingredients, including meat, cheese, beans, potatoes, vegetables, seafood or combinations.

Etymology

The Real Academia Española defines the word *enchilada*, as used in Mexico, as a rolled maize tortilla stuffed with meat and covered with a tomato and chile sauce. *Enchilada* is the past participle of Spanish *enchilar*, "to add chile pepper to", literally to "season (or decorate) with chile."

History

Enchiladas originated in Mexico, where the practice of rolling tortillas around other food dates back at least to Mayan times. The people living in the lake region of the Valley of Mexico traditionally ate corn tortillas folded or rolled around small fish. Writing at the time of the Spanish conquistadors, Bernal Díaz del Castillo documented a feast enjoyed by Europeans hosted by Hernán Cortés in Coyoacán, which included foods served in corn tortillas. (Note that the native Nahuatl name for the flat corn bread used was *tlaxcalli*; the Spanish give it the name *tortilla*.) The Nahuatl word for enchilda is *chīllapītzalli* [tʃiːlːapiːˈtsalːi] which is formed of the Nahuatl word for "chili", *chīlli* [ˈtʃiːlːi] and the Nahuatl word for "flute", *tlapītzalli* [tɬapiːˈtsalːi]. In the 19th century, as Mexican cuisine was being memorialized, enchiladas were mentioned in the first Mexican cookbook, *El cocinero mexicano* ("The Mexican Chef"), published in 1831, and in Mariano Galvan Rivera's *Diccionario de Cocina*, published in 1845. An early mention, in English, is a 1914 recipe found in *California Mexican-Spanish Cookbook*, by Bertha Haffner Ginger.

Varieties

In their original form as Mexican street food, enchiladas were simply corn tortillas dipped in chili sauce and eaten without fillings. They now have taken many varieties, which are distinguished primarily by their sauces, fillings and, in one instance, by their form. Various adjectives may be used to describe the recipe content or origin, e.g. *enchilada tapatia* would be a recipe from Jalisco.

Varieties include:

Enchiladas con chile colorado (with red chile) are made with traditional red enchilada sauce, composed of dried red chili peppers soaked and ground into a sauce with other seasonings. However, red enchilada sauce may also be tomato-based with red chilis added.

Enchiladas con mole, instead of chili sauce, are served with *mole*, and are also known as *enmoladas*.

Enchiladas placera are Michoacán plaza-style, made with vegetables and poultry.

Enchiladas poblanas are soft corn tortillas filled with chicken and poblano peppers, topped with oaxaca cheese.

Enchiladas potosinas originate from San Luis Potosi, Mexico and are made with cheese-filled, chili-spiced masa.

Enchiladas San Miguel are San Miguel de Allende-style enchiladas flavored with guajillo chilies by searing the flavor into the tortillas in a frying pan.

Enchiladas suizas (Swiss-style) are topped with a white, milk or cream-based sauce, such as *béchamel*. This appellation is derived from Swiss immigrants to Mexico who established dairies to produce cream and cheese.

Enchiladas verdes (green enchiladas) are made with green enchilada sauce composed of tomatillos and green chilis.

Enfrijoladas are topped with refried beans rather than chili sauce; their name come from *frijol*, meaning "bean".

Entomatadas are made with tomato sauce instead of chile sauce.

Gravy-style enchiladas are the dominant variety found throughout South and Central Texas. These have a gravy-like chili sauce over either cheese-filled or beef-filled corn tortillas, and are topped with a layer of cheese.

Enchiladas montadas, stacked enchiladas, are a New Mexico variation in which corn tortillas are fried flat until softened but not tough, then stacked with red or green sauce, chopped onion and shredded cheese between the layers and on top of the stack. Ground beef or chicken can be added to the filling, but meat is not traditional. The stack is often topped (*montada*) with a fried egg. Shredded lettuce and sliced black olives may be added as a garnish.

Fillings, toppings and garnishes

Fillings include meat, such as chicken, beef or pork, seafood, cheese, potatoes, vegetables, and any combination of these. Enchiladas are commonly topped or garnished with cheese, sour cream, lettuce, olives, chopped onions, chili peppers, salsa, or fresh cilantro.

Enchilada variations

Three enchiladas from Cartago, Costa Rica
Homestyle Honduran enchiladas

Enchiladas suizas

Costa Rican enchilada

In Costa Rica, the enchilada is a common, small, spicy pastry made with puff pastry and filled with diced potatoes spiced with a common variation of tabasco sauce or other similar sauces. It is typically eaten in the afternoons in the coffee break, and available in almost every bakery in the country. Other variations include fillings made of spicy chicken or minced meat.

Honduran enchilada

In Honduras, enchiladas look and taste very different from those in Mexico; they are not corn tortillas rolled around a filling, but instead are flat, fried, corn tortillas topped with ground beef, salad toppings (usually consisting of cabbage and tomato slices), a tomato sauce (often ketchup blended with butter and other spices such as cumin), and crumbled or shredded cheese. They look and taste much like what many people call a tostada.

Nicaraguan enchilada

In Nicaragua, enchiladas are different from the other ones in Central America and resemble those in Mexico; they are corn tortillas filled with a mixture of ground beef and rice with chilli, they are then folded and covered in egg batter and deep fried. It is commonly served with a cabbage and tomato salad (either pickled salad or in cream and tomato sauce). The Nicaraguan enchilada resembles the Empanada of other countries.

Guatemalan enchilada

In Guatemala, enchiladas look much like Honduran enchiladas but the recipe is different. Usually starts with a leaf of fresh lettuce, next a layer of picado de carne, which includes a meat (ground beef, shredded chicken, or pork) and diced vegetables (carrot, potato, onion, celery, green bean, peas, red bell pepper, garlic, bay leaf, a you can season with a little salt and black pepper) next is the curtido layer which includes more vegetables (cabbage, beets, onions, and carrots) next is about two or three pieces of sliced hard boiled egg, next layer is thin sliced white onion, next layer is a drizzle of red (not spicy) salsa, next topped with either queso seco or queso fresco and lastly topped with cilantro.

Source http://en.wikipedia.org/wiki/Enchilada

Esquites

Esquites being fried in butter

Esquites *(or ezquites) (or troles or trolelotes in Northern Mexico)* is a Mexican snack or antojito. Shops and market stalls selling corn also tend to sell Esquites. Festival and fair stalls may sell them too. The word esquites comes from the Nahuatl word *ízquitl*, which means "toasted corn".

In one recipe, the grains of corn are first boiled in salted water. Then they are sauteed in butter with onions, chopped pequin chiles, epazote and salt. It is served hot, in small cups and topped with varying combinations of lime juice, chile powder or hot sauce, salt and mayonnaise.

Source http://en.wikipedia.org/wiki/Esquites

Falafel

Falafel balls

Origin

Region or state	Believed to have originated in Egypt before spreading north to the Levant

Details

Course	Street food
Serving temperature	Hot
Main ingredient(s)	Fava beans or chickpeas

Falafel (/fəˈlɑːfəl/; Arabic: فلافل, [falaːfɪl] (listen)) is a deep-fried ball or patty made from ground chickpeas, fava beans, or both. Falafel is a traditional Arab food, usually served in a pita, which acts as a pocket, or wrapped in a flatbread known as lafa; "falafel" also frequently refers to a wrapped sandwich that is prepared in this way. The falafel balls are topped with salads, pickled vegetables, hot sauce, and drizzled with tahini-based sauces. Falafel balls may also be eaten alone as a snack or served as part of a meze.

Generally accepted to have first been made in Egypt, falafel has become a dish eaten throughout the Middle East. The Copts of Egypt claim to have first made the dish as a replacement for meat during Lent. The fritters are now found around the world as a replacement for meat and as a form of street food.

Etymology

The word *falafel* can refer to the fritters themselves or to sandwiches filled with them. Some sources trace the name to the Arabic word *falāfil* (فلافل), the plural of *filfil* (فلفل), meaning "pepper", from Persian *pilpil* (پلپل), probably from the Sanskrit word *pippalī* (पिप्पली), meaning "long pepper". A Coptic origin has recently been proposed from *pha la phel* (Φα Λα Φελ), meaning "of many beans". However, the locus of the word's use is in the Levant rather than Egypt (where falafel are generally known as *ṭaʿmiyya* (طعمية), and in fact an etymology from internal Levantine sources is possible. Levantine colloquial Arabic *falāfil* is grammatically a mass noun that must be counted with the word *ḥubba* (حبة), "grain, piece" (as the English word bread must be counted with *loaf* or *slice*). It may represent a frozen plural of an earlier unattested *filfal*, from Aramaic *pilpāl*, "small round thing, peppercorn," derived from *palpēl*, "to be round, roll". Thus in origin, falafel would be "rollers, little balls." In its vocabulary, grammar, and phonology, the colloquial Arabic of the Levant reflects the deep influence of Aramaic, the language from which the population of the Levant shifted after the Muslim conquest of Syria in 634–638. In this way, an Aramaic origin for the colloquial term is not problematic, although the late date of attestation of the word in Arabic renders it somewhat tentative—a problem from which the proposed Coptic etymology, also invoking an unattested Coptic phrase, suffers from in equal measure. (In connection with the proposed origin of falafel in Lenten practices of the Copts, it should be remembered that since the days of the Apostles, the Levant to this day has a very large Aramaic-speaking, and later Arabic-speaking, Christian population.) The Arabic word *falāfil* has been borrowed into many other languages and spread around the rest of the world as the general name for this food. In English, it is first attested in 1941.

Falafel is known as *taʿamiya* (Egyptian Arabic: طعمية *taʿmiyya*, IPA: [tˤɑʕˈmejjɑ]) in Egypt, with the exception of Alexandria. The word is derived from a diminutive form of the Arabic word *ṭaʿām* (طعام, "food"); the particular form indicates "a unit" of the given root in this case Ṭ-ʿ-M (ط ع م, having to do with taste and food), thus meaning "a little piece of food" or "small tasty thing".

History

The origin of falafel is unknown and controversial. A common theory is that the dish originated in Egypt, possibly eaten by Copts as a replacement for meat during Lent. As Alexandria is a port city, it was possible to export the dish and name to other areas in the Middle East. The dish later migrated northwards to the Levant, where chickpeas replaced the fava. It has also been theorized to a lesser extent that falafel originated during Egypt's Pharaonic Period or in the Indian subcontinent.

Falafel sandwich

Middle East

Falafel grew to become a common form of street food or fast food in the Middle East. The croquettes are regularly eaten as part of meze. During Ramadan, falafel balls are sometimes eaten as part of the *iftar*, the meal that breaks the daily fast after sunset. Falafel became so popular that McDonald's now serves a "McFalafel" in some countries. It is still popular with the Copts, who cook large volumes during religious holidays. Debates over the origin of falafel have sometimes devolved into political discussions about the relationship between Arabs and Israelis. In modern times, falafel has been considered a national dish of Egypt, Palestine, and of Israel. Resentment exists amongst many Palestinians for what they see as the appropriation of their dish by Israelis. Additionally, the Lebanese Industrialists' Association has raised assertions of copyright infringement against Israel concerning falafel.

Falafel plays an iconic role in Israeli cuisine and is wildly considered to be the national dish of the country. While falafel is not a specifically Jewish dish, it was eaten by Mizrahi Jews in their countries of origin. Later, it was adopted by early Jewish immigrants to Palestine. Due to its being entirely plant based, it is considered parve under Jewish dietary laws and gained acceptance with Jews because it could be eaten with meat or dairy meals.

North America
In North America, prior to the 1970s, falafel was found only in Middle Eastern and Jewish neighborhoods and restaurants, and also eaten by vegans, who used it as a meat analogue. Today, the dish is a common and popular street food in many cities throughout North America.

Vegetarianism
Falafel has become popular among vegetarians and with those in the vegan movement, where it is celebrated as an alternative to meat-laden street foods, and is now sold in packaged mixes in health-food stores. While traditionally thought of as being used to make veggie burgers, its use has expanded as more and more people have adopted it as a source of protein. A versatile ingredient, it has allowed for the reformulating of recipes for meatloaf, sloppy joes and spaghetti and meatballs into vegetarian dishes.

Today, falafel is eaten all over the world.

Preparation and variations
Falafel is made from fava beans or chickpeas, or a combination of the two. The use of chickpeas is predominant in most Middle Eastern countries. The dish is usually made with chickpeas in Syria, Jordan, Lebanon, Israel and Palestine. This version is the most popular in the West. The Egyptian variety uses fava beans.

When chickpeas are used, they are not cooked prior to use (cooking the chickpeas will cause the falafel to fall

A man using an *aleb falafel* while frying falafel

apart, requiring adding some flour to use as a binder). Instead they are soaked (sometimes with baking soda) overnight, then ground together with various ingredients such as parsley, scallions, and garlic. Spices such as cumin and coriander are often added to the beans for added flavor. Fava beans must be cooked, for medical reasons. The mixture is shaped into balls or patties. This can be done by hand or with a tool called an *aleb falafel* (falafel mould). The mixture is usually deep fried, or it can be oven baked.

When not served alone, falafel is often served with unleavened bread when it is wrapped within lafa or stuffed in a hollow pita. Tomatoes, lettuce, cucumbers, and other garnishes can be added. Falafel is commonly accompanied by tahini.

Falafel is typically ball-shaped, but is sometimes made in other shapes, particularly donut-shaped. The inside of falafel may be green (from green herbs such as parsley or green onion), or tan.

Nutrition

Nutritional value per 100 g (3.5 oz)

Energy	1,393 kJ (333 kcal)
Carbohydrates	31.84 g
Fat	17.80 g
Protein	13.31 g
Water	34.62 g
Vitamin A	13 IU
Thiamine (vit. B)	0.146 mg (13%)
Riboflavin (vit. B)	0.166 mg (14%)
Niacin (vit. B)	1.044 mg (7%)
Pantothenic acid (B)	0.292 mg (6%)
Vitamin B	0.125 mg (10%)
Folate (vit. B)	78 µg (20%)
Vitamin B	0.00 µg (0%)
Calcium	54 mg (5%)
Iron	3.42 mg (26%)
Magnesium	82 mg (23%)
Manganese	0.691 mg (33%)
Phosphorus	192 mg (27%)
Potassium	585 mg (12%)
Sodium	294 mg (20%)
Zinc	1.50 mg (16%)

Percentages are relative to US recommendations for adults.

Source: USDA Nutrient Database

When made with chickpeas, falafel is high in protein, complex carbohydrates, and fiber. Chickpeas are also low in fat and salt and contain no cholesterol. Key nutrients are calcium, iron, magnesium, phosphorus, potassium, zinc, copper, manganese, Vitamin C, thiamine, pantothenic acid, Vitamin B, and folate. Phytochemicals include beta-carotene. Falafel is high in soluble fiber, which has been shown to be effective in lowering blood cholesterol.

Falafel can be baked to reduce the high fat content associated with frying. Although baking alters the texture and flavour, it is a preparation technique often recommended to people suffering from health problems like diabetes.

World records

Largest falafel ball
The current record, 74.75 kg (164.4 lb), was set on 28 July 2012 in Amman, Jordan. The previous record was 23.94 kg (52.8 lb), 1.17 m in circumference and 0.3 m in height, set at the Santa Clarita Valley Jewish Food and Cultural Festival (USA), at the College of the Canyons in Valencia, California, USA, on 15 May 2011.

Largest serving of falafel
The record, 5,173 kg (11,404 lb 8 oz), was set by Chef Ramzi Choueiri and the students of Al-Kafaat University (Lebanon) in Beirut on 9 May 2010.
Source http://en.wikipedia.org/wiki/Falafel

Farinata

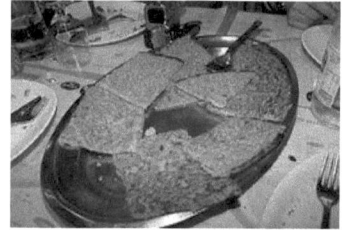

Origin	
Alternative name(s)	Socca, cecina
Place of origin	Italy
Region or state	Genoa
Details	
Type	Pancake
Main ingredient(s)	Chickpea flour, water, olive oil

Farinata, **socca**, or **cecina** is a sort of thin, unleavened pancake or crêpe of chickpea flour originating in Genoa and later a typical food of the Ligurian Sea coast, from Nice to Pisa.

Names

In standard Italian, the dish is called "farinata" 'made of flour', in Genoese dialect **fainâ**. In Nice and the Côte d'Azur, it is called "socca", and in Tuscany, "cecina" 'made of chickpeas'. In Argentina and Uruguay it is known as fainá or faina.

Cooking method

It is made by stirring chickpea flour into a mixture of water and olive oil to form a loose batter, and baking it in the open oven. A tin-plated copper baking-pan is used. *Farinata* may be seasoned with fresh rosemary, pepper and sea salt. Traditionally farinata is cut into irregularly shaped triangular slices, and enjoyed (with no toppings) on small plates with optional black pepper. Elsewhere in Italy (traditionally in Tuscany, where it is called *cecina* (from the Italian word for chickpea, *ceci*), it is served stuffed into small focaccia (mainly in Pisa) or between two slices of bread, as it is traditional in Livorno. It is sold in pizzerias and bakeries.

Italian variations

On the Tuscan coast, south of Liguria, especially in the province of Pisa, Livorno, Lucca, Massa Carrara *cecina* or, in Livorno, *Torta (di ceci)* (Chickpea pie) is baked (with no rosemary used for toppings).

In Sassari, Sardinia, due to the historical ties with Genoa, la **fainé genovese** (*genoese fainé*), is a typical dish.

In Savona province (near Genoa), a version of farinata called *farinata bianca* (white farinata) is used. It is made with wheat flour instead of chickpeas flour.

The name Panissa or Paniscia in Genoese indicates a solidified polenta-like paste, made with the same ingredients as farinata, which can then be cut into strips to be fried, assuming the name *panissette*.

In Genoa, variants of the farinata include sometimes onions or artichokes, but the most famous derivative recipe is the *fainâ co i gianchetti* (farinata with whitebait), at times hard to find due to fishing regulations, but traditionally seen as the quintessential fainâ.

France

Socca of Nice also known as *La Cade* in Toulon

Socca is a specialty of southeastern French cuisine, particularly in and around the city of Nice. Its primary ingredients are chickpea flour and olive oil. After being formed into a flat cake and baked in an oven, often on a cast iron pan more than a meter in diameter, the socca is seasoned generously with black pepper and eaten while hot with

Socca, just coming out of the oven, in the old town of Nice, on the French Riviera

Slices of socca at a Nice market

the fingers.

Beyond the Ligurian Sea

In Algeria, **karantita** is a similar dish which is very popular. It is served hot and dressed with cumin and harissa.

In Argentina and Uruguay (where many thousands of Ligurian people emigrated between the 19th and the 20th centuries) farinata is known as **fainá**, similar to the original Genoese name *fainâ*. It is often eaten on top of pizza (*a caballo*).

In Uruguay, olive oil is very seldom or never used to make fainá. It is very expensive and not used much in Uruguayan cooking, so more common types of oil such as sunflower, canola, corn, and soybean oils are used. For people accustomed to olive oil fainá, the taste can be quite different.

In Gibraltar, where a significant portion of its population is of Genoese origin, it is known as **calentita** when it is baked or **panissa** when it is fried.

They are typically eaten plain, without any toppings. These are considered to be Gibraltar's national dishes.

In India, the dal (the word for pulses) "chila" (pronounced "cheela") or besan (the word for chickpea flour) "puda" (pronounced "poora"), depending on the region, is a similar dish made by cooking chickpea (or another pulse) flour and water on an oiled skillet. Vegetables such as onions, green chillies, cabbage and herbs and spices such as coriander are also added in certain versions of the preparation.

Source http://en.wikipedia.org/wiki/Farinata

Fish ball

Fish ball

Fishball closeup

Traditional Chinese	魚蛋 or 魚旦
Simplified Chinese	鱼蛋 or 鱼旦
Literal meaning	fish egg
Alternative Chinese name	
Traditional Chinese	魚丸
Simplified Chinese	鱼丸
Literal meaning	fish ball

Fish balls are a common food in southern China and overseas Chinese communities made from surimi (魚漿, *yújiāng*). They are also common in Scandinavia, where they are usually made from cod or haddock.

Terminology

The term 魚蛋 (literally "fish eggs") is used at street hawker stalls and *dai pai dong* in Hong Kong, while 魚丸 (*yú wán*) and 魚圓 (*yú yuán*) are more commonly used in Singapore and Malaysia.

Production

Fish balls made in Scandinavia are similar to meatballs, only with fish instead of pork or beef.

Meatballs made in Asia differ significantly in texture from their European counterparts. Instead of grinding and forming meats, meat used for making meatballs is pounded, which lends a smooth texture to the meatballs. This is also often the case for fillings in steamed dishes. Pounding, unlike grinding, uncoils and stretches previously wound and tangled protein strands in meat.

Regional variations

Steamed rice rolls with fish balls

Fish balls and *kwek kwek* (hard-boiled quail eggs fried in batter) in the Philippines

Faroe Islands

In Faroe Islands, fish balls are called *knettir* and made with ground fish and

Fish balls with vermicelli sold in Bukit Batok, Singapore

Swedish *fiskbullar*, here served with dill sauce and pasta

Kaeng khiao wan luk chin pla: Green curry with fish balls

fat.

Fuzhou

In the Fuzhou area, "Fuzhou fish ball" (福州鱼丸) is made from fish and has minced pork filling within the fish ball.

Hong Kong

Yellow Fish Ball (Street Food)

There are two kinds of fish balls sold in Hong Kong. One is smaller in size, yellow in colour and made from a cheaper fish. They are usually sold at food stalls with five to seven fish balls on a bamboo skewer. Many of these stall owners sole support comes from selling this type of fish ball, similar to the hot dog stands in the United States. The fish balls are usually boiled in a spicy curry sauce. It is one of the most popular and representative "street foods" (街頭熟食) of Hong Kong.

They are completely different from the white fish balls sold in restaurants in terms of texture and flavor. White fish balls are a little expensive to produce and it requires much preparation and work on the part of the chef to ensure the quality of the fish balls that are produced every morning. Therefore, mass production of hand-made fish balls is quite difficult.

In order to cater to the large consumptive needs of the people in Hong Kong, the production costs of making fish balls had to be lowered. The yellow fish balls sold by these street food stalls consist of very little fish and a larger proportion of flour. Therefore consumers might notice a difference in texture, due to the increased flour content. The ingredient "fish" accounts for less than 20% in a fish ball and they are all mass produced in large quantities by machines. Also, the fish used in these factory produced fish balls are not very carefully selected and monosodium glutamate (MSG) is added for flavor.

The street stalls order their fish balls from these factories and almost every store then creates their own recipes of curry satay sauce to make their fish balls unique from other sellers.

History

Diet is never only used to allay one's hunger and slake one's thirst. Since factors like one's economic situation, geographical location and religion vary among countries, the diet of each has its own special characteristics. The characteristic of each country's food is reflected in the areas' unique cultural background. In Hong Kong, the first fish ball was made and sold by hawkers between the 50's to 60's. Fish balls were produced and sold in this manner as a cheap, yet tasty and filling snack for the people. Although society has drastically changed since then, fish balls are still closely related to Hong Kong and its people in terms of its ubiquity, the flavour, the method of sales and their production. Subsequently, fish balls have spread throughout other parts of Asia.

The Changes Between Years

Before the 1960's, people were faced with financial difficulties so they changed their occupation into becoming a hawker. However, since 1972, Hong Kong implemented "The Hong Kong Cleanup" action (清潔香港運動) in order to establish the sense of belonging for the local people and to keep a clean environment. After the improvement of the public's spirit and the environment, the uncleanliness and hygienic problems caused by hawkers became a focal point. From 1979 onward, the government stopped licensing hawkers for the reason of road blocking, and requested hawkers to relinquish their licenses through compensatory means in order to lessen the number of existing hawkers. In 1995, the government established two new policies which officially prohibited the existence of hawkers and fined those with licenses. In 2000, despite the fact that the government had loosened its supervisory control of hawkers in New Territories, the recent incident caused by arresting hawkers revealed their determination in executing this policy.

The historical developments related to hawkers would directly affect the development of the fish ball. The ban against hawkers had changed the operation mode from vendors to street stalls. Nowadays, most of the people would prefer to buy them from the street stalls as opposed to the vendors.

Ingredients of Fish Balls

The ingredients are basically fish and sometimes flour and flavorings such as salt and sugar is used. The proportion of fish and flour depends on the quality and type of fish balls to be made. The white fish balls found in some traditional Hong Kong restaurants are made using only fresh fish. While the street fried fish balls are made by using cheap fish and a mixture of flour in order to reduce costs from the wholesale business. In the past, a wide variety and good quality of fish was used. But now the supply quality has become tensed for some reasons. The commonly used fish to make fish balls now are 九棍、或仔魚和門鱔 etc.

Fish ball, the most popular and most common street food, was founded between the 50's and 60's. At that time, in order reduce costs, the process of making fish balls was most likely done by mixing and frying the remaining materials of ChouZhou fish ball 潮州白魚丸 or stale fishes. Nowadays, fish balls sold in Hong Kong are mainly imported by wholesale businesses. Therefore, the texture of fish ball does not have too much difference. In recent years, fish balls are sold with different hot or curry sauces.

Prices of Fish Ball

Selling Price

In general, the current market price in 2012 ranges from $6 to $9 per stick (with 5 fish balls); from $15 to $20 per small bowl (with 10 fish balls); and around $30 per big bowl (with about 20 fish balls). Based on the current situation, we calculate that the price per fish ball is about $1.5, which has increased by 50% compared to 5 years ago. For some stalls, the price has increased even more. For instance, in Tai Wai, the price jumped from $5 to $8 or an increase of 60% within two years.

Wholesale Price

When you consider the wholesale price of $16/kg (about 80 fish balls), the cost per fish ball is $0.2. By selling one fish ball, a stall owner can earn $1.3. According to the owner of Jinwei 津味, a famous fish ball stall operating its business in Mong Kok, Tsim Sha Tsui and Causeway Bay, he stated that the number of fish balls sold per day is 15,000. So the estimated net profit per day is almost $20,000, which is quite a pleasing amount.

Unprevailing Price

Some stalls in Hong Kong are selling fish balls at an unexpected high price to tourists. For each bowl of fish balls sold to customers, the number of fish balls can vary. This just depends on the type of customer, i.e. local people or tourists. According to a reporter of SUN Life, he visited one of these stalls in Mong Kok and reported that an Australian tourist paid $40 for a big bowl containing 25 fish balls; while a local person paid $20 for a small bowl but had 30 fish balls. Obviously, the stall owner was unethical and cheated the tourist. This stall only sells 'a bowl of fish balls' and no 'fish balls on a stick'. In this way, customers will have a difficult time discovering the truth that there is no standardized number of fish balls to be sold in each bowl. Indeed, the stall workers just randomly put fish balls in the bowl thus the number contained in each bowl varies from time to time. Even for two separate local customers, they were still given different numbers of fish balls for the same price.

Rent

The main reason behind the increased pricing of fish balls is because of the continuous and crazy rise of rental cost. Particularly, the rent is extremely high in some tourist-prone areas such as Causeway Bay, Mong Kok and Tsim Sha Tsui. One example is the fish ball stall located in Yee Woo Street, Causeway Bay. The rent in 2010 increased to $300,000 per month. Although there was a large flow of paying customers at this stall, the revenue earned was not enough to cover the rental cost. In the end, the owner had no choice and was forced to shut down the business.

In some special places, such as flower market, the rental cost is even higher. According to the reporter of Sharp Daily, the weekly rent of a fish ball stall increased from $380,000 in 2011 to $510,000 in 2012, which was a 34% increase. Based on the market situation in 2012, the net profit for each fish ball sold was approximately $1.1, that means the stall owner needed to sell at least 70,000 fish balls per day in order to break-even. Considering the cost of labor, ingredients and other expenses, the stall owner estimated that he has to sell a stick of fish balls every 5 seconds to break-even.

Target Customers

The targeted group of customers include lower class, working class and middle class. The price level is still acceptable and affordable by these groups of people. Most of the working-class people are accustomed to eating fish balls after work or after dinner. They care less about manners and hygienic issues. They don't mind eating on the street nor concerned about the seemingly unhygienic street food. On the other hand, due to the low quality of fish ball ingredients, perceived bad eating manners and unsafe hygienic operations and the eating environment, the high income classed people or celebrities seldom or never buy from the stalls on the street. They need to protect their social status and avoid breaking the shared norm or values created among the collective groups in Hong Kong, as described in the sociological imagination. Once they break this social norm, they will appear in the news or in a magazine within a few days. For instance, Fiona Sit, Ken Hung and Vincy Chan were once being photographed by a paparazzi while they were eating fish balls on the street. From this example, we can see that the social media inserts a great deal of influence on shaping human behavior and social norms. It indirectly conveys a message that the high, social status of people such as government executives, CEO's of public companies or famous celebrities should not buy and eat fish balls on the street. Otherwise, their social status or public image will be seriously damaged.

Innovative way in engaging fish ball business

To cope with the challenge of rising rental costs in Hong Kong, fish ball stall owners try to use different strategies in an attempt to increase their profit margin. In 2004, Ng Han Wai, successfully innovated a fish ball vending machine and in the same year started his own business. The first fish ball vending machine was located in the Sha Tin MTR station. Customers can buy a cup of fish balls by inserting a $5 coin or using the Octopus card which is quite convenient. All the processes are machine-automated to ensure a good quality of hygiene. From this innovative way of selling fish balls, we can see that Ng had changed the traditional way of doing business, a rationalized and humanized mode (fish ball stalls) to a new rationalized and mechanical mode (fish ball vending machine)of doing business. Under this new system, everything is done electronically with standardized selling and processing procedures. Human error can be greatly avoided.

The rent for these machines are definitely lower than the street stall's. According to Ng, each machine sold about 80 cups of fish ball per day, together with the revenue from advertisement and franchisee fees, he estimated that it only took half and a year to break-even. Unfortunately, he tried to commit suicide in 2005 due to some personal reasons, causing all his business come to a standstill.

White Fish Ball

White fish balls are larger in size and made with only fish, no other ingredients are added, and then boiled till done. As a result of this cooking method, these fish balls are white in color. A good fish ball should have an elastic (bouncy) and fluffy texture and a strong taste of fish. They are made using a more costly fish, and has a considerably different texture and taste. This kind is usually eaten as a compliment with noodles at Chiuchow-style noodle restaurants, and at some *cha chaan tengs*, which also sellbeef balls (牛丸) and cuttlefish balls (墨魚丸). Readily available in traditional markets and supermarkets, fish balls are also a popular ingredient for hot pot.

Traditional Hong Kong fish ball restaurants (老字號魚蛋店) all agree that "good fish" is the key in making good fish balls. They insist on using certain kinds of fresh fish and not adding flour. 九棍 fish are said to be good for giving it a strong taste of fish (魚味). However, these fish are now becoming rare and hard to catch. Other fish, such as 紅衫 fish, are becoming more expensive. These traditional restaurants are all facing the same problem, limited, specific fish supplies and increasing ingredient costs. The cost of these fish supplies have increased two to threefold in recent years. White fish balls from the traditional fish ball restaurants are regarded as the true fish ball because they have a higher quality. They are only made from fresh fish and only fresh fish. These fish balls are normally hand-made (手打) by the owners using traditional techniques. The price of these fish balls is usually higher. However, using the same ingredients, hand-made fish balls are still far better than the machine-made ones.

Indonesia

In Indonesia, fish balls are called *bakso ikan* (fish *bakso*). The most popular bakso are made of beef, but fish bakso is also available, served with tofu and fish *otak-otak* in clear broth soup as *tahu kok*, or thinly sliced as additional ingredients in *mie goreng*, *kwetiau goreng*, and *cap cai*. A similar dish made of fish is called *pempek*.

Peninsular Malaysia and Singapore

Fish balls are cooked in many ways in Peninsular Malaysia and Singapore. They can be served with soup and noodles like the Chiuchow style or with *yong tau foo*. There is also a type called fish ball *mee pok*.

Philippines

The most commonly eaten type of fish balls is colloquially known simply as fishballs. It is somewhat flat in shape and most often made from the meat of cuttlefish or pollock and served with a sweet and spicy sauce or with a thick, black, sweet and sour sauce.

Fish balls in the Philippines are sold by street vendors pushing wooden deep-frying carts. The balls are served skewered, offered with a choice of three kinds of dipping sauces: spicy (white/orange colored) - vinegar, water, diced onions and garlic, sweet (brown gravy colored) - corn starch, banana ketchup, sugar and salt, and sweet/sour (amber or deeper orange colored) - the sweet variety with lots of small hot chilis added. Dark sauces are rare, as these are soy sauce-based and soy sauce is expensive in terms of food cost for street food. A recent trend in the Philippine fishball industry is the introduction of 'ball' varieties: chicken, squid (cuttlefish actually), and *kikiam*. The last are low cost renditions vaguely resembling the original Chinese delicacy of the same (soundwise) name.

Scandinavia

Fiskbullar in Sweden and *fiskeboller* in Norway are usually bought in cans. In Sweden, they are normally served with mashed potatoes or rice, boiled green peas and dill, caviar or seafood sauces. In Norway, they are commonly served with potatoes and white sauce made with the stock from the can, sometimes with added curry.

Thailand

In Thai cuisine, fish balls are also very popular. They are usually fried or grilled to be eaten as a snack. In Chinese-influenced restaurants, fish balls are cooked in noodle soups and come in many varieties. They can also be eaten in a Thai curry. *Kkaeng khiao wan luk chin pla* is green curry with fish balls.

Fish ball store and Social media

Fish ball stores appeared in social media with multiple images. They do not only represent the unique eating culture of Hong Kong but also act as famous attractions in Hong Kong.

Famous Attractions

Big Golden Fish Ball - Cheung Chau

This is a very famous snack in Cheung Chau. It is a must-have item for tourists visiting Cheung Chau. Many visitors have shared their comments on Cheung Chau's fish balls in online forums, such as Open Rice.

Selling Price

Due to the inflation in Hong Kong, the price has risen more than 60% within 2 years. In 2010, two Big Golden fish balls were sold at $6. In 2012, they were selling for $10.

Unique Selling Points

There are several unique selling points of Big Golden fish balls compared to the normal ones sold on the street.

1. Large in size

As reflected from its name, the size is larger; they can be fist-sized.

2. Special sourcing

Big Golden fish ball is served with a special curry sauce.

3. Texture is al dente

Big Golden fish ball is mainly made from fresh fish which makes the texture more al dente than the cheap fish ball usually sold.

Examples - Famous Fish Ball Stores

1. Kam Wing Tai Fish Ball Store G/F, 106 San Hing Street, Cheung Chau
2. Sun Jiu Kee Snacks Store 3 Tung Wan Street, Cheung Chau
3. Cheung Chau Cheung Kee 83A Praya Street, Cheung Chau

Source http://en.wikipedia.org/wiki/Fish_ball

Focaccia

Homemade Focaccia with olives and herbs

Origin

Place of origin	Italy

Details

Type	Flatbread
Main ingredient(s)	High-gluten flour, oil, water, salt, yeast

Focaccia (Italian pronunciation: [foˈkattʃa]) is a flat oven-baked Italian bread, which may be topped with herbs or other ingredients.

Focaccia is popular in Italy and is usually seasoned with olive oil and salt, and sometimes herbs, and may be topped with onion, cheese and meat, or flavored with a number of vegetables.

Focaccia doughs are similar in style and texture to pizza doughs, consisting of high-gluten flour, oil, water, salt and yeast. It is typically rolled out or pressed by hand into a thick layer of dough and then baked in a stone-bottom or hearth oven. Bakers often puncture the bread with a knife to relieve bubbling on the surface of the bread.

Also common is the practice of dotting the bread. This creates multiple wells in the bread by using a finger or the handle of a utensil to poke the unbaked dough. As a way to preserve moisture in the bread, olive oil is then spread over the dough, by hand or with a pastry brush prior to rising and baking. In the northern part of Italy, lard will sometimes be added to the dough, giving the focaccia a softer, slightly flakier texture. Focaccia recipes are widely available, and with the popularity of bread machines, many cookbooks now provide versions of dough recipes that do not require hand kneading.

Focaccia can be used as a side to many meals, as a base for pizza, or as sandwich bread.

Etymology and regional variants

In ancient Rome, *panis focacius* was a flat bread baked on the hearth. The word is derived from the Latin *focus* meaning "hearth, place for baking." The basic recipe is thought by some to have originated with the Etruscans or ancient Greeks, but today it is widely associated with Ligurian cuisine.

As the tradition spread, the different dialects and diverse local ingredients resulted in a large variety of bread (some may even be considered cake). Due to the number of small towns and hamlets dotting the coast of Liguria, the focaccia recipe has fragmented into countless variations (from the biscuit-hard focaccia of Camogli to the oily softness of the one made in Voltri), with some bearing little resemblance to its original form. The most extreme example is the specialty "focaccia col formaggio" (focaccia with cheese) which is made in Recco, near Genoa. Other than the name, this Recco version bears no resemblance to other focaccia varieties, having a caillé and cheese filling sandwiched between two layers of paper-thin dough. It is even being considered for European Union PGI status. Regional variations also exist, such as *focaccia dolce* (sweet focaccia), popular in some parts of north-western Italy, consisting of a basic focaccia base and sprinkled lightly with sugar, or including raisins, honey, or other sweet ingredients.

Focaccia is present in many variants in Italy itself, for example the *focaccia alla genovese*, originated in Genoa, the *focaccia alla barese*, from Bari, or the *focaccia alla messinese*, from Messina. Another widespread variation is the *Focaccia Barese*, common in the provinces of Bari, Brindisi, Lecce and Taranto. It usually comes in three variations: classic *focaccia* with fresh tomatoes and olives, *potato focaccia* with potato slices 5 mm thick and *white Focaccia* with salt grains and rosemary. Some other variations include peppers, onions, eggplant or other vegetables.

In Burgundy, focaccia is called "foisse" or "fouaisse", and in Catalonia, Provence and Languedoc it's "fogassa" or, more commonly, the French "fougasse". In Argentina, it is widely consumed under the name *fugazza*, derived from *fugàssa* in the native language of Argentina's many Ligurian immigrants. The Spaniards call it "hogaza".

In American-English, it is sometimes referred to as *focaccia bread*. The Sicilian-style pizza, and the Roman *pizza bianca* (white pizza) can be considered a variant of focaccia. Focaccia is used extensively as a sandwich bread outside of Italy.

Source http://en.wikipedia.org/wiki/Focaccia

French fries

A dish of French fries

Origin

Alternative name(s)	Belgian fries, chips, hot chips, finger chips, fries, steak fries, wedges, potato wedges, frites
Place of origin	Belgium

Details

Course	Side dish or snack, rarely as a main dish
Serving temperature	Hot, generally salted, often served with ketchup, vinegar, barbecue sauce, mayonnaise, other sauce on the side
Main ingredient(s)	Potatoes and oil

French fries (American English, with "French" often capitalized), or **chips**, **fries**, **finger chips**, or **French-fried potatoes** are batons of deep-fried potato. North Americans refer to any elongated pieces of fried potatoes as *fries*, while in the United Kingdom, Australia, Ireland and New Zealand, long, thinly cut slices of fried potatoes are sometimes called *fries* to distinguish them from the more thickly cut strips called **chips**.

French fries are served hot and generally eaten as an accompaniment with lunch or dinner, or eaten as a snack, and they are a common fixture of fast food. French fries are generally salted, and in their simplest and most common form, are served with ketchup, though in many countries they are topped instead with other things, including vinegar, mayonnaise, or other local specialities. Fries can also be topped more elaborately, as is the case with the dishes of poutine and chili cheese fries. Sometimes fries are made with sweet potatoes instead of potatoes, are baked instead of fried, or are cut into unusual shapes, as is the case with curly fries, wavy fries or tornado fries.

Etymology

Oven-baked fries

Thomas Jefferson had "potatoes served in the French manner" at a White House dinner in 1802. The expression "French Fried Potatoes" first occurs in print in English in the 1856 work *Cookery for Maids of All Work* by E. Warren: "French Fried Potatoes. – Cut new potatoes in thin slices, put them in boiling fat, and a little salt; fry both sides of a light golden brown colour; drain." In the early 20th century, the term "French fried" was being used in the sense of "deep-fried", for other foods such as onion rings or chicken.

It is unlikely that "French fried" refers to *frenching* in the sense of *julienning*, which is not attested until after *French fried potatoes*. Previously, Frenching referred only to trimming meat off the shanks of chops.

Culinary origin

Belgium

Belgian journalist Jo Gérard claims that a 1781 family manuscript recounts that potatoes were deep-fried prior to 1680 in what was then the Spanish Netherlands (present-day Belgium), in the Meuse valley: "The inhabitants of Namur, Andenne, and Dinant, had the custom of fishing in the Meuse for small fish and frying, especially among the poor, but when the river was frozen and fishing became hazardous, they cut potatoes in the form of small fish and put them in a fryer like those here." Gérard has not produced the manuscript that supports this claim, which, even if true, is unrelated to the later history of the French fry, as the potato did not arrive in the region until around 1735. Also, given 18th century economic conditions: "It is absolutely unthinkable that a peasant could have consecrated large quantities of fat for cooking potatoes. At most they were sautéed in a pan...." Some Belgians believe that the term "French" was introduced when American soldiers arrived in Belgium during World War I, and consequently tasted Belgian fries. They supposedly called them "French," as it was the official language of the Belgian Army at that time. At this time French fries were growing popular. However, in the south of Netherlands, bordering Belgium, they were, and still are, called *Vlaamse Frieten* or *Flemish fries*.

"Pommes frites", "frites" (French) or "frieten" (Dutch) became the national snack and a substantial part of several national dishes.

France and French-speaking countries

A popular Canadian dish is poutine, such as this one from La Banquise restaurant in Montreal. It is made with French fries, cheese curds and gravy.

In France and French-speaking countries, fried potatoes are formally *pommes de terre frites*, but more commonly *pommes frites*, *patates frites*, or simply *frites*. The word "*aiguillettes*" or *allumettes* is used when the chips are very small and thin.

Eating potatoes was promoted in France by Parmentier, but he did not mention fried potatoes in particular. Many Americans attribute the dish to France and offer as evidence a notation by U.S. President Thomas Jefferson. *"Pommes de terre frites à cru, en petites tranches"* ("Potatoes deep-fried while raw, in small cuttings") in a manuscript in Thomas Jefferson's hand (circa 1801–1809) and the recipe almost certainly comes from his French chef, Honoré Julien. In addition, from 1813 on, recipes for what can be described as French fries occur in popular American cookbooks. By the late 1850s, one of these uses the term *French fried potatoes*.

Frites are the main ingredient in the Canadian dish of Québécois descent known in both Canadian English and French as poutine, comprising fried potatoes covered with cheese curds and gravy, a dish with a growing number of variations.

Spain

In Spain, fried potatoes are called *patatas fritas* or *papas fritas*. Another common form, in which the potatoes are cut into irregular shapes and seasoned with a spicy tomato sauce, is called *patatas bravas*.

Some speculate that the dish may have been invented in Spain, the first European country in which the potato appeared via the New World colonies, and assumes the first appearance to have been as an accompaniment to fish dishes in Galicia, from which it spread to the rest of the country and further to the Spanish Netherlands, which became Belgium more than a century later.

Professor Paul Ilegems, curator of the Friet-museum in Antwerp, Belgium, believes that Saint Teresa of Ávila fried the first chips, referring also to the tradition of frying in Mediterranean cuisine.

Spreading popularity

French fry production at a restaurant with thermostatic temperature control.

Frozen fries

The J. R. Simplot Company is credited with successfully commercializing French fries in frozen form during the 1940s. Subsequently, in 1967, Ray Kroc of McDonald's contracted the Simplot company to supply them with frozen fries, replacing fresh-cut potatoes.

In 2004, 29% of the United States' potato crop were used to make frozen fries – 90% consumed by the food services sector and 10% by retail. It is estimated that 80% of households in the UK buy frozen fries each year.

Canada's McCain Foods is the world's leading producer of frozen fries. In addition to household products, they supply frozen fries to fast food companies such as McDonald's and KFC.

Belgium and the Netherlands

A *patatje speciaal*, with *frietsaus*, *curry ketchup* or tomato ketchup, and chopped raw onions, is popular in the Netherlands.

Fries are very popular in Belgium and the Netherlands. In Belgium fries are sold in shops called *friteries* in French and *frietkot/ fritkot/ frituur* in Dutch. They are served with a large variety of sauces and eaten either on their own or with other snacks such as fricandelle or burgers. Traditionally, they are served in a *cornet de frites* (French) or *frietzak/ fritzak* (Dutch), a white cardboard cone, then wrapped in paper, with a good spoonful of sauce on the top. With the fries they serve many traditional fast-food products, such as frikandel/ fricadelle, gehaktbal/boulet or kroket/ croquette. In the Netherlands, you can find them in a snack bar. They are served mostly with mayonnaise or curry ketchup.

In most of the Netherlands, French Fries are called *patat*, whereas in the southern Netherlands and in Belgium, they are named 'friet'. In the Netherlands 'Flemish Fries' (Vlaamse friet) is sometimes used for thick fries of good quality.

Friteries and other fast-food establishments tend to offer a number of different sauces for the fries and meats. In addition to ketchup and mayonnaise, popular options include:
Aioli, garlic mayonnaise.
Sauce Andalouse – mayonnaise with tomato paste and peppers.
Sauce Americaine – mayonnaise with tomato chervil onions, capers and celery.
Bicky Dressing (Gele Bicky-sauce), a commercial brand made from mayonnaise, white cabbage, tarragon, cucumber, onion, mustard and dextrose.
Curry mayonnaise.
Mammoet-sauce – mayonnaise, tomato, onion, glucose, garlic, soy sauce.
Peanut sauce – when combined with mayonnaise and optionally raw onion, this is called *patat oorlog* ("war fries").
Samurai-sauce – mayonnaise with sambal oelek.
Sauce "Pickles" – a yellow mayonnaise-based sauce with turmeric, mustard and crunchy vegetable chunks, similar to Piccalilli.
Pepper-sauce – mayonnaise with green pepper, garlic, glucose.
Tartar sauce.
Zigeuner sauce, A "gypsy" sauce of tomatoes, paprika and chopped bell peppers, borrowed from Germany.
À la zingara
These sauces are generally also available in supermarkets. Occasionally hot sauces are offered by friteries, including hollandaise sauce, sauce provençale, Béarnaise sauce or even a splash carbonade flamande stew from an constantly simmering pot, in the spirit of British *Chips and Gravy*.

United Kingdom

Fish and chips

Traditionally, *chips* in the United Kingdom are cut much thicker, i.e., are "chipped" from the potatoes and described in some recipes as *chipped pota-*

toes, not simply *chips*, and are typically between 10 and 15 mm (3/8–1/2 inches) wide. Since the surface-to-volume ratio is lower, they have a lower fat content. Thick-cut, or beefsteak, British chips are occasionally made from unpeeled potatoes to enhance their flavor and nutritional value. Chips are not necessarily served as crisp as the European French fry due to their relatively high water content.

As with all members of the deep-fried chip family, they are cooked twice, once at a relatively low temperature (blanching) to cook the potato, and then at a higher temperature to crisp the surface, making them crunchy on the outside and fluffier on the inside.

In the UK, chips are part of the popular take-out dish fish and chips and few towns are without a fish and chip shop.

The first chips fried in the UK were on the site of Oldham's Tommyfield Market in 1860. A blue plaque in Oldham marks the origin of the fish and chip shop and fast food industries in Britain. In Scotland, chips were first sold in Dundee, "...in the 1870s, that glory of British gastronomy – the chip – was first sold by Belgian immigrant Edward De Gernier in the city's Greenmarket."

United States

Wavy French fries sold in a Canadian supermarket

Although chips were already a popular dish in most Commonwealth countries, the thin style of French fries has been popularized worldwide in part by U.S.-based fast food chains such as McDonald's, Burger King, Wendy's, and Arby's.

Pre-made French fries have been available for home cooking since the 1960s, usually having been pre-fried (or sometimes baked), frozen and placed in a sealed plastic bag.

Some later varieties of French fries are battered and breaded, and many U.S. fast food chains dust the potatoes with kashi, dextrin, and other flavor coatings for crispier fries with particular tastes. Results with batterings and breadings, followed by microwaving, have not achieved widespread critical acceptance. Oven frying delivers a dish different from deep-fried potatoes.

Variants

Animal fries (covered with cheese, grilled onions, and spread) from In-N-Out Burger's secret menu

Variants of French fries include *thick-cut fries*, *steak fries*, *shoestring fries*, *jojos*, *crinkle fries*, *curly fries*, *hand-cut fries* and *tornado fries*. Fries cut thickly with the skin left on are called *potato wedges*, and fries without the skin are called *steak fries*, essentially the American equivalent of the British *chip*. They can also be coated with breading, spices, or other ingredients, which include garlic powder, onion powder, black pepper, paprika, and salt to create *seasoned fries*, cheese to create *cheese fries*, or chili to create *chili fries*. Sometimes, French fries are cooked in the oven as a final step in the preparation (having been coated with oil during preparation at the factory): these are often sold frozen and are called *oven fries* or *oven chips*. Some restaurants and groceries in North America offer French fries made from sweet potatoes instead of traditional white potatoes.

In France, the thick-cut fries are called *Pommes Pont-Neuf* or simply *pommes frites*, about 10 mm; thinner variants are *pommes allumettes* (match-

Chili cheese fries

stick potatoes), ±7 mm, and *pommes paille* (potato straws), 3–4 mm (roughly ⅜, ¼ and ⅛ inch respectively). The two-bath technique is standard (Bocuse). *Pommes gaufrettes* or *waffle fries* are not typical French fried potatoes, but actually crisps obtained by quarter-turning the potato before each next slide over a grater and deep-frying just once.

Sweet potato fries served in a restaurant in Harvard Square.

Fries in the pot

In an interview, Burger King president Donald Smith said that his chain's fries are sprayed with a sugar solution shortly before being packaged and shipped to individual outlets. The sugar caramelizes in the cooking fat, producing the golden color customers expect.

Curly fries

McDonald's was assumed to fry their fries for a total time of about 15 to 20 minutes, and with fries fried at least twice.

Curly fries

Curly fries are characterized by their spring-like shape. They are generally made from whole potatoes that are cut using a specialized spiral slicer. They are also typically characterized by the presence of additional seasonings (which give the fries a more orange appearance when compared to the more yellow appearance of standard fries), although this is not always the case. This seasoning also gives the fries a slightly spicier taste than standard fries.

Sometimes they are packaged for preparation at home, often in frozen packs. In the US they can also be found at a number of restaurants and fast food outlets like Arby's, Hooters, and Hardee's, where they are served with condiments such as ketchup, cheese, fry sauce, or sweet chili sauce and sour cream.

Tornado fries

Tornado fries are made by skewering the whole potato, and then cutting with a specialized spiral slicer. The potato is spread evenly along the skewer and deep fried. The cooking process fuses the potato to the skewer and holds it in place. It is then sprinkled with dry seasonings or served with dipping sauce. The Tornado fry gets its name from the tornado-like shape that the potato has on the skewer.

Tornado fries

Accompaniments

Fries tend to be served with a variety of accompaniments, e.g., salt and vinegar (malt, balsamic or white), pepper, grated cheese, melted cheese, mushy peas, heated curry sauce, curry ketchup (mildly spiced mix of the former), hot or chili sauce, mustard, mayonnaise, bearnaise sauce, tartar sauce, tzatziki, feta cheese, garlic sauce, fry sauce, ranch dressing, barbecue sauce, gravy, aioli, brown sauce, ketchup, lemon juice, piccalilli, pickled cucumber, pickled gherkins, pickled onions or pickled eggs.

Health aspects

Fries frying in oil.

French fries can contain a large amount of fat from frying. For example, fat accounts for 45% of the caloric value of French fries at McDonald's in the United States; since raw potatoes are virtually fat-free, almost all of it comes from the cooking oil that was absorbed by potatoes while frying. A 13 year long observation performed by the University of Maastricht, the Netherlands, on 120,000 subjects between 55 and 70, has shown that increased intake of acrylamide (formed when potatoes are baked or fried) is correlated with a 60% higher rate of kidney cancer. However, researchers from the Harvard School of Public Health and Karolinska Institutet in Stockholm, Sweden, found no association between the consumption of foods high in acrylamide and increased risk of three forms of cancer: bladder, large bowel and kidney.

Frying French fries in beef tallow, lard, or other animal fats adds saturated fat to the diet. Replacing animal fats with tropical vegetable-oils, such as palm oil, simply substitutes one saturated fat for another. Replacing animal fats with partially hydrogenated oil reduces cholesterol but adds trans fat, which has been shown to both raise LDL cholesterol and lower HDL cholesterol. Canola/Rapeseed oil, or sunflower-seed oil are also used, as are mixes of vegetable oils, but beef tallow is generally more popular, especially amongst fast food outlets that use communal oil baths. Many restaurants now advertise their use of unsaturated oils. Five Guys and Chick-fil-A, for example, both advertise that their fries are prepared in peanut oil, while In-N-Out advertises that their fries are made using vegetable oil.

Legal issues

In June 2004, the United States Department of Agriculture, with the advisement of a federal district judge from Beaumont, Texas, classified batter-coated French fries as a vegetable under the Perishable Agricultural Commodities Act. This was primarily for trade reasons. French fries do not meet the standard to be listed as a processed food.

In 2002, the McDonald's Corporation agreed to donate $10 million to Hindu and other groups to settle lawsuits filed against the chain for mislabeling French fries and hash browns as vegetarian, because their French fries and hash browns were found to contain beef extract added during production.

Source http://en.wikipedia.org/wiki/French_fries

Fried chicken

Pieces of fried chicken

Details

Course	Main meal
Serving temperature	Hot
Main ingredient(s)	Chicken

Fried chicken (also referred to as **Southern fried chicken**) is a dish consisting of chicken pieces usually from broiler chickens which have been floured or battered and then pan-fried, deep fried, or pressure fried. The breading adds a crisp coating or crust to the exterior. What separates fried chicken from other fried forms of chicken is that generally the chicken is cut at the joints and the bones and skin are left intact. Crisp well-seasoned skin, rendered of excess fat, is a hallmark of well made fried chicken.

Preparation

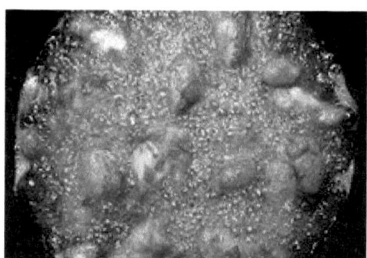

Frying chicken upper wings in corn oil

Generally, chickens are not fried whole; instead, the chicken is divided into its four main constituent pieces: the two white meat sections are the breast and the wing from the front of the chicken, while the dark meat sections are from the rear of the chicken. To prepare the chicken pieces for frying, they are dredged in flour or a similar dry substance (possibly following marination or dipping in milk or buttermilk) to coat the meat and to develop a crust. Seasonings such as salt, pepper, cayenne pepper, paprika, garlic powder, onion powder, or ranch dressing mix can be mixed in with the flour. As the pieces of chicken cook, some of the moisture that exudes from the chicken is absorbed by the coating of flour and browns along with the flour, creating a flavorful crust. Traditionally, lard is used to fry the chicken, but corn oil, peanut oil, canola oil, or vegetable oil are also frequently used. The flavor of olive oil is generally considered too strong to be used for traditional fried chicken, and its low smoke point makes it unsuitable for use.

There are three main techniques for frying chickens: pan frying, deep frying and broasting. Pan frying (or shallow frying) requires a frying pan of sturdy construction and a source of fat that does not fully immerse the chicken. The chicken pieces are prepared as above, then fried. Generally the fat is heated to a temperature hot enough to seal (without browning, at this point) the outside of the chicken pieces. Once the pieces have been added to the hot fat and sealed, the temperature is reduced. There is debate as to how often to turn the chicken pieces, with one camp arguing for often turning and even browning, and the other camp pushing for letting the pieces render skin side down and only turning when absolutely necessary. Once the chicken pieces are close to being done the temperature is raised and the pieces are browned to the desired color (some cooks add small amounts of butter at this point to enhance browning). The moisture from the chicken that sticks and browns on the bottom of the pan become the fonds required to make gravy. Chicken Maryland is made when the pan of chicken pieces, and fat, is placed in the oven to cook, for a majority of the overall cooking time, basically "fried in the oven".

Deep frying requires a deep fryer or other device in which the chicken pieces can be completely submerged in hot fat. The pieces are floured as above or battered using a batter of flour and liquid (and seasonings) mixed together. The batter can/may contain ingredients like eggs, milk, and leavening. The fat is heated in the deep fryer to the desired temperature. The pieces are added to the fat and a constant temperature is maintained throughout the cooking process.

Broasting uses a pressure cooker to accelerate the process. The moisture inside the chicken becomes steam and increases the pressure in the cooker, lowering the cooking temperature needed. The steam also cooks the chicken through, but still allows the pieces to be moist and tender while maintaining a crisp coating. Fat is heated in a pressure cooker. Chicken pieces are then floured or battered and then placed in the hot fat. The lid is placed on the pressure cooker, and the chicken pieces are thus fried under pressure.

History

Fritters have existed in Europe since the middle ages. The Scots, and later Scottish immigrants to the southern United States, had a tradition of deep frying chicken in fat, unlike their English counterparts who baked or boiled chicken.

A number of West African cuisines featured dishes where chicken was fried, typically in palm oil, sometimes having been battered before. These would be served on special occasions in some areas, or sometimes sold in the streets as snacks in others. This provided some means of independent economy for enslaved and segregated African American women, who became noted sellers of poultry (live or cooked) as early as the 1730s. Because of this and the expensive nature of the ingredients, it was, despite popular perception, a rare and special dish in the African-American community.

After the development of larger and faster-growing hogs (due to crosses between European and Asian breeds) in the 18th and 19th century, in the United States, backyard and small-scale hog production provided an inexpensive means of converting waste food, crop waste, and garbage into calories (in a relatively small space and in a relatively short period of time). Many of those calories came in the form of fat and rendered lard. Lard was used for almost all cooking and was a fundamental component in many common homestead foods (many that today are still regarded as holiday and comfort foods) like biscuits and pies. The economic/caloric necessity of consuming lard and other saved fats may have led to the popularity of fried foods, not only in the US, but worldwide. In the 19th century cast iron became widely available for use in cooking. The combination of flour, lard, a chicken and a heavy pan placed over a relatively controllable flame became the beginning of today's fried chicken.

When it was introduced to the American South, fried chicken became a common staple. Later, as the slave trade led to Africans being brought to work on southern plantations, the slaves who became cooks incorporated seasonings and spices that were absent in traditional Scottish cuisine, enriching the flavor. Since most slaves were unable to raise expensive meats, but generally allowed to keep chickens, frying chicken on special occasions continued in the African American communities of the South. It endured the fall of slavery and gradually passed into common use as a general Southern dish. Since fried chicken traveled well in hot weather before refrigeration was commonplace, it gained further favor in the periods of American history when segregation closed off most restaurants to the black population. Fried chicken continues to be among this region's top choices for "Sunday dinner" among both blacks and whites. Holidays such as Independence Day and other gatherings often feature this dish.

Since the American Civil War, traditional slave foods like fried chicken, watermelon, and chitterlings have suffered a strong association with African American stereotypes and blackface minstrelsy. This was commercialized for the first half of the 20th century by restaurants like Sambo's and Coon Chicken Inn, which selected exaggerated depictions of blacks as mascots, implying quality by their association with the stereotype. Although also being acknowledged positively as "soul food" today, the affinity that African American culture has for fried chicken has been considered a delicate, often pejorative issue. While the perception of fried chicken as an ethnic dish has been fading for several decades, with the ubiquity of fried chicken dishes in the US, it persists as a racial stereotype.

Before the industrialization of chicken production, and the creation of broiler breeds of chicken, only young spring chickens (pullets or cockerels) would be suitable for the higher heat and relatively fast cooking time of frying, making fried chicken a luxury of spring and summer. Older, tougher birds require longer cooking times at lower temperatures. To compensate for this, sometimes tougher birds are simmered till tender, allowed to cool and dry, and then fried. (This method is common in Australia.) Another method is to fry the chicken pieces using a pan fried method. The chicken pieces are then simmered in liquid, usually, a gravy made in the pan that the chicken pieces were cooked in. This process (of flouring, frying and simmering in gravy) is known as "smothering" and can be used for other tough cuts of meat, such as swiss steak. Smothered chicken is still consumed today, though with the exception of people who raise their own chickens, or who seek out stewing hens, it is primarily made using commercial broiler chickens.

The derivative phrases "country fried" and "chicken fried" often refer to other foods prepared in the manner of fried chicken. Usually, this means a boneless, tenderized piece of meat that has been floured or battered and cooked in any of the methods described above or simply chicken which is cooked outdoors. Chicken fried steak and "country fried" boneless chicken breast are two common examples.

Global variants

Nashville-style hot chicken with traditional accompaniments

Tori no Karaage, Japanese fried chicken

Throughout the world, different seasoning and spices are used to augment the flavor of fried chicken. Because of the versatility of fried chicken, it is not uncommon to flavor the chicken's crisp exterior with a variety of spices ranging from spicy to savory. Depending on regional market ubiquity, local spice variations may be labeled as distinct from traditional Southern U.S. flavors, or may appear on menus without notation. With access to chickens suitable for frying broadening on a global scale with the advent of industrialized poultry farming, many localities have added their own mark on fried chicken, tweaking recipes to suit local preferences.

North America

Buffalo wings: Named for their place of

Savory Restaurant fried chicken (Philippines)

origin, Buffalo, New York, this is one of the few kinds of fried chicken that is not traditionally battered before frying.

Buffalo strips, fingers, crisp wings and boneless wings: using the same cayenne-pepper sauce as Buffalo Wings, these chicken products are battered before frying. See also: chicken fingers and chicken nuggets.

Chicken fingers: also known as *chicken tenders* or *chicken strips*, this is one of the most common forms of fried chicken, generally pieces of chicken breast (sometimes with rib meat) cut into long strips, breaded or battered dipped, and deep fried.

Chicken fries: chicken nuggets in the shape of French fries, popularized by the fast-food chains Burger King and KFC. These may also be referred to as *chicken sticks*.

Chicken Maryland, a form of pan-fried chicken, often marinated in buttermilk, served with cream gravy and native to the state of Maryland. The recipe spread beyond the United States to the *haute cuisine* of Auguste Escoffier and, after heavy modification, found a place in the cuisines of Britain and Australia.

Chicken nuggets: an industrially reconstituted boneless chicken product invented by Cornell poultry science professor Robert C. Baker in the 1950s.

Popcorn chicken: occasionally known as *chicken bites* or other similar terms, small morsels of boneless chicken, battered and fried, resulting in little nuggets that resemble popcorn.

Chicken patties: breaded, fried patties of chicken meat used in sandwiches.

Country Fried Chicken: chicken meat that has been coated with flour or breaded, fried and served topped with country cream gravy. Related tangentially to Chicken fried steak.

Chicken and waffles, a combination platter of foods traditionally served at breakfast and dinner in one meal, common to soul food restaurants in the American South and beyond.

Hot chicken: common in the Nashville, Tennessee area, a pan-fried variant of fried chicken coated with lard and cayenne pepper paste.

Asia

Crispy fried chicken: a dish from the regional Cantonese cuisine of China.

Chicken karaage- a Japanese marinated and fried method of preparing fried chicken.

Chicken katsu- (チキンカツ), a Japanese panko-breaded, deep fried chicken cutlet, adapted from tonkatsu, a pork chop variant.

Korean fried chicken: fried chicken pieces flavored with Korean ganjang sauce with garlic.

Buldak: fried chicken with Korean seasonings like gochujang.

Prawn paste chicken or "shrimp paste chicken": popular in Hong Kong-style restaurants in Singapore and Malaysia. Incorporates puréed shrimp and ginger juice into its breading mixture.

Sweet and sour chicken: deep-fried balls of chicken breast in batter.

Toriten: Japanese tempura style fried chicken

Chicken with chilies: (辣子鸡), a Sichaun-style dish with small deep-fried pieces of chicken that are then stir-fried with chilies.

Chicken lollipop: An Indian snack of fried chicken drumettes, coated in a spiced batter and fried.

Racial stereotype

In the United States, fried chicken has stereotypically been associated with African Americans. The reasons for this are various. Chicken dishes were popular among slaves before the Civil War, as chickens were generally the only animals slaves could raise on their own.

In 2009, when a Bangladeshi immigrant renamed his restaurant to "Obama Fried Chicken" in honor of recently inaugurated President Barack Obama, it caused some controversy. Despite this, the owner refused to change the name back, and the restaurant still operates today with the name.

In 2012, Burger King received criticism over a commercial for a fried chicken wrap served by the restaurant which was seen as using negative racial stereotypes in relation to fried chicken.

Source http://en.wikipedia.org/wiki/Fried_chicken

Ginanggang

Ginanggang*, *guinanggang*, or *ginanggang (Cebuano; English pronunciation: /gɪˈnɒŋgɒŋ/) is a snack food of grilled skewered bananas brushed with margarine and sprinkled with sugar. It originates from the island of Mindanao in the Philippines.

Ginanggang is made from a type of banana in the Philippines called *saba* (A cooking banana also known as the Cardaba banana). The banana is peeled, skewered and then grilled over charcoals. When the outer surface is lightly charred, it is then taken off the grill, brushed with margarine, and sprinkled with sugar. It differs from banana cue in that the banana is actually grilled on the stick. The sugar used on it is also white table sugar and is not caramelized (being applied after cooking).

Source http://en.wikipedia.org/wiki/

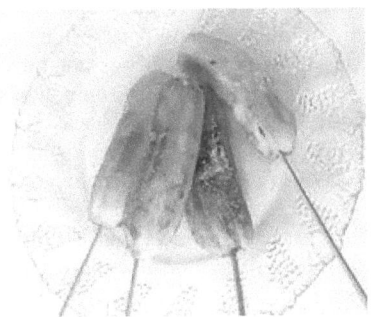

Ginanggang

Hamburger

A hamburger

Origin
Place of origin Germany, United States
Creator(s) Multiple claims (see text)
Details
Course Entree
Serving temperature Hot
Main ingredient(s) Ground beef, bread

A **hamburger** (also called a **hamburger sandwich**, **burger** or **hamburg**) is a sandwich consisting of a cooked patty of ground meat usually placed inside a sliced hamburger bun. Hamburgers are often served with lettuce, bacon, tomato, onion, pickles, cheese and condiments such as mustard, mayonnaise, ketchup and relish.

The term "burger", can also be applied to the meat patty on its own, especially in the UK where the term "patty" is rarely used. The term may be prefixed with the type of meat as in "turkey burger".

Etymology

The hamburger is named after Hamburg, Germany

The term *hamburger* originally derives from Hamburg, Germany's second largest city, from which many people emigrated to the United States. In High German, *Burg* means fortified settlement or fortified refuge; and is a widespread component of place names. *Hamburger* can be a descriptive noun in German, referring to someone from Hamburg (compare London → Londoner) or an adjective describing something from Hamburg. Similarly, *frankfurter* and *wiener*, names for other meat-based foods, are also used in Germany and Austria as descriptive nouns for people and as adjectives for things from the cities of Frankfurt and Wien (Vienna), respectively. The term "burger" is associated with many different types of sandwiches similar to a (ground beef) hamburger, using different meats, such as a buffalo burger, venison, kangaroo, turkey, elk, lamb, salmon burger or veggie burger.

History

The hamburger, a ground beef patty between two slices of bread, was first created in America in 1900 by Louis Lassen, owner of Louis' Lunch in New Haven, Connecticut. There have been rival claims by Charlie Nagreen, Frank and Charles Menches, Oscar Weber Bilby, and Fletcher David. White Castle traces the origin of the hamburger to Hamburg, Germany with its invention by Otto Kuase. However, it gained national recognition at the 1904 St. Louis World's Fair when the New York Tribune namelessly attributed the hamburger as, "the innovation of a food vendor on the pike." No conclusive claim has ever been made to end the dispute over the inventor of the hamburger with a variety of claims and evidence asserted since its creation.

Claims of invention

Louis Lassen

The Library of Congress has officially declared that Louis Lassen of Louis' Lunch, a small lunch wagon in New Haven, Connecticut, sold the first hamburger and steak sandwich in the U.S. in 1900. *New York* magazine states that, "The dish actually had no name until some rowdy sailors from Hamburg named the meat on a bun after themselves years later", noting also that this claim is subject to dispute. A customer ordered a quick hot meal and Louis was out of steaks. Taking ground beef trimmings, Louis made a patty and grilled it, putting it between two slices of toast. Though some critics, like Josh Ozersky, a food editor for New York Magazine claims that this sandwich was not a hamburger because the bread is toasted.

Charlie Nagreen

One of the earliest claims comes from Charlie Nagreen, who in 1885 sold a meatball between two slices of bread at the Seymour Fair now called the Outagamie County Fair in some attributions. The Seymour Community Historical Society of Seymour, Wisconsin, credits Charlie Nagreen, now known as "Hamburger Charlie", with the invention of the hamburger. Nagreen was fifteen when he reportedly made sandwiches out of porks that he was selling at the 1885 Seymour Fair (now the Outagamie County Fair), so that customers could eat while walking. The Historical Society explains that Nagreen named the hamburger after the Hamburg steak with which local German immigrants were familiar.

Otto Kuase

According to White Castle, Otto Kuase was the inventor of the hamburger. In 1891 he created a beef patty cooked in butter, topped with a fried egg. German sailors would later omit the fried egg.

Oscar Weber Bilby

Another claim attributes the invention of the hamburger to Oscar Weber Bilby in 1891.</ref> The family of Oscar Weber Bilby claim the first-known hamburger on a bun was served on Grandpa Oscar's farm using a yeast bun on the Fourth of July. In 1995, Governor Frank Keating proclaimed that the first true hamburger on a bun was created and consumed in Tulsa, Oklahoma in 1891; calling Tulsa, "The Real Birthplace of the Hamburger."

Frank and Charles Menches

Another claim from 1885 comes from Frank and Charles Menches who claims to have sold a ground beef sandwich at the Erie County Fair in Hamburg, New York. During the fair, they ran out of pork sausage for their sandwiches and substituted beef. Kunzog, who spoke to Frank Menches, says they exhausted their supply of sausage, so purchased chopped up beef from a butcher, Andrew Klein. Though historian Joseph Streamer wrote that the meat was from Stein's market not Klein's; despite Stein having sold the market in 1874. The story notes that the origin of the hamburger comes from Hamburg, New York not Hamburg Germany. Yet Frank Menches's obituary in The New York Times states that these events took place at the 1892 Summit County Fair in Akron, Ohio.

Fletcher Davis

Fletcher Davis of Athens, Texas claimed to have invented the hamburger. According to oral histories, in the 1880s, he opened a lunch counter in Athens and served a 'burger' of fried ground beef patties with mustard and Bermuda onion between two slices of bread; with a pickle on the side. The claim is that in 1904, Davis and his wife Ciddy ran a sandwich stand at the St. Louis World's Fair. Historian Frank X. Tolbert, noted that Athen's resident Clint Murchison said his grandfather dated the hamburger to the 1880s with 'Old Dave' a.k.a. Fletcher Davis. A photo of "Old Dave's Hamburger Stand" from the 1904 connection was sent to Tolbert as evidence of the claim. Also the New York Tribune namelessly attributed the innovation of the hamburger to the stand on the pike.

Other hamburger-steak claims

Various non-specific claims of the hamburgers invention relates to the term hamburger steak, but no mention of it being a sandwich. The first printed American menu which listed hamburger was claimed to be an 1826 menu from Delmonico's in New York. However, the printer of the original menu was not in business in 1834. In 1889, a menu from Walla Wall Union in Washington offered hamburger steak as a menu item.

Between 1871–1884, "Hamburg Beefsteak" was on the "Breakfast and Supper Menu" of the Clipper Restaurant at 311/313 Pacific Street in San Fernando. It cost 10 cents—the same price as mutton chops, pig's feet in batter, and stewed veal. It was not, however, on the dinner menu, only "Pig's Head" "Calf Tongue" and "Stewed Kidneys" were listed.

Another claim ties the hamburger to Summit County, New York or Ohio. Summit County, Ohio exists, but Summit County, New York does not.

Early major vendors

The McDonald's Big Mac

1921 — White Castle, Wichita, Kansas. Due to widely prevalent anti-German sentiment in the U.S. during World War I, an alternative name for hamburgers was Salisbury steak. Following the war, hamburgers became unpopular until the White Castle restaurant chain marketed and sold large numbers of small 2.5-inch square hamburgers, known as *sliders*. They started to punch five holes in each patty, which help them cook evenly and eliminates the need to flip the burger. White Castle began in 1995 selling frozen hamburgers in convenience stores and vending machines.

1940 — McDonald's restaurant, San Bernardino, California, opened by Richard and Maurice McDonald. Their introduction of the "Speedee Service System" in 1948 established the principles of the modern fast-food restaurant. The McDonald brothers began franchising in 1953. In 1961, Ray Kroc (the supplier of their multi-mixer milkshake machines) purchased the company from the brothers for $2.7 million and a 1.9% royalty.

Hamburgers today

A fast food hamburger from Sonic Drive-In.

Hamburger preparation in a fast food establishment.

Hamburgers are usually a feature of fast food restaurants. The hamburgers served in major fast food establishments are usually mass-produced in factories and frozen for delivery to the site. These hamburgers are thin and of uniform thickness, differing from the traditional American hamburger prepared in homes and conventional restaurants, which is thicker and prepared by hand from ground beef. Generally most American hamburgers are round, but some fast-food chains, such as Wendy's, sell square-cut hamburgers. Hamburgers in fast food restaurants are usually grilled on a flat-top, but some firms, such as Burger King, use a gas flame grilling process. At conventional American restaurants, hamburgers may be ordered "rare", but normally are served medium-well or well-done for food safety reasons. Fast food restaurants do not usually offer this option.

The McDonald's fast-food chain sells the Big Mac, one of the world's top selling hamburgers, with an estimated 550 million sold annually in the United States. Other major fast-food chains, including Burger King (also known as Hungry Jack's in Australia), A&W, Culver's, Whataburger, Carl's Jr./Hardee's chain, Wendy's (known for their square patties), Jack in the Box, Cook Out, Harvey's, Shake Shack, In-N-Out Burger, Five Guys, Fatburger, Vera's, Burgerville, Back Yard Burgers, Lick's Homeburger, Roy Rogers, Smashburger and Sonic also rely heavily on hamburger sales. Fuddruckers and Red Robin are hamburger chains that specialize in the mid-tier "restaurant-style" variety of hamburgers.

Some North American establishments offer a unique take on the hamburger beyond what is offered in fast food restaurants, using upscale ingredients such as sirloin or other steak along with a variety of different cheeses, toppings, and sauces. Some examples would be the Bobby's Burger Palace chain founded by well-known chef and Food Network star Bobby Flay.

Hamburgers are often served as a fast dinner, picnic or party food, and are usually cooked outdoors on barbecue grills.

Raw hamburger may contain harmful bacteria that can produce food-borne illness such as *Escherichia coli* O157:H7, due to the occasional initial improper preparation of the meat, so caution is needed during handling and cooking. Because of the potential for food-borne illness, the USDA recommends hamburgers be cooked to an internal temperature of 170 °F (80 °C). If cooked to this temperature, they are considered well-done.

A high-quality hamburger patty is made entirely of ground (minced) beef and seasonings; this may be described as an "all-beef hamburger" or "all-beef patties" to distinguish them from inexpensive hamburgers made with added flour, textured vegetable protein, ammonia treated defatted beef trimmings which the company Beef Products Inc, calls "lean finely textured beef", advanced meat recovery or other fillers to decrease their cost. In the 1930s ground liver was sometimes added to the patties. Some cooks prepare their patties with binders, such as eggs or breadcrumbs. Seasonings may be included with the hamburger patty including salt and pepper, and others such as parsley, onions, soy sauce, Thousand Island dressing, onion soup mix, or Worcestershire sauce. Many name brand seasoned salt products are also used.

A restaurant dish consisting of smaller versions of three different hamburgers available in the restaurant, each with different toppings, accompanied with French fries, coleslaw, jalapeños, ketchup and sweet chili sauce.

In Finland, night-time fast food kiosks sell hamburgers to take away and eat at home. These hamburgers are intended mostly as quick nourishment instead of a culinary experience.

Variations

Burgers can also be made with patties made from ingredients other than beef. For example, a *turkey burger* uses ground turkey meat, a *chicken burger* uses ground chicken meat. A *buffalo burger* uses ground meat from a bison, and an *ostrich burger* is made from ground seasoned ostrich meat. A deer burger uses ground venison from deer.

A *veggie burger*, *garden burger*, or *tofu burger* uses a meat analogue, a

An extremely spicy hamburger containing Naga Morich chili sauce.

meat substitute such as tofu, TVP, seitan (wheat gluten), quorn, beans, grains or an assortment of vegetables, ground up and mashed into patties.

United States and Canada

North American homemade hamburger

In the United States and Canada, burgers may be classified as two main types: fast food hamburgers and individually prepared burgers made in homes and restaurants. The latter are traditionally prepared "with everything", which includes lettuce, tomato, onion, and often sliced pickles (or pickle relish). Coleslaw and french fries usually accompany the burger. Cheese (usually processed cheese slices but often Cheddar, Swiss, pepper jack, or blue), either melted on the meat patty or crumbled on top, is generally an option.

Condiments might be added to a hamburger or may be offered separately on the side including mustard, mayonnaise, ketchup, salad dressings and barbecue sauce.

Other toppings include bacon, avocado or guacamole, sliced sautéed mushrooms, cheese sauce and/or chili (usually without beans), fried egg, scrambled egg, feta cheese, blue cheese, salsa, pineapple, jalapenos and other kinds of chili peppers, anchovies, slices of ham or bologna, pastrami or teriyaki-seasoned beef, tartar sauce, french fries, onion rings or potato chips.

Standard toppings on hamburgers may depend upon location, particularly at restaurants that are not national or regional franchises. A "Texas burger" uses mustard as the only sauce, and comes with or without vegetables, jalapeno slices, and cheese. In the Upper Midwest, particularly Wisconsin, burgers are often made with a buttered bun, butter as one of the ingredients of the patty or with a pat of butter on top of the burger patty. This is called a "butter burger". In the Carolinas, a hamburger "with everything" may be served with cheese, chili, onions, mustard, and coleslaw. National chain Wendy's sells a "Carolina Classic" burger with these toppings in these areas. In Hawaii hamburgers are often topped with teriyaki sauce, derived from the Japanese-American culture, and locally grown pineapple. Waffle House claims on its menus and website to offer 70,778,880 different ways of serving a hamburger. In portions of the Midwest and East coast, a hamburger served with lettuce, tomato, and onion is called a "California burger". This usage is sufficiently widespread to appear on the menus of Dairy Queen. In the Western U.S., a "California" burger often means a cheeseburger, with guacamole and bacon added. Pastrami burgers may be served in Salt Lake City, Utah.

A hamburger with two patties is called a "double decker" or simply a "double", a hamburger with three patties is called a "triple". Doubles and triples are often combined with cheese and sometimes with bacon, yielding a "double cheeseburger" or a "triple bacon cheeseburger", or alternatively, a "bacon double or triple cheeseburger".

A hamburger smothered in red or green chile is called a slopper.

A patty melt consists of a patty, sautéed onions and cheese between two slices of rye bread. The sandwich is then buttered and fried.

A slider is a very small square hamburger patty sprinkled with diced onions and served on an equally small bun. According to the earliest citations, the name originated aboard U.S. Navy ships, due to the way greasy burgers slid across the galley grill while the ship pitched and rolled. Other versions claim the term "slider" originated from the hamburgers served by flight line galleys at military airfields, which were so greasy they slid right through you; or because their small size allows them to "slide" right down your throat in one or two bites.

The term "steakburger" is commonly used to describe a hamburger made with patties from meat considered to be of higher quality, such as ground steak or other lean ground beef. It is known mostly for the burgers named as "steakburgers" on the menu of restaurants such as Freddy's Frozen Custard and Steak 'n Shake.

In Alberta, Canada a "kubie burger" is a hamburger made with a pressed Ukrainian sausage (kubasa).

In Minnesota, a "Juicy Lucy", or "Jucy Lucy", is a hamburger having cheese inside the meat patty rather than on top. A piece of cheese is surrounded by raw meat and cooked until it melts, resulting in a molten core of cheese within the patty. This scalding hot cheese tends to gush out at the first bite, so servers frequently warn patrons to let the sandwich cool for a few minutes before consumption.

A low carb burger is a hamburger where the bun is omitted and large pieces of lettuce are used in its place, with mayonnaise and/or mustard being the sauces primarily used.

Mexico

In Mexico, burgers (called *hamburguesas*) are served with ham and slices of American cheese (locally called *queso americano*) fried on top of the meat patty. The toppings include avocado, jalapeño slices, shredded lettuce, onion and tomato. The bun has mayonnaise, ketchup and mustard. In certain parts are served with bacon, which can be fried or grilled along with the meat patty. A slice of pineapple is also a usual option, and the variation is known as a

"Hawaiian hamburger".

Some restaurants' burgers also have barbecue sauce, and others also replace the ground patty with sirloin, Al pastor meat, barbacoa or a fried chicken breast. Many burger chains from the United States can be found all over Mexico, including Carl's Jr., Sonic, as well as global chains such as McDonald's and Burger King.

United Kingdom and Ireland

Hamburgers in the UK and Ireland are very similar to their US cousins, and the High Street is dominated by the same big two chains as in the U.S. — McDonald's and Burger King. The menus offered to both countries are virtually identical, although portion sizes tend to be smaller in the UK. In Ireland the food outlet Supermacs is widespread throughout the country serving burgers as part of its menu. In Ireland, Abrakebabra (started out selling kebabs) and Eddie Rockets are also major chains.

An original and indigenous rival to the big two U.S. giants was the quintessentially British fast-food chain Wimpy, originally known as Wimpy Bar (opened 1954 at the Lyon's Corner House in Coventry Street London), which served its hamburgers on a plate with British-style chips, accompanied by cutlery and delivered to the customer's table. In the late 1970s, to compete with McDonald's, Wimpy began to open American-style counter-service restaurants and the brand disappeared from many UK high streets when those restaurants were re-branded as Burger Kings between 1989–90 by the then-owner of both brands, Grand Metropolitan. A management buyout in 1990 split the brands again and now Wimpy table-service restaurants can still be found in many town centers whilst new counter-service Wimpys are now often found at motorway service stations.

Hamburgers are also available from mobile kiosks, particularly at outdoor events such as football matches. Burgers from this type of outlet are usually served without any form of salad — only fried onions and a choice of tomato ketchup, mustard or brown sauce.

Chip shops, particularly in the West Midlands, North-East, Scotland and Ireland, serve battered hamburgers called batter burgers. This is where the burger patty, by itself, is deep-fat-fried in batter and is usually served with chips.

Hamburgers and veggie burgers served with chips and salad, are standard pub grub menu items. Many pubs specialize in "gourmet" burgers. These are usually high quality minced steak patties, topped with items such as blue cheese, brie, avocado et cetera. Some British pubs serve burger patties made from more exotic meats including venison burgers (sometimes nicknamed Bambi Burgers), bison burgers, ostrich burgers and in some Australian themed pubs even kangaroo burgers can be purchased. These burgers are served in a similar way to the traditional hamburger but are sometimes served with a different sauce including redcurrant sauce, mint sauce and plum sauce.

In the early 21st century "premium" hamburger chain and independent restaurants have arisen, selling burgers produced from meat stated to be of high quality and often organic, usually served to eat on the premises rather than to take away. Chains include Gourmet Burger Kitchen, Ultimate Burger, Hamburger Union and Byron Hamburgers in London. Independent restaurants such as Meatmarket and Dirty Burger developed a style of rich, juicy burger in 2012 which is known as a *dirty burger* or *third-wave burger*.

In recent years Rustlers has sold pre-cooked hamburgers re-heat able in a microwave oven in the United Kingdom.

In the UK, as in North America and Japan, the term "burger" can refer simply to the patty, be it beef, some other kind of meat, or vegetarian.

Australia and New Zealand

Fast food franchises sell American style fast food hamburgers in Australia and New Zealand. The traditional Australasian hamburgers are usually bought from fish and chip shops or milk bars. The hamburger meat is almost always ground beef, or "mince" as it is more commonly referred to in Australia and New Zealand. They commonly include tomato, lettuce, grilled onion and meat

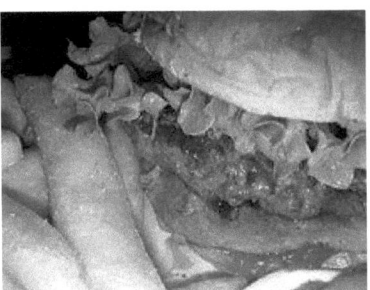

This hamburger in a fast food restaurant in Auckland, New Zealand contains beetroot for flavor.

as minimum, and can optionally include cheese, beetroot, pineapple, a fried egg and bacon. If all these optional ingredients are included it is known in Australia as "The Lot".

The only variance between the two countries' hamburgers is that New Zealand's equivalent to the "The Lot" often contains a steak (beef) as well. The condiments regularly used are barbecue sauce and tomato sauce. The McDonald's "McOz" Burger is partway between American and Australian style burgers, having beetroot and tomato in an otherwise typical American burger, however it is no longer a part of the menu. Likewise McDonald's in New Zealand created a Kiwiburger, similar to a Quarter Pounder, but features salad, beetroot and a fried egg. The Hungry Jack's (Burger King) "Aussie Burger" has tomato, lettuce, onion, cheese, bacon, beetroot, egg, ketchup and a meat patty.

China

In China, restaurants such as McDonald's and KFC have been proliferating all across the country. In many parts of China, small hamburger chains have opened up.

In supermarkets and corner stores, customers can buy unrefrigerated "hamburgers" (*hanbao*) off the bread shelf. These are ultra-sweet buns cut open with a thin slice of pork or ham placed inside without any condiments or vegetables. These hanbao are a half-westernised form of the traditional Cantonese buns called "*char siu bao*" (BBQ Pork Bun). The Chinese word for hamburger (hanbao) often refers to all sandwiches containing hamburger buns and cooked meat, regardless of the meat's origin including chicken burgers.

Japan

Hamburg steak

MOS Burger "Rice Burger"

In Japan, hamburgers can be served in a bun, called *hanbāgā* (ハンバーガー), or just the patties served without a bun, known as *hanbāgu* (ハンバーグ) or "hamburg", short for "hamburg steak".

Hamburg steaks (served without buns) are similar to what are known as Salisbury steaks in the USA. They are made from minced beef, pork or a blend of the two, mixed with minced onions, egg, breadcrumbs and spices. They are served with brown sauce (or demi-glace in restaurants) with vegetable or salad sides, or occasionally in Japanese curries. It is may be served in casual, western style suburban restaurant chains known in Japan as "family restaurants".

Hamburgers in buns, on the other hand, are predominantly the domain of fast food chains such as American chains known as McDonald's and Wendy's. Japan has home grown hamburger chain restaurants such as MOS Burger, First Kitchen and Freshness Burger. Local varieties of burgers served in Japan include teriyaki burgers, *katsu* burgers (containing tonkatsu) and burgers containing shrimp korokke. Some of the more unusual examples include the "Rice Burger", where the bun is made of rice, and the luxury 1000-yen (US$10) "Takumi Burger" (meaning "artisan taste"), featuring avocados, freshly grated wasabi, and other rare seasonal ingredients. In terms of the actual patty, there are burgers made with Kobe beef, butchered from cows that are fed with beer and massaged daily. McDonald's Japan also recently launched a McPork burger, made with U.S. pork. McDonald's has been gradually losing market share in Japan to these local hamburger chains, due in part to the preference of Japanese diners for fresh ingredients and more refined, "upscale" hamburger offerings. Burger King once retreated from Japan, but re-entered the market in Summer 2007 in cooperation with the Japanese fast-food chain Lotteria.

Other countries

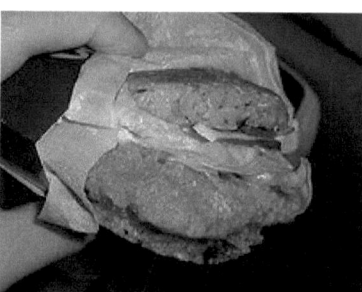

Chicken burger with rice bun (sold in Taiwan, Korea, Hong Kong, Macao, the Philippines, Thailand and Singapore). Note that the "bun" is composed of cooked rice

Rice burgers, mentioned above, are also available in several East Asian countries such as Taiwan and South Korea. Lotteria is a big hamburger franchise in Japan owned by the South Korean Lotte group, with outlets also in China, South Korea, Vietnam, and Taiwan. In addition to selling beef hamburgers, they also have hamburgers made from squid, pork, tofu, and shrimp. Variations available in South Korea include Bulgogi burgers and Kimchi burgers.

In the Philippines a wide range of major U.S. fast-food franchises are well represented, together with local imitators, often amended to the local palate. The chain McDonald's (locally nicknamed "McDo") have a range of burger and chicken dishes often accompanied by plain steamed rice and/or French fries. The Philippines boasts its own burger-chain called Jollibee, which offers burger meals and chicken, including a signature burger called "Champ". Jollibee now has a number of outlets in the United States, the Middle East and East Asia.

Vada pav or "Indian Burger" is made of Potatoes and spices.

In India, burgers are usually made from chicken or vegetable patties due to cultural beliefs against eating beef (which stem from Hindu religious practice) and pork (which stems from Islamic religious practice). Because of this, the majority of fast food chains and restaurants in India do not serve beef. McDonald's in India, for instance, do not serve beef, offering the "Maharaja Mac" instead of the Big Mac, substituting the beef patties with chicken. Another version of the Indian vegetarian burger is the Wada Pav consisting deep-fried potato patty dipped in gramflour batter. It is usually served with mint chutney and fried green chili.

In Pakistan, apart from American fast food chains, burgers can be found in stalls near shopping areas, the best known being the "shami burger". This is made from "shami kebab", made by mixing lentil and minced lamb. Onions, scrambled egg and ketchup are the most may be toppings.

Beef burger with fried egg, cabbage and some french fries in Kota Kinabalu, Malaysia.

In Malaysia there are 300 McDonald's restaurants. The menu in Malaysia also includes eggs and fried chicken on top of the regular burgers. Burgers are also easily found at nearby mobile kiosks, especially Ramly Burger.

In Mongolia, a recent fast food craze due to the sudden influx of foreign influence has led to the prominence of the hamburger. Specialized fast food restaurants serving to Mongolian tastes have sprung up and seen great success.

In Turkey, in addition to the internationally familiar variations of burgers, localized variations of the hamburger such as the Islak Burger (lit. "Wet-Burger"), lamb-burgers and offal-burgers are offered by global chains McDonald's and Burger King and local fast food businesses alike. The Islak Hamburger, which is typically assembled with just the patty and bun, coated with seasoned tomato sauce and stemed within a glass chamber, has its origins in the Turkish fast food retailer Kizilkayalar. Furthermore, hamburger shops have also adopted a pizzaria-like approach when it comes to delivering and almost all major fast food chains deliver.

Unusual hamburgers

At $499, the world's largest hamburger commercially available tips the scales at 185.8 pounds (84.3 kg) and is on the menu at Mallie's Sports Grill & Bar in Southgate, Michigan. It is called the "Absolutely Ridiculous Burger", which takes about 12 hours to prepare. It was cooked and adjudicated on May 30, 2009.

A $777 Kobe beef and Maine lobster burger, topped with caramelized onion, Brie cheese and prosciutto, was reported available at Le Burger Brasserie, inside the Paris Las Vegas casino.

New York chef Daniel Boulud created an intricate dish composed of layers of ground sirloin, foie gras, and wine-braised short ribs, assembled to look exactly like a fast-food burger. It is available with truffles in season.

On September 2, 2012, the Black Bear Casino Resort near Carlton, Minnesota made the world-record bacon cheeseburger that weighed 2,014 pounds (914 kg). Guinness World Records verified the record for biggest burger.

In Las Vegas, Nevada at the Heart Attack Grill there is a Quadruple Bypass Burger. The burger weighs two pounds and the name is derived from the fact that the burger is unhealthy. The restaurant is known for being honest about the fact that their food is unhealthy. Interestingly, they allow people that weigh over 350 pounds (160 kg) to eat for free.

Slang

"$100 hamburger" ("hundred-dollar hamburger") is aviation slang for a general aviation pilot needing an excuse to fly. A $100 hamburger trip typically involves flying a short distance (less than two hours), eating at an airport restaurant, and flying home.

Source http://en.wikipedia.org/wiki/Hamburger

Hot dog

A cooked hot dog on a bun garnished with mustard

Origin
Alternative name(s)	Frankfurters, Frankfurts, franks, wieners, weenies

Details
Serving temperature	Hot
Main ingredient(s)	Pork, beef, chicken, or combinations thereof, and bread
Variations	Multiple
Other information	Hot dogs are often pink, but may be brown

A **hot dog** is a fully cooked sausage, traditionally grilled or steamed. typically served in a sliced bun, As a Corn dog dipped in corn batter and deep fried, or as an ingredient in other dishes like beanie weenies.It is often garnished with mustard, ketchup, onions, mayonnaise, relish, cheese, chili and/or sauerkraut.

History

Claims about hot dog invention are difficult to assess, as stories assert the creation of the sausage, the placing of the sausage (or another kind of sausage) on bread or a bun as finger food, the popularization of the existing dish, or the application of the name "hot dog" to

Carts selling frankfurters in New York City, circa 1906. The price is listed as "3 cents each or 2 for 5 cents".

a sausage and bun combination most commonly used with ketchup or mustard and sometimes relish.

The word **frankfurter** comes from Frankfurt, Germany, where pork sausages similar to hot dogs originated. These sausages, *Frankfurter Würstchen*, were known since the 13th century and given to the people on the

A "home-cooked" hot dog with ketchup, mustard, raw onion, fried onion, artificial bacon bits, and pickle-relish

Hot dog vendor in Amsterdam

event of imperial coronations, starting with the coronation of Maximilian II, Holy Roman Emperor as King. **Wiener** refers to Vienna, Austria, whose German name is "Wien", home to a sausage made of a mixture of pork and beef (cf. Hamburger, whose name also derives from a German-speaking city). Johann Georg Lahner, a 18th/19th century butcher from the Franconian city of Coburg, is said to have brought the *Frankfurter Würstchen* to Vienna, where he added beef to the mixture and simply called it *Frankfurter*. Nowadays, in German speaking countries, except Austria, hot dog sausages are called *Wiener* or *Wiener Würstchen* (*Würstchen* means "little sausage"), in differentiation to the original pork only mixture from Frankfurt. In Swiss German, it is called *Wienerli*, while in Austria the terms *Frankfurter* or *Frankfurter Würstel* are used.

Around 1870, on Coney Island, German immigrant Charles Feltman began selling sausages in rolls.

Others have supposedly invented the hot dog. The idea of a hot dog on a bun is ascribed to the wife of a German named Antonoine Feuchtwanger, who sold hot dogs on the streets of St. Louis, Missouri, United States, in 1880, because his customers kept taking the white gloves handed to them for eating without burning their hands. Anton Ludwig Feuchtwanger, a Bavarian sausage seller, is said to have served sausages in rolls at the World's Fair–either the 1893 World's Columbian Exposition in Chicago or the 1904 Louisiana Purchase Exposition in St Louis–again allegedly because the white gloves he gave to customers so that they could eat his hot sausages in comfort began to disappear as souvenirs.

The association between hot dogs and baseball began as early as 1893 with Chris von der Ahe, a German immigrant who owned not only the St. Louis Browns, but also an amusement park.

Another claim of inventing the hot dog is told by Harry M. Stevens, an American sports concessionaire whose vendors sold German sausages and rolls to spectators at the old New York Polo Grounds during the winter. He called them "Dachshund sandwiches", but a New York Post cartoonist "couldn't spell dachshund, so when he drew the cartoon, he called them hot dogs."

In 1916, a Polish American employee of Feltman's named Nathan Handwerker was encouraged by Eddie Cantor and Jimmy Durante, both working as waiters/musicians, to go into business in competition with his former employer. Handwerker undercut Feltman's by charging five cents for a hot dog when his former employer was charging ten.

At an earlier time in food regulation, when the hot dog was suspect, Handwerker made sure that men wearing surgeon's smocks were seen eating at Nathan's Famous to reassure potential customers.

Etymology

The term *dog* has been used as a synonym for sausage since 1884 and accusations that sausage makers used dog meat date to at least 1845. In the early 20th century, consumption of dog meat in Germany was common. The suspicion that sausages contained dog meat was "occasionally justified".

According to a myth, the use of the complete phrase *hot dog* in reference to sausage was coined by the newspaper cartoonist Thomas Aloysius "TAD" Dorgan around 1900 in a cartoon recording the sale of hot dogs during a New York Giants baseball game at the Polo Grounds. However, TAD's earliest usage of *hot dog* was not in reference to a baseball game at the Polo Grounds, but to a bicycle race at Madison Square Garden, in *The New York Evening Journal* December 12, 1906, by which time the term *hot dog* in reference to sausage was already in use. In addition, no copy of the apocryphal cartoon has ever been found.

The earliest known usage of *hot dog* in clear reference to sausage, found by Fred R. Shapiro, appeared in the December 31, 1892 issue of the *Paterson (New Jersey) Daily Press*. The story concerned a local traveling vendor, Thomas Francis Xavier Morris, also known as "Hot Dog Morris".

Somehow or other a frankfurter and a roll seem to go right to the spot where the void is felt the most. The small boy has got on such familiar terms with this sort of lunch that he now refers to it as "hot dog." "Hey, Mister, give me a hot dog quick," was the startling order that a rosy-cheeked gamin hurled at the man as a Press reporter stood close by last night. The "hot dog" was quickly inserted in a gash in a roll, a dash of mustard also splashed on to the "dog" with a piece of flat whittled stick, and the order was fulfilled.

Other early uses of *hot dog* in reference to sausage appeared in the *New Brunswick* (New Jersey) *Daily Times* (May 20, 1893), the *New York World*

(May 26, 1893), and the *Knoxville* (Tennessee) *Journal* (September 28, 1893).

General description

Grilled hot dogs

Ingredients

Common hot dog ingredients include:
Meat trimmings and fat
Flavorings, such as salt, garlic, and paprika
Preservatives (cure) - typically sodium erythorbate and sodium nitrite
Pork and beef are the traditional meats used in hot dogs. Less expensive hot dogs are often made from chicken or turkey, using low cost mechanically separated poultry. Hot dogs often have high sodium, fat and nitrite content, ingredients linked to health problems. Changes in meat technology and dietary preferences have led manufacturers to use turkey, chicken, vegetarian meat substitutes, and to lower the salt content.

If a manufacturer produces two types of hot dogs, "wieners" tend to contain pork and are blander, while "franks" tend to be all beef and more strongly seasoned.

Commercial preparation

Hot dogs are prepared commercially by mixing the ingredients (meats, spices, binders and fillers) in vats where rapidly moving blades grind and mix the ingredients in the same operation. This mixture is forced through tubes into casings for cooking. Most hot dogs sold in the US are "skinless" as opposed to more expensive "natural casing" hot dogs.

Natural casing hot dogs

As with most sausages, hot dogs must be in a casing to be cooked. Traditional casing is made from the small intestines of sheep. The products are known as "natural casing" hot dogs or frankfurters. These hot dogs have firmer texture and a "snap" that releases juices and flavor when the product is bitten.

Kosher casings are expensive in commercial quantities in the US, so kosher hot dogs are usually skinless or made with reconstituted collagen casings.

Skinless hot dogs

One of the more recent developments in hot dog preparation: The hot dog toaster.

"Skinless" hot dogs must use a casing in the cooking process when the product is manufactured, but the casing is usually a long tube of thin cellulose that is removed between cooking and packaging. This process was invented in Chicago in 1925 by Erwin O. Freund, founder of Visking which would later become Viskase Companies.

The first skinless hot dog casings were produced by Freund's new company under the name "Nojax", short for "no jackets" and sold to local Chicago sausage makers.

Skinless hot dogs vary in the texture of the product surface but have a softer "bite" than natural casing hot dogs. Skinless hot dogs are more uniform in shape and size than natural casing hot dogs and less expensive.

Home cooking hot dogs

Hot dogs are prepared and eaten in a variety of ways. The wieners may be boiled, grilled, fried, steamed, broiled, baked, or microwaved. The cooked wiener may be served on a bun (usually topped with condiments), or it may be used as an ingredient in another dish.

Health effects

Unlike other sausages which may be sold uncooked, hot dogs are cooked before packaging. Hot dogs can be eaten without additional cooking, although they are usually warmed before serving. Because an unopened, packaged hot dog can have *Listeria* bacteria that cause listeriosis, it is safer to heat them, especially for pregnant women and those with suppressed immune systems.

An American Institute for Cancer Research report found that consuming one 50-gram serving of processed meat — about one hot dog — every day increases risk of colorectal cancer by 20 percent. The Cancer Project group filed a class-action lawsuit demanding warning labels on packages and at sporting events. Hot dogs are high in fat and salt and have preservatives sodium nitrate and nitrite, which are possible contributors to nitrate-containing chemicals believed to cause cancer. According to the AICR, the average risk of colorectal cancer is 5.8 percent, but 7 percent when a hot dog is consumed daily over years.

Hot dogs have relatively low heterocyclic amines (HCA) levels compared to other types of ready-to-eat meat products, because they are manufactured at low temperatures.

Choking risk

Hot dogs present a significant choking risk, especially for children. A study in the US found that 17% of food-related asphyxiations among children younger than 10 years of age were caused by hot dogs. Their size, shape and texture make them difficult to expel from the windpipe. This risk can be reduced by cutting a hot dog into small pieces or lengthwise strips before serving to young children. It is suggested that redesign of size, shape and texture would reduce the risk. One pediatric emergency doctor comments that a stuck hot dog is "almost impossible" to dislodge from a child's windpipe.

In the United States

In the US, "hot dog" may refer to just the sausage or to the combination of

A roadside hot dog stand near Huntington, West Virginia

a sausage in a bun. Many nicknames for hot dogs have popped up over the years. A hot dog can often be seen under the names of frankfurter, frank, red hot, wiener, weenie, durger, coney, or just "dog".

Hot dog restaurants

Hot dog stands and trucks sell hot dogs at street and highway locations. Wandering hot dog vendors sell their product in baseball parks. At convenience stores, hot dogs are kept heated on rotating grills. 7-Eleven sells the most grilled hot dogs in North America — 100 million annually. Hot dogs are also common on restaurants' children's menus.

Condiments

A Detroit Coney Island hot dog with chili, onion and mustard

Hot dogs may be served plain, but are commonly served with a variety of condiments, including ketchup, mustard, chile con carne, pickle relish, sauerkraut, onion, mayonnaise, lettuce, tomato, cheese, and chili peppers.

In 2005, the US-based National Hot Dog & Sausage Council (part of the American Meat Institute) found mustard to be the most popular condiment, with 32% of respondents preferring it; 23% of Americans said they preferred ketchup; chili con carne came in third at 17%, followed by relish at 9% and onions at 7%. Southerners showed the strongest preference for chili, while Midwesterners showed the greatest affinity for ketchup.

Condiments vary across the country. All-beef Chicago-style hot dogs are topped with mustard, fresh tomatoes, onions, sport peppers, bright green relish, dill pickles, and celery salt, but they exclude ketchup.

Many variations are named after regions other than the one in which they are popular. Italian hot dogs popular in New Jersey include peppers, onions, and potatoes. Meaty Michigan hot dogs are popular in upstate New York (as are white hots), while beefy Coney Island hot dogs are popular in Michigan. In New York City, conventional hot dogs are available on Coney Island, as are bagel dogs. Hot wieners, or weenies, are a staple in Rhode Island. Texas hot dogs are spicy variants found in upstate New York and Pennsylvania (and as "all the way dogs" in New Jersey), but not Texas.

Some baseball parks have signature hot dogs, such as Fenway Franks at Fenway Park in Boston and Dodger Dogs at Dodger Stadium in Los Angeles. The Fenway signature is that the hot dog is boiled and grilled Fenway-style, and then served on a New England-style bun, covered with ketchup and relish. Often during Red Sox games, vendors traverse the stadium selling the hot dogs plain, giving customers the choice of adding the condiments.

Hot dogs outside North America

In most of the world, "hot dog" is recognized as a sausage in a bun, but the type varies considerably. The name is applied to something that would not be described as a hot dog in North America. For example, in New Zealand, it refers to a battered sausage, often on a stick (which is known as a corn dog in North America), and the version in a bun is called an "American hot dog".

Records

The world's longest hot dog created was

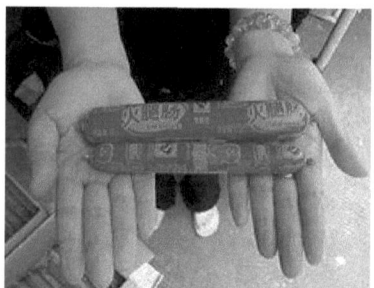

A common brand of hot dog available throughout China

60 metres (197 ft), which rested within a 60.3-metre (198 ft) bun. The hot dog was prepared by Shizuoka Meat Producers for the All-Japan Bread Association, which baked the bun and coordinated the event, including official measurement for the world record. The hot dog and bun were the center of a media event in celebration of the Association's 50th anniversary on August 4, 2006, at the Akasaka Prince Hotel, Tokyo, Japan.

A hot dog prepared by head chef Joe Calderone in Manhattan sold for US$69 during the National Hot Dog Day in 2010, making it the most expensive hot dog sold at the time. The hot dog was topped with truffle oil, duck foie gras, and truffle butter.

On May 31, 2012, Guinness World Records certified the world record for most expensive hot dog at $145.49. The "California Capitol City Dawg", served at Capitol Dawg in Sacramento, California, features a grilled 18" all-beef in natural casing frank from Chicago, served on a fresh baked herb and oil focaccia roll, spread with white truffle butter, then grilled. The record breaking hot dog is topped with a whole grain mustard from France, garlic & herb mayonnaise, sauteed chopped shallots, organic mixed baby greens, maple syrup marinated/fruitwood smoked uncured bacon from New Hampshire, chopped tomato, expensive moose cheese from Sweden, sweetened dried cranberries, basil olive oil/pear-cranberry-coconut balsamic viniagrette, and ground peppercorn. Proceeds from the sale of each 3 lb. super dog are donated to the Shriners Hospitals for Children.   Source http://en.wikipedia.org/wiki/ Hot_dog

Hot dog cart

Hot dog cart in New York City

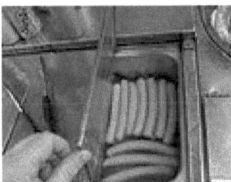

Hot dog cart hot dogs in heated water

A **hot dog cart** is a specialized mobile food stand for preparing and selling street food, specifically hot dogs, to passersby. A cart operator must meet stringent health regulations designed to protect the public. Hot dog carts are quick and easy food services, supplying millions of people with food every day. The U.S. Hot Dog Council estimates that 15% of the approximately 10 billion hot dogs consumed by Americans last year were purchased from a mobile hot dog vendor cart.

Overview

A hot dog cart is generally a compact cart, fully self-contained and designed to serve a limited menu. An on-board cooler is used to keep the hot dogs safely chilled until ready for reheating. It also provides cold storage for beverages, such as sodas, and multiple sinks for washing and cleaning utensils. Most hot dog carts use propane to heat the foods, making them independent of electrical power. Some carts may also be fitted with a propane grill, griddle, deep fryer, or other such cooking appliance. A colorful umbrella is often installed to protect the food preparation area from contamination, provide some shade, and advertise the cart's location. The purpose of the umbrella is to offer shade to the operator and customers and as well to keep airborne dirt from falling onto the cart.

Construction

Hot dog carts are generally built from materials that resist corrosion, are hygiene friendly, and are easy to clean. This generally means that they are made of stainless steel, but some carts also have components made from plastic, wood, or fiberglass. The food preparation body of the cart is often mounted on a chassis that can be easily towed, to a vendor's location by a vehicle or pushed to a location by hand. Types of carts may vary from a lightweight push cart of only about 200 lbs (90 kg), to fully enclosed walk-in carts weighing 1/2 a ton or more. A good hot dog cart must generally be equipped with the following components. Stainless steel easily cleanable construction ; 1 7/8 hitch; standard wiring ; 20 lb propane tank (NSF Approved); full-size umbrella; insulated soda cooler; although it is not a good idea due to the high heat generated by the cart. You will end up using an ice chest; hot & cold water hand sink (NSF Parts); display case with doors; standard tail lamps; 5–7 gallon fresh-water tank; waste tank (7–9 gallon); three individually operated burners; adjustable controls; bottom storage compartment; safe to use pilots on stove.

Issues

Although hot dog carts can be equipped to cook a variety of other meats and foods from fresh or raw states, local health code regulations in the U.S. and Canada governing food safety and the types of food that can be sold from mobile food stands usually limit hot dog carts to selling reheated pre-cooked wieners and sausages. These health code regulations vary widely from state to state and county to county. In addition, health regulations often limit what side dishes, condiments, and garnishes may be sold from a mobile food cart, which are potentially hazardous foods, foods at high risk for spoilage due to rapid bacterial growth at certain temperatures. For example, and it is rarely done, but some stands may offer eggs and dairy products. Meats that are considered to be hazardous, such as pork and poultry, may also be banned from sale at mobile foods stands. Bacon Wrapped dogs are typically forbidden, however a common workaround is offering pre-cooked bacon bits as a condiment. Wieners are only served on buns with certain approved condiments such as, but not limited to: mustards, pickles, pickled relishes, chopped onions, and tomato ketchup.

Health regulations

Health code regulations are usually dictated by county health departments, and as a result, they vary widely across the United States and Canada. In addition to determining what types of foods are allowed to be served, these local codes often specify mandates of what equipment should be installed on a mobile food cart. Such codes also ensure that the food cart has built-in facilities for achieving appropriate hygiene levels for the cart, the equipment and utensils being used, and the operator handling the food. This may include hot and cold running water, an insulated ice box, and a number of separate sinks for washing hands and utensils. Some areas specify that a cart have as many as four of these sinks. Local or state codes may also require that a hot dog cart be approved by a quality assurance agency such as NSF International (National Sanitation Foundation). In addition, local health codes may require the cart to be physically inspected by the local health department, and that a cart operator attend a training course in safe food handling and preparation.

California

California recently passed new legislation that greatly affected the operation of hot dogs carts in that state. The new California Retail Food Code (Cal Code) was introduced in July 2010. This is, in effect, the strictest and most comprehensive set of laws governing the use of hot dog carts in the United States. While these new regulations are thought to be stricter than the previous rules they are in fact merely made more difficult with the intent to keep new hot dog cart operators from opening. Indeed the new regulations are so onerous as to be nearly impossible to implement without paying such a high cost for a cart as to be unfeasible.

The Cal Code mandates that hot dog cart operators must follow a strict operational procedure that includes formal approved training in food safety. Under this new framework of food laws, hot dog carts in California must also operate from an approved commissary, often an approved restaurant, delicatessen, grocery store, or other food facility providing a safe, clean base of operations for the hot dog cart. At the commissary, the cart is to be cleaned, loaded with food and fresh water each day, drained of waste water and emptied of unused food at day's end, and stored overnight. The commissary also provides services such as storing and preparing foods for the hot dog cart operator. This would include chopping the vegetables, such as onions and tomatoes, being used as condiments. The Cal Code specifies the list of facilities, equipment, and procedures that an approved commissary must have in place. Preparing food in a private home for retail sale to the public is strictly forbidden by the Cal Code. The local county health department usually has a list of approved commissaries for their jurisdiction.

The Cal Code also specifies the necessary equipment that hot dog carts must have on board for legal operations. This mandatory equipment list includes four sinks for ware washing and hand washing, a large volume of on-board water and appropriate sized waste water tanks, a refrigerator for storing potentially hazardous foods, such as meats, thermometers for monitoring food temperatures, and sneeze guards to protect the food display and preparation areas of the cart.

Manufacturing and sales

A large number of manufacturers of hot dog carts exist in the U.S. and Canada.

There is a surprisingly large number of regional recipes and presentation styles for hot dogs. These styles may range from specific condiments, such as a Michigan hot dog or a Montreal hot dog, to sauces that are added to the wiener and bun such as chili sauce and red onion sauce. Wieners are offered in a wide variety of sizes and types of meats including beef, chicken, turkey, and even vegetarian. Sausages reflect the various American and European styles such as Polish, Hot Italian, and Kosher. The bun itself can be offered in a number of varieties of sizes and bread types.

Although the hot dog is considered an American food invention dating back to New York in the late 19th century, cart manufacturers ship hot dog carts all around the world, including Europe, Asia, South America, and even the Middle East.

Source http://en.wikipedia.org/wiki/Hot_dog_cart

Isaw

Isaw

Isaw is a street food from the Philippines, made from barbecued pig or chicken intestines. The intestines are cleaned, turned inside out, and cleaned again, repeating the process several times. They are then either boiled, then grilled, or immediately grilled on sticks. They are usually dipped in kurat (Filipino term for vinegar with onions, peppers, and other spices) then eaten. They are usually sold by vendors on the street corners in afternoons.

While popular throughout the Philippines, Isaw has taken on an iconic status as a campus staple at the University of the Philippines Diliman. The UP Isawan (Isaw stall) is used as a regular setting comic book artist Manix Abrera, in his daily KikoMachine comic strip on the Philippine Daily Inquirer.

Source http://en.wikipedia.org/wiki/Isaw

Jiaozi

Ten steamed jiaozi *(zhengjiao)* and a peanut butter dipping sauce

Origin

Place of origin	China, Nepal

Details

Type	Dumpling
Main ingredient(s)	Dough, ground meat or vegetables

Jiaozi

Chinese name

Traditional Chinese	餃子
Simplified Chinese	饺子
Hanyu Pinyin	jiǎozi

Alternative Chinese name

Traditional Chinese	鍋貼
Simplified Chinese	锅贴
Literal meaning	pot sticker

Second alternative Chinese name

Traditional Chinese	扁食
Literal meaning	flat food

Korean name

Hangul	교자

Japanese name

Kanji	餃子
Kana	ギョーザ, ギョウザ

Nepali name

Nepali	म:म: or ममचा

Jiǎozi (simplified Chinese: 饺子; traditional Chinese: 餃子; Japanese: 餃子 (gyōza); Vietnamese: *bánh chẻo*; Nepali: म:म: or ममचा) or **pot sticker** is a Chinese dumpling widely spread to Nepal, Japan, Eastern and Western Asia.

Jiaozi typically consists of a ground meat and/or vegetable filling wrapped into a thinly rolled piece of dough, which is then sealed by pressing the edges together or by crimping. Jiaozi should not be confused with wonton; jiaozi has a thicker skin and a relatively flatter, more oblate, double-saucer like shape (similar in shape to ravioli), and is usually eaten with a soy-vinegar dipping sauce (and/or hot chili sauce); while wontons have thinner skin, have square skins, and are usually served in broth. The dough for the jiaozi and wonton wrapper also consist of different ingredients.

Types

A plate of boiled dumplings *(shuijiao)* and sauce.

Chinese dumplings *(jiaozi)* may be divided into various types depending on how they are cooked:

Boiled dumplings: *(shuijiao)* literally "water dumpling" (水餃; pinyin: *shuǐjiǎo*).

Steamed dumplings: *(zhengjiao)* literally "steam dumpling" (蒸餃; pinyin: *zhēngjiǎo*).

Pan fried dumplings: *(guotie)* literally "pan stick", known as "potstickers" in N. America, (鍋貼; pinyin: *guōtiē*), also referred to as "dry-fried dumplings" (煎餃; pinyin: *jiānjiǎo*).

Dumplings that use egg rather than dough to wrap the filling are called "egg dumplings" or (蛋餃; pinyin: *dànjiǎo*). Cantonese style Chinese dumplings (gaau) are standard fare in dim sum. *Gaau* is simply the Cantonese pronunciation for 餃 (pinyin: *jiǎo*). The immediate noted difference to *jiǎozi* is that they are smaller and wrapped in a thinner translucent skin, and usually steamed. In other words, these are steamed dumplings. The smaller size and the thinner pastry make the dumplings easier to cook through with steaming. Fillings include shrimp, scallop, chicken, tofu, mixed vegetables, and others. The most common type are shrimp dumplings (har gow). In contrast to *jiǎozi*, *gaau* are rarely home-made. Similar to *jiaozi*, many types of fillings exist, and dim sum restaurants often feature their own house specials or innovations. Dim sum chefs and artists often use ingredients in new or creative ways, or draw inspiration from other Chinese culinary traditions, such as Chiuchow, Hakka, or Shanghai. More creative chefs may even incorporate a fusion from other cultures, such as Japanese (teriyaki) or Southeast Asian (satay, curry), while upscale restaurants may use expensive or exotic ingredients such as lobster, shark fin and bird's nest. Another Cantonese dumpling is the jau gok.

Fillings in dumplings

Common dumpling meat fillings include pork, mutton, beef, chicken, fish, and shrimp, which are usually mixed with chopped vegetables. Popular vegetable fillings include napa cabbage, scallion (spring onions), leek, celery and garlic chives. Dumplings are eaten with a soy sauce-based dipping sauce that may include vinegar, garlic, ginger, rice wine, hot sauce, and sesame oil.

Origin

A plate of potstickers *(guotie)*, and dipping sauce.

Jiaozi are one of the major foods eaten during the Chinese New Year and year round in the northern provinces. They look like the golden ingots *yuan bao* used during the Ming Dynasty for money and the name sounds like the word for the earliest paper money, so serving them is believed to bring prosperity. Many families eat these at midnight on Chinese New Year's Eve. Some cooks will even hide a clean coin for the lucky to find.

Jiaozi were so named because they were horn shaped. The Chinese for "horn" is *jiǎo* (角), and jiaozi was originally written with the Chinese character for "horn", but later it was replaced by a specific character 餃, which has the food radical on the left and the phonetic component *jiāo* (交) on the right.

According to folk tales, jiaozi were invented by Zhang Zhongjing, one of the greatest practitioners of traditional Chinese medicine in history. They were originally called "tender ears" (嬌耳; pinyin: *jiao'er*) because they were used to treat frostbitten ears.

Jiaozi are eaten all year round, and can be eaten at any time of the day – breakfast, lunch or dinner. They can constitute one course, starter or side dish, or the main meal. In China, jiaozi are sometimes served as a last course during restaurant meals. As a breakfast dish, jiaozi are prepared alongside xiaolongbao at inexpensive, roadside restaurants. Typically, they are served in small steamers containing ten pieces each. Although mainly consumed at breakfast, these small restaurants keep them hot on steamers, and ready to eat all day.

As a dish prepared at home, each family has its own preferred method of making them, using favourite fillings, with types and methods of preparation varying widely from region to region.

Japanese version

Hamamatsu Gyōza

The Japanese word *Gyōza* (ギョーザ, ギョウザ) was derived from the reading of 餃子 in the Shandong Chinese dialect (giaozi) and is written using the same Chinese characters pronounced with Japanese sounds. The selection of characters indicates that the word is of non-Japanese origin.

The most prominent differences of Japanese-style gyōza from Chinese style jiaozi are the rich garlic flavor, which is less noticeable in the Chinese version, and the fact that Japanese gyōza are very lightly flavored with salt, soy, and that the gyōza wrappers are much thinner. Of course, jiaozi vary greatly across regions even within China, so these differences are not always substantial. They are usually served with soy-based tare sauce seasoned with rice vinegar and/or Rāyu (known as chili oil in English, *làyóu* (辣油) in China). The most common recipe found is a mixture of minced pork, cabbage, and *Nira* (Chinese chives), and sesame oil, and/or garlic, and/or ginger, which is then wrapped into thinly rolled dough skins. In essence, gyōza are similar in shape to pierogi.

Gyōza can be found in supermarkets and restaurants throughout Japan. Panfried *Gyōza* are sold as a side dish in many *ramen* and Chinese restaurants.

The most popular preparation method is the pan-fried style called *Yaki-gyōza* (焼き餃子), in which the dumpling is first fried on one flat side, creating a crispy skin. Then, water is added and the pan sealed with a lid, until the upper part of the *gyōza* is steamed. Other popular methods include boiled *Sui-gyōza* (水餃子) and deep fried *Age-gyōza* (揚げ餃子).

Store bought frozen dumplings are often prepared at home by first placing them in a pot of water which is brought to a boil, and then transferring them to a pan with oil to fry the skin.

Momo

The Nepali version is known as momo (म:म). The word "momo" comes from a Chinese loanword "momo" (饃饃). which translates to "steamed bread". When preparing momo, flour is filled, most commonly with ground water buffalo meat. Often, ground lamb or chicken meats are used as alternate to water buffalo meat. Finely chopped onion, minced garlic, fresh minced ginger, cumin powder, salt, coriander/cilantro, etc. are added to meat for flavoring. Sauce made from cooked tomatoes flavored with timur (Szechwan pepper), minced red chilies is often served along with momo.

Guotie

Making *guotie*.

Guotie (simplified Chinese: 锅贴; traditional Chinese: 鍋貼; pinyin: *guōtiē*; literally "pot stick") is pan-fried *jiaozi*, also known as **potstickers** in North America, or **yaki-gyoza** in Japan. They are a Northern Chinese style dumpling popular as a street food, appetizer, or side order in Chinese. This dish is sometimes served on a dim sum menu, but may be offered independently. The filling for this dish usually contains pork (sometimes chicken, or beef in Muslim areas), cabbage (or Chinese cabbage and sometimes spinach), scallions (spring or green onions), ginger, Chinese rice wine or cooking wine, and sesame seed oil.

Guotie are shallow-fried in a wok (Mandarin "guo"). A small quantity of water is added and the wok is covered. While the base of the dumplings is fried, the upper part is steamed and this gives a texture contrast typical of Chinese cuisine.

An alternative method is to steam in a wok and then fry to crispness on one side in a shallow frying pan.

Exactly the same dumpling is boiled in plenty of water to make jiaozi and both are eaten with a dipping sauce or chilli paste.

Three or five folds are made on one side of the round wrapper that is rolled so that the edges are thinner than the middle. This gives the base a large surface area that helps to give the dumpling stability to stand up in the pan.

The Chinese method of preparing the dough is to pour boiling water onto the flour and letting stand for five minutes and then adding a small quantity of cold water. This helps to activate the gluten in the dough.

Other names for *guotie*:

Peking ravioli – In Boston, *guotie* are known as "Peking ravioli", a name first coined at the Joyce Chen Restaurant in Cambridge, MA, in 1958.

Wor tip (Cantonese Jyutping: *wo1 tip3*) is the Cantonese name for *guotie'*

History

Guotie is said to date back over four millennia. However, the first mention in literature dates back to the Song Dynasty (960-1280 AD) in ancient China reporting *guotie* as being exceptionally good for the human soul.

Source http://en.wikipedia.org/wiki/Jiaozi

Kaassoufflé

A *broodje kaassoufflé* showing the melted cheese filling

Kaassoufflé (plural: *kaassoufflés*; diminutive form: *kaassouffleetje*) normally refers to a Dutch snack of melted cheese inside a thin dough-based wrap which has been breaded and then deep-fried.

Overview

A *kaassoufflé* is thought to originate from Indonesian street food. It is either bought ready-made frozen and deep-fried at home, or ordered at *snackbars* in the Netherlands, where it is one of the few vegetarian fast-food snacks available. At certain Dutch fastfood outlets, such as FEBO or Smullers, it is possible to purchase a *kaassoufflé* without having to order it at the counter; instead it can be had directly from an *automatiek*, a coin-operated vending machine. *Kaassoufflé* is also a popular snack to be served at a *borrel*, an informal Dutch gathering with drinks and snacks (the word *"borrel"* originally referred to a small glass in which distilled beverages, usually jenever, is served).

Typically this snack comes in two different shapes: either as a large rectangle measuring approximately 10 cm by 5 cm (4" by 2"), or shaped like a half moon of about 10 cm (5") in length. Smaller versions, called *mini kaassoufflés*, are usually sold for consumption at home, or for at the aforementioned *borrel* where they are usually eaten as part of a *bittergarnituur*, a selection of snacks to go with drinks. *Kaassoufflés* are not limited to having only a Gouda-like cheese as a filling. Additional flavourings can be added to the cheese, such as ham and spinach, or it can also be made with different types of cheese. Another variety of *kaassoufflé* is the oven-baked type. This is simply done by wrapping a slice of cheese, with or without additional spices, inside puff pastry and then baking it in an oven.

Although the name of this snack contains the word "soufflé", it has very little in common with a real soufflé which, indeed, can contain cheese and can therefore also be called a *kaassoufflé* in the Dutch language.

Consumption practices

A *kaassoufflé* is usually eaten on its own, or with mustard or a sweet chilli sauce on the side. A *broodje kaassoufflé* is the snack served in a bun.

Source http://en.wikipedia.org/wiki/Kaassoufflé

Kapsalon

A serving of Kapsalon

Kapsalon is a Dutch food item consisting of fries, topped with döner or shawarma meat, grilled with a layer of Gouda cheese until melted and then subsequently covered with a layer of dressed salad greens. The dish is often served with garlic sauce and sambal. Kapsalon is quite high in calories, with each serving containing approximately 1800 kcal. The term *kapsalon* literally means, "barbershop" in Dutch, alluding to one of the inventors of the dish.

The dish was conceived in 2003 by Nathaniël Gomes, a Capeverdian hairdresser in Rotterdam who in collaboration with the neighboring shawarma store "El Aviva" combined all his favorite ingredients into one dish. The dish has since spread around the Netherlands into Belgium and is commonly found in restaurants serving shawarmas.

Source http://en.wikipedia.org/wiki/Kapsalon

Kebab

Roast chicken kebab in Iran

Origin

Place of origin	Middle East

Details

Course	Main course
Serving temperature	Hot
Main ingredient(s)	Meat

Sturgeon kebabs being cooked in Turkmenistan

A sandwich of döner

Kebab (**kebap**, **kabab**, **kebob**, **kabob**, **kibob**, **kebhav**, or **kephav**) is a wide variety of skewered meals originating in the Middle East and later on adopted in the Balkans, the Caucasus, other parts of Europe, as well as Central and South Asia, that are now found worldwide. In English, *kebab* with no qualification generally refers more specifically to shish kebab (Turkish: "şiş kebap") cooked on a skewer. In the Middle East, however, kebab refers to meat that is cooked over or next to flames; large or small cuts of meat, or even ground meat; it may be served on plates, in sandwiches, or in bowls. The traditional meat for kebab is lamb, but depending on local tastes and religious prohibitions, it may now be beef, goat, chicken or fish. Like other ethnic foods brought by travellers, the kebab has become a part of everyday cuisine in many countries.

History

Pair of firedogs with zoomorphic finials, 17th century BC, Akrotiri.

The origin of kebab may lie in the short supply of cooking fuel in the Near East. Tradition has it that the dish was invented by medieval Persian soldiers who used their swords to grill meat over open-field fires. "Kebab", or the way the meat turns, is derived from Arabic word "cabob", a distortion of the Aramaic word "kabbaba" or "kababu" meaning to burn or char. According to Ibn Battuta, a Moroccan traveller, in India, kebab was served in the royal houses during the Delhi Sultanate period (1206-1526 CE), and even commoners would enjoy it for breakfast with naan. The dish has been native to the Near East and ancient Greece since antiquity; an early variant of kebab (Ancient Greek: ὀβελίσκος - *obeliskos*) is attested in Greece since 8th century BCE (archaic period) in Homer's *Iliad* and *Odyssey* and in classical Greece, amongst others in the works of Aristophanes, Xenophon and Aristotle. Excavations held in Akrotiri on the Greek island of Santorini by professor Christos G. Doumas, unearthed firedogs (stone sets of barbecue for skewers; Ancient Greek: κρατευταί - *krateutai*) used before the 17th century BCE. In each pair of the supports, the receptions for the spits are found in absolute equivalence, while the line of small openings in the base constitutes a mechanism for supplying the coals with oxygen so that they are kept alight during use.

National varieties

Cağ kebabı, a related dish. Note that the meat is horizontally stacked.

A serving of pork **souvlakia** with fried garlic bread and lemons

In Afghanistan

The main varieties include kabob e chopan, chapli kabob, teka kabob, shaami kabob, and rudi kabob.

In Armenia

Kebabs in Armenia are referred to as khorovats (խորոված). The choice of meats used in Armenia are pork, beef, chicken, lamb, and also include fish. With these meats many times there are additions of tomato, peppers, eggplant. The meat and vegetables are usually barbecued on metal skewers. Before barbecuing the meat, it is usually marinated and usually left to sit for 24–48 hours.

At the same time, kebab in Armenia is used to name a dish prepared of ground meat spiced with pepper, parsley and other herbs and roasted on skewers.

In Azerbaijan

Tika kabab and lyula kabab from mutton, as served in Qəçrəş, Quba Rayon, north-eastern Azerbaijan.

The main varieties include tika kabab, lyula kabab (doyma kabab in some places), tas kababy and tava kabab. The meat for tika kabab is sometimes prepared in basdirma (an onion gravy and thyme) and then goes onto the ramrods. When served, it could be adorned with sauce-like pomegranate addon (narsharab) and other condiments, and may also be served wrapped in Lavash.

In Bulgaria

In Bulgaria, the word кебап (kebap) refers to meat stews with relatively few or no vegetables. Dishes which are known in English as different kinds of "kebab" are not perceived as a distinct group of dishes. The Döner kebab is wide spread as fast food and is called merely дюнер (döner) thus not relating it to the Bulgarian кебап at all. Шиш кебап (Shish kebap) or Шашлик (Shahlik) is also common and has the same name as in Turkish.

In China

Chuan-style lamb kebab sticks sold by a street vendor.

كاۋاپ (Kawap) in Uyghur or Chuanr 串 called "chuàn" in Mandarin, often referred to as "Chua'r" in Pekingese throughout the North, is a variation of kebab originating from the Uyghurs in the Western province of Xinjiang, and a popular dish in Chinese Islamic cuisine.

It has since spread across the rest of the country and become a popular street food.

Small pieces of meat are skewered and either roasted or deep-fried. Common spices and condiments include cumin called "ziran", pepper, sesame, and sesame oil.

Although the most traditional form of chuanr uses lamb or mutton, other types of meat, such as chicken, beef, pork, and seafood, can be used as well.

During Chinese New Year, it is common to find fruit kebabs candied and covered with a hard candy sugar coating. At the famous Wángfǔjǐng in Beijing, it is very common to find many kinds of fruit kebabs of everything from bananas, strawberries, and seasonal Chinese fruits, as well as scorpions, squids, and various Japanese flavored kebabs all year long.

In Greece

Souvlaki is a popular Greek fast food consisting of small pieces of meat and sometimes vegetables grilled on a skewer. It may be served on the skewer for eating out of hand, in a pita sandwich with garnishes and sauces, or on a dinner plate, often with fried potatoes. The meat usually used in Greece and Cyprus is pork, although chicken may also be used. Hardly ever is lamb used.

In India

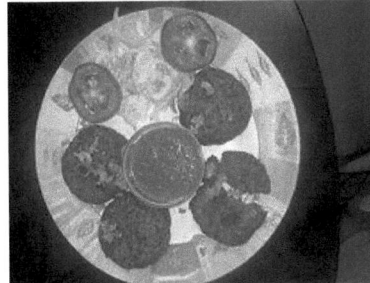

Shami kebab from Lucknow, India

Kebabs in India are more or less similar to most other kebab preparations along with their distinct taste which can be credited to the spices native to the Indian subcontinent. All the varieties such as Sheekh, Doner (known as Shawarma), Shammi Tikka, and other forms of roasted and grilled meats are savoured in South Asia. Some popular kebabs are:
Kakori Kebab
Shami Kabab
Kalmi Kebab
Kacche gosht ke chapli kabab
Tunda Kabab (prepared with pumpkin)
Sambhali Kabab
Galawati Kebab
Boti Kebab
Hara Bhara Kabab
Kathi Kabab
Reshmi Kabab
Lasoni Kabab
Chicken Malai Kabab
Tikka Kabab
Tangdi Kabab (Tangdi meaning leg of the chicken)
Kaleji Kabab
Hariali Chicken Kabab
Bihari Kabab

In Iran

Kabab (Persian: کباب) is a national dish of Iran. It is either served with steamed, saffroned basmati or Persian rice (chelow), in this case it is called "Chelow Kabab" (Persian: چلو کباب)) or served with Persian naan (bread).There are several distinct Persian varieties of Kabab.

It is served with the basic Iranian meal accompaniments, in addition to grilled tomatoes on the side of the rice,

Iranian kabab

Iranian Kabab Koobideh

and butter on top of the rice. It is an old northern tradition (probably originating in Tehran) that a raw egg yolk should be placed on top of the rice as well, though this is strictly optional, and most restaurants will not serve the rice this way unless it is specifically requested. "Somagh", powdered sumac, is also made available and its use varies based on tastes to a small dash on the rice or a heavy sprinkling on both rice and meat, particularly when used with red (beef/veal/lamb) meat. At Persian restaurants, the combination of one Kabab Barg and one Kabab Koobideh is typically called Soltani, meaning 'Sultan's Feast.' The traditional beverage of choice to accompany kebab is doogh, a sour yogurt drink with mint and salt.

In the old bazaar tradition, the rice (which is covered with a tin lid) and accompaniments are served first, immediately followed by the kebabs, which are brought to the table by the waiter, who holds several skewers in his left hand, and a piece of flat bread (typically nan-e lavash) in his right. A skewer is placed directly on the rice and while holding the kebab down on the rice with the bread, the skewer is quickly pulled out. With the two most common kebabs, barg and koobideh, two skewers are always served. In general, bazaar kebab restaurants only serve these two varieties, though there are exceptions.

Kabab koobideh

Kabab koobideh (Persian: کباب کوبیده) or *kūbide* (Persian: کوبیده) is an Iranian minced meat kabab which is made from ground lamb, beef, or chicken, often mixed with parsley and chopped onions.

Kabab Koobideh contains: ground meat, onion, salt, pepper, turmeric, and seasoning. These ingredients are mixed together until the mixture becomes smooth and sticky. One egg is added to help the mix stick together. The mixture is then pressed around a skewer. Koobideh Kabab is typically 7–8 inches (18–20 cm) long.

Kabab barg

Kabāb-e Barg (Persian: کباب برگ) is a Persian style barbecued lamb, chicken or beef kebab dish. The main ingredients of *Kabab Barg* - a short form of this name are fillets of beef tenderloin, lamb shank or chicken breast, onions and olive oil.

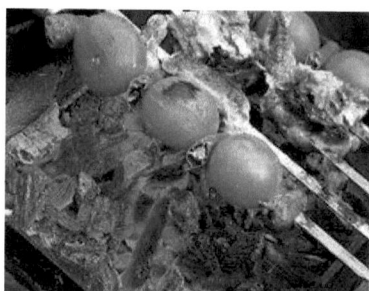

Jujeh Kabab - An Iranian chicken kebob

Marinade is prepared by the mixture of half a cup of olive oil, three onions, garlic, half teaspoon saffron, salt and black pepper. One kilogram of lamb is cut into 1 cm thick and 4–5 cm long pieces. It should be marinated overnight in refrigerator, and the container should be covered. The next day, the lamb is threaded on long, thin metal skewers. It is brushed with marinade and is barbecued for 5–10 minutes on each side. Kabab-e Barg

Jujeh kabab

Jūje-kabāb (Persian: جوجه‌کباب) consists of pieces of chicken first marinated in minced onion and lemon juice with saffron then grilled over a fire. It is sometimes served with grilled tomato and pepper. Jujeh kabab is one of the most popular Persian dishes.

Kabab bakhtiari

Combination of Jujeh Kabab and Kabab Barg in a decussate form.

In the Levant

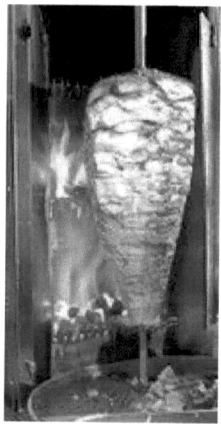

Döner kebap in Istanbul

Shawarma and other varieties of kebabs can be found at most restaurants representing this region. The preparation of Shawarma consists of chicken, turkey, beef, veal, or mixed meats being placed on a spit (commonly a vertical spit in restaurants), and being grilled for as long as a day. Shavings are cut off the block of meat for serving, and the remainder of the block of meat is kept heated on the rotating spit. Although it can be served in shavings on a plate (generally with accompaniments), shawarma also refers to a pita bread sandwich or wrap made with shawarma meat.

In Norway

In Norway, the kebab was introduced by Pakistani and Turkish immigrants during the 1980s. It soon became a very popular meal after a night out, gaining a cult status among young people during the 1990s . The kebab has become a symbol of immigration from the Muslim world, and speaking Norwegian with an Arab accent or with a lot of words and expressions borrowed from the Pakistani, Turkish, Arabic, and Persian languages is sometimes referred to as "Kebabnorsk" (Kebab Norwegian).

The kebabs in Norway are served in a variety of ways, commonly in fast-food shops selling both hamburgers and kebabs. The kebab roll has become increasingly popular, with the kebab not served in pita bread, but rather wrapped in pizza dough (making it look like a spring roll) for easy consumption. The most "Norwegian" kebab to date is probably the whalemeat kebab sold at the Inferno Metal Festival. As of 2008, the average price of the kebab in Norway lies around 65 kroner, or about €8. In Bergen the average price of a kebab is around 50 kr. In Bergen kebab is most commonly served in the dürüm variety, with two types of sauces, one standard and one optional hot chili variety.

The Norwegian Food Safety Authority in 2007 issued a warning about cheap kebabs. According to *Verdens Gang* they estimated that more than 80% of kebab shops in Oslo use illegally produced meat. It was warned that such meat could be dangerous to eat because it could contain salmonella or other bacteria, and that it could be connected to organised crime.

In Pakistan

Pakistani-style seekh kebabs being grilled on a skewer

Pakistani cuisine is rich with different kebabs. Meat including beef, chicken, lamb and fish is used in kababs. Some popular Kebabs are:
Adreki Murgh Kebab
Bihari Kebab (Urdu: بہاری کباب)
Bun kebab (Urdu: بن کباب)
Chapli Kebab (Urdu: چپلی کباب)
Chargha
Chicken Kebab (Urdu: مرغ کباب)
Dhaga Kabab
Doner kebab
Fish Kebab
Fry Kebab
Gola Kebab
Kache Qeema Kebab
Lamb Kebab (Urdu: کباب برہ گوشت)
Pasinday (Urdu: پسندے)
Peshawari Kebab
Reshmi Kebab (Urdu: ریشمی کباب)
Sajji
Seekh Kebab (Urdu: سیخ کباب)
Shami Kebab (Urdu: شامی کباب)
Tikka Kebab (Urdu: تکہ کباب)

In Malaysia

Kebabs in Malaysia are generally sold at pasar malam (night markets) and in shopping mall food courts. Normally the meat, after being cut from the spit is pan fried with onions and hot sauce then placed into a pita bread pocket before being filled with condiments such as tomatoes, mayonnaise, onion and lettuce.

In Turkey

İskender kebap

Before taking its modern form, as mentioned in Ottoman travel books of the 18th century, the doner used to be a horizontal stack of meat rather than vertical, probably sharing common ancestors with the Cağ Kebabı of the Eastern Turkish province of Erzurum.

In his own family biography, İskender Efendi of 19th century Bursa writes that "he and his grandfather had the idea of roasting the lamb vertically rather than horizontally, and invented for that purpose a vertical mangal". Since then Hacı İskender is known as the inventor of Turkish Döner Kebap. With time, the meat took a different marinade, got leaner, and eventually took its modern shape. The Greek gyro, along with the similar Arab Shawarma and Mexican Tacos al Pastor, are derived from this dish.

Shish

Shish kebab ("Şiş", pronounced shish, meaning "skewer" is a Turkish word.) is a dish consisting of meat threaded on a skewer and grilled. Any kind of meat may be used; cubes of fruit or vegetables are often threaded on the spit as well. Typical vegetables include tomato, bell pepper, onions, and mushrooms.

In English, the word "kebab" usually refers to shish kebab.

Döner

İskender kebap, the original döner kebab with yoghurt and tomate sauce, invented in Bursa, Turkey.

Döner kebab, literally "rotating kebab" in Turkish, is sliced lamb, beef or chicken, slowly roasted on a vertical rotating spit. The Middle Eastern shawarma, Mexican tacos al pastor and Greek gyros are all derived from the **Turkish döner kebab** which was invented in Bursa in the 19th century by a cook named Hacı İskender. Döner kebab is most popularly served in pita bread, as it is best known, with salad, but is also served in a dish with a salad and bread or French fries on the side, or used for Turkish pizzas called pide or "kebabpizza". Take-out döner kebab or shawarma restaurants are common in many parts of Europe. Döner kebab is popular in many European countries, Canada, New Zealand and Australia.

In parts of Europe 'kebab' usually

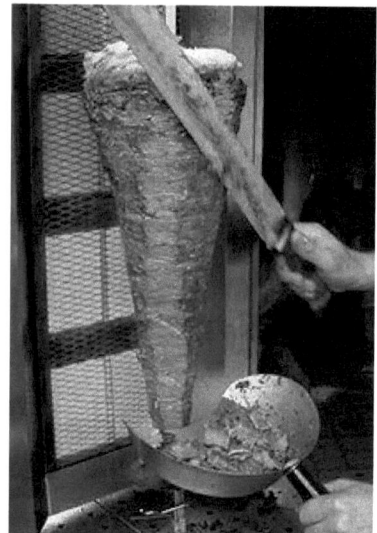

Slicing "döner kebap" off a rotating vertical spit.

refers to döner kebab in pita. Australian Doner Kebabs are usually served in wraps which are toasted before eating.

In Australia and the UK, kebabs (or döner meat and chips) are most popularly eaten after a night out, representing a large part of nightlife culture. As a result, many kebab shops (and vans) will do their main business in the hours around closing time for local pubs and clubs (usually from 10 pm to 4 am). The same applies for Belgium, the Netherlands, Poland, Ireland, New Zealand, Canada, Scandinavia and Italy. It is therefore not uncommon to find similar late-night kebab vending shops in holiday-clubbing destinations such as Ibiza and Thailand.

Health concerns about döner kebab, including unacceptable salt and fat levels and improper labeling of meat used, are repeatedly reported in UK media. The German-style döner kebab was supposedly invented by a Turkish immigrant in Berlin in the 1970s, and became a popular German take-away food during the 1990s, but is almost exclusively sold by Turks and considered a Turkish specialty in Germany.

Adana

Adana kebabı (or kıyma kebabı) is a long, hand-minced meat kebab mounted on a wide iron skewer and grilled over charcoal. It is generally "hot." A version "less hot" is generally called Urfa kebabı.

Steam kebab

Steam kebab (Turkish Buğu kebabı) is a Turkish kebab dish which is prepared in an earthenware casserole. The casserole's lid is sealed with dough in order to cook the meat in its own juices. The dish is prepared with pearl onions, garlic, thyme, and other spices. In Tekirdağ, it is served with cumin; in Izmir, it is served with mastic.

Testi kebabı

Testi kebab as served in Goreme, Turkey

A dish from Central Anatolia and the Mid-Western Black Sea region, consisting of a mixture of meat and vegetables cooked in a clay pot or jug over fire (testi means jug in Turkish). The pot is sealed with bread dough or foil and is broken when serving.

Other variants

Left to right: Chenjeh Kebab, Kebab Koobideh, Jujeh Kebab in an Afghan restaurant.

Kebab Kenjeh کباب کنجه

Kenjeh is a popular meat dish in the Middle East. It originated in Iran and was later adopted in Asia Minor. Kebab Kenjeh is now found worldwide. Lamb is traditionally the meat used in this dish. The ingredients include lamb, olive oil, lemon juice, salt, and pepper. It is usually served with rice, grilled tomato, and raw onion. There are also local variations in the pronunciation of Kenje Kebab کنجه کباب.

Kebab Halabi

Kebab Hindi from Aleppo

A kind of kebab served with a spicy tomato sauce and Aleppo pepper, very common in Syria and Lebanon, named after the city of Aleppo (*Halab*). Kebab halabi has around 26 variants including:
Kebab karaz for cherry kebab in Arabic - meatballs (lamb) along with cherries and cherry paste, pine nuts, sugar and pomegranate molasses. It is considered one of Aleppo's main dishes especially among Armenians.
Kebab kashkhash - rolled lamb or beef with chili pepper paste, parsley, garlic and pine nuts.
Kebab Hindi - rolled meat with tomato paste, onion, capsicum and pomegranate molasses.
Kebab kamayeh - soft meat with truffle pices, onion and various nuts.
Kebab siniyye for tray kebab in Arabic - lean minced lamb in a tray added with chili pepper, onion and tomato.

Kakori

Kakori kebab is a South Asian kebab attributed to the city of Kakori in Uttar Pradesh, India. There is much folklore about this famous kebab that takes its name from a small hamlet called Kakori on the outskirts of Lucknow.

One such story says that the kakori kebab was created by the Nawab of Kakori, Syed Mohammad Haider Kazmi, who, stung by the remark of a British officer about the coarse texture of the kebabs served at dinner, ordered his rakabdars (gourmet cooks) to evolve a more refined seekh kebab.

After ten days of research, they came up with a kebab so soft and so juicy it won the praise of the very British officer who had scorned the Nawab.

The winning formula his rakabdars came upon included mince obtained from no other part but the raan ki machhli (tendon of the leg of mutton), khoya, white pepper and a mix of powdered spices.

Chapli

Chapli Kebab served in a Birmingham Balti restaurant

Chapli kebab is a patty made from beef mince, and is one of the popular barbecue meals in Pakistan and Afghanistan. The word Chapli comes from the Pashto word Chaprikh which means flat. It is prepared flat and round and served with naan. The kebab originates from Mardan and is a common dish in Pashtun cuisine. Mardan is famous for chapli kabab not only locally but also internationally. Chapli Kebab is made of minced meat or chicken, onions, tomatoes, green chilies, coriander seeds, cumin seeds, salt, black pepper, lemon juice or promegranate seeds, eggs, cornstarch and coriander leaves.

Burrah

Burrah kebab is another kebab from Mughlai Cuisine, fairly popular in South Asia. This is usually made of goat meat, liberally marinated with spices and charcoal grilled.

Kalmi

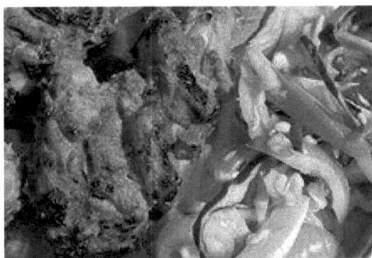

Kalmi Kebab served with onions and cabbage in Delhi, India.

Kalmi kebab a popular snack in Indian cuisine. The dish is made by marinating chicken drumsticks and placing them in a tandoor. Various kinds of freshly ground Indian spices are added to the yogurt used for the marination of the chicken. When prepared, the drumsticks are usually garnished with mint leaves and served with onions and Indian bread.

Galouti

Galouti Kabab as served in Lucknow, India

One of the more delicate kebabs from South Asia, made of minced goat / bison / buffalo meat. Legend has it that the galawati kebab was created for an aging Nawab Wajid Ali Shah of Lucknow who lost his teeth, but not his passion for meat dishes.

'Galawati' means "melt in your mouth" and was perfect for the toothless Nawab who continued savouring this until his last days.

Traditionally, green papaya is used to make it tender. After being mixed with a few select herbs and spices (great chefs rarely reveal what they are exactly), the very finely ground meat is shaped into patties and fried in pure ghee until they are browned.

The original recipe that brought many a smile on the Nawab's face, albeit toothless, and many a sigh of satisfaction, is supposed to have more than 100 aromatic spices.

The Galouti Kebab is part of the "Awadhi Cuisine". Along with the Lucknowi biryani and Kakori Kebab, this is one of the outstanding highlights of the great food tradition from the Awadh region in Uttar Pradesh, India.

Many leading Indian hotel chains have taken to popularising the Awadhi food tradition, with the Galouti Kebab being a Pièce de résistance.

The home of this kebab is Lucknow. It is most famously had at the almost iconic eatery "Tundey Miyan" at Old Lucknow.

Kebab chain

The world's largest kebab chain is Kebab Turki Baba Rafi, which founded in 2003 by young entrepreneur, Hendy Setiono, and since 2005, it was franchised. Now, it operates more than 1000 outlets in Indonesia, Malaysia, and Philippines. It continues the expansion to another countries around the world.

Similar dishes

Europe, Eastern Europe, Caucasus, and Eurasia
Kebakko (Finnish)
Brochette (French)
Pinchitos (Spanish Andalusian)
Espetada (Portuguese)
Spiedino (Italian)
Rablóhús (Hungarian)
Ćevapi (Balkan)
Souvlaki (Σουβλάκι - Greek)
Frigărui and Mititei (Romanian)
Mtsvadi (მწვადი - Georgian)
Khorovatz (Armenian)
Shashlik (Russian)

Asia
Kawap (Uyghur)
Chuanr (Chinese)
Satay (Southeast Asian)
Kkochi (Korean)

Kushiyaki and Yakitori (Japanese)
Americas
Donair (Canadian)
City Chicken (Ohio Valley-Upstate New York)
Spiedies (New York State)
Banderilla (México)
Anticuchos (Andean)
Espetinho (Brazilian)

Africa
Suya (Nigerian)
Sosatie (South African)
Source http://en.wikipedia.org/wiki/Kebab

Knish

A classic potato knish

Origin
Alternative name(s): Knysh
Details
Type: Snack, Side Dish
Main ingredient(s): Mashed potatoes, ground meat, sauerkraut, onions, kasha or cheese

A **knish** (pron.: /ˈknɪʃ/) or **knysh** is an Eastern European, and Jewish snack food made popular in North America by Eastern European immigrants, eaten widely by both Jewish and non-Jewish people.

History

Eastern European immigrants who arrived sometime around 1900 brought knishes to North America. Knish (קניש) is a Yiddish word that was derived from the Ukrainian or Russian "knysh" (Книш), meaning dumpling or cake. The first knish bakery was founded in New York in 1910." Generally recognized as a food made popular in New York by immigrants in the early 1900s, the United States underwent a knish renaissance in the 2000s driven by knish specialty establishments such as the Knish Shop in Baltimore, Maryland, Buffalo and Bergen in Washington, DC, or My Mother's Knish, in Westlake Village, California.

A knish consists of a filling covered with dough that is either baked, grilled, or deep fried. Knishes can be purchased from street vendors in urban areas with a large Jewish population, sometimes at a hot dog stand or from a butcher shop.

In the most East European traditional versions, the filling is made entirely of mashed potato, ground meat, sauerkraut, onions, kasha (buckwheat groats), or cheese. Other varieties of fillings include sweet potatoes, black beans, fruit, broccoli, tofu, or spinach.

Many cultures have variations of baked, grilled, or fried dough-covered snacks to which epicurean family the knish belongs including the Cornish pasty, the Scottish Bridie, the Jamaican patty, the Spanish and Latin American empanada, the Middle Eastern fatayer, the Portuguese *rissol* (rissole), the Italian calzone, the Indian samosa, the Polish pierogi, the Russian Pirozhki, and the Ukrainian Pyrizhky.

Knishes may be round, rectangular, or square. They may be entirely covered in dough or some of the filling may peek out of the top. Sizes range from those that can be eaten in a single bite hors d'oeuvre to sandwich-sized.

Source http://en.wikipedia.org/wiki/Knish

Korean taco

Korean tacos from the "Seoul on Wheels" truck in San Francisco

Korean tacos are a fusion dish popular in the United States, which originated in Los Angeles, often as street food, consisting of Korean-style fillings, such as bulgogi and kimchi, placed on top of small traditional Mexican corn tortillas. **Korean burritos** are a similarly themed dish, using larger flour tortillas as a wrap.

Background

Although nearly any savory dish can and has been used as filling for a taco, burrito, or sandwich wrap, and other restaurants have occasionally served dishes they called Korean tacos, the enduring popularity of the dish is generally traced to the use of Twitter by the proprietors of the Kogi Korean BBQ, a food truck in Los Angeles, California, to announce their schedule and itinerary. The idea of making Korean tacos came to owner Mark Manguera after an unsuccessful search of Los Angeles' Koreatown for carne asada tacos. In its first year of operation, Kogi generated an estimated $2 million of revenue.

Korean taco trucks later appeared in Portland, Oregon (the "KOI Fusion" truck), Austin, Texas (the Chi'Lantro BBQ truck), and Seattle, Washington ("Marination Mobile", whose spicy pork Korean taco earned them Good Morning America's Best Food Truck in America). In San Francisco the dish was popularized in 2009 by Namu Restaurant's Happy Belly food cart in Golden Gate Park, later moving to a farmers market food stand at the San Francisco Ferry Building. The dish's popularity lead mainstream fast food chain Baja Fresh to test market Korean tacos as a menu item in California, with plans to introduce the dish to hundreds of locations nationwide.

By 2010, restaurants and food trucks serving Korean tacos had appeared across the country including Austin, Chicago, and the East Coast of the United States.

In April 2010, *Food & Wine* magazine named Roy Choi, the chef of the original Kogi's, one of its annual "Best New Chefs". It was the first time a food truck chef had been nominated for the award.

Source http://en.wikipedia.org/wiki/Korean_taco

Laksa

Origin	
Place of origin	Malaysia
Region or state	Malaysia, Singapore, Indonesia
Creator(s)	Peranakan culture
Details	
Course	Lunch
Main ingredient(s)	Laksa noodles or rice vermicelli, coconut milk, curry soup base
Variations	Curry laksa, Asam laksa
Laksa	
Chinese	叻沙
Alternative Chinese name	
Chinese	喇沙

Laksa is a popular spicy noodle soup from the Peranakan culture, which is a merger of Chinese and Malay elements found in Malaysia and Singapore, and Indonesia.

Origin

The origin of the name "laksa" is unclear. One theory traces it back to Hindi/Persian *lakhshah*, referring to a type of vermicelli, which in turn may be derived from the Sanskrit *lakshas* (लकशस) meaning "one hundred thousand" (lakh). It has also been suggested that "laksa" may derive from the Chinese word 辣沙 (Cantonese: [lɛt.sáː]), meaning "spicy sand" due to the ground dried prawns which gives a sandy or gritty texture to the sauce. The last theory is that the name comes from the similar sounding word "dirty" in Hokkien due to its appearance.

Types

There are two basic types of laksa: *curry laksa* and *asam laksa*. Curry laksa is a coconut curry soup with noodles, while asam laksa is a sour fish soup with noodles. Thick rice noodles also known as **laksa noodles** are most commonly used, although thin rice vermicelli (*bee hoon* or *mee hoon*) are also common and some variants use other types.

Curry laksa

Katong laksa and banana leaf otak-otak

Curry laksa

Curry laksa (in many places referred to as simply as "laksa") is a coconut-based curry soup. The main ingredients for most versions of curry laksa include

A bowl of Penang laksa, a variant of asam laksa.

Johor laksa

Laksa sold in Bukit Batok, Singapore

bean curd puffs, fish sticks, shrimp and cockles. Some vendors may sell chicken laksa. Laksa is commonly served with a spoonful of sambal chilli paste and garnished with Vietnamese coriander, or *laksa leaf*, which is known in Malay as *daun kesum.*

This is usually known as curry mee in Penang rather than curry laksa, due to the different kind of noodles used (yellow mee or bee hoon, as opposed to the thick white laksa noodles). Curry mee in Penang uses congealed pork blood, a delicacy to the Malaysian Chinese community.

The term "curry laksa" is more commonly used in Kuala Lumpur or Singapore. Laksa is popular in Singapore and Malaysia, as are laksa yong tau foo, lobster laksa, and even plain laksa, with just noodles and gravy.

Variants of curry laksa include:

Laksa lemak, also known as **nyonya laksa** (Malay: *Laksa nyonya*), is a type of laksa with a rich coconut gravy. *Lemak* is a culinary description in the Malay language which specifically refers to the presence of coconut milk which adds a distinctive richness to a dish. As the name implies, it is made with a rich, slightly sweet and strongly spiced coconut gravy. Laksa lemak is usually made with a fish-based gravy (with vegetarian food stalls omitting fish) and is heavily influenced by **Thai laksa** (Malay: *Laksa Thai*), perhaps to the point that one could say they are one and the same.

Laksam, a speciality of the Northeastern Malaysian states of Kelantan, Terengganu and Kedah, is made with very thick flat white rice flour noodles in a rich, full-bodied white gravy of boiled fish and coconut milk. Though usually made of fish flesh, it is sometimes made with eels. Traditionally laksam is eaten with hands rather than with eating utensils due to the gravy's thick consistency.

Katong laksa (Malay: *Laksa Katong*) is a variant of laksa lemak from the Katong area of Singapore. In Katong laksa, the noodles are normally cut up into smaller pieces so that the entire dish can be eaten with a spoon alone, without chopsticks or a fork. Katong laksa is a strong contender for the heavily competed title of Singapore's national dish.

Asam laksa

Asam laksa is a sour, fish-based soup. It is listed at number 7 on *World's 50 most delicious foods* complied by *CNN Go* in 2011. *Asam* (or *asam jawa*) is the Malay word for tamarind, which is commonly used to give the stock its sour flavor. It is also common to use *asam keping* (also known as *asam gelugor*), dried slices of sour mangosteen, for added sourness. The modern Malay spelling is *asam*, though the spelling *assam* is still frequently used.

The main ingredients for asam laksa include shredded fish, normally *kembung* fish or mackerel, and finely sliced vegetables including cucumber, onions, red chillies, pineapple, lettuce, common mint, "daun kesum" (Vietnamese mint or laksa mint) and pink *bunga kantan* (ginger buds). Asam laksa is normally served with either thick rice noodles or thin rice noodles (vermicelli). And topped off with "petis udang" or "hae ko" (蝦羔), a thick sweet prawn/shrimp paste.

Variants of asam laksa include:

Penang laksa (Malay: *Laksa Pulau Pinang*), also known as *asam laksa* from the Malay for tamarind, comes from the Malaysian island of Penang. It is made with mackerel (*ikan kembung*) soup and its main distinguishing feature is the *asam* or tamarind which gives the soup a sour taste. The fish is poached and then flaked. Other ingredients that give Penang laksa its distinctive flavour include lemongrass, galangal (*lengkuas*) and chilli. Typical garnishes include mint, pineapple slices, thinly sliced onion, hɛ-ko, a thick sweet prawn paste and use of torch ginger flower. This, and not 'curry mee' is the usual 'laksa' one gets in Penang.

Perlis laksa (Malay: *Laksa Perlis*) is similar to Penang Laksa but differs in garnishing used such as catfish and eel fish. The famous Perlis laksa can be found in Kuala Perlis.

Kedah laksa (Malay: *Laksa Kedah*) is very similar to Penang laksa and only differs in the garnishing used. Sliced boiled eggs are usually added to the dish. Kedah laksa used rice to make a laksa noodle. The famous laksa in Kedah is Laksa Telok Kechai.

Ipoh laksa (Malay: *Laksa Ipoh*), from the Malaysian city of Ipoh, is similar to Penang laksa but has a more sour (rather than sweet) taste, and contains prawn paste.

Kuala Kangsar Laksa (Malay: *Laksa Kuala Kangsar*), made of wheat flour (usually hand made). The soup is rather lighter than the common laksa taste and so much different from Ipoh Laksa in shape, taste and smell. The local municipal council even built a complex called "Kompleks Cendol dan Laksa" near the river bank of the Perak River. It is the main attraction for tourists in Kuala Kangsar.

Other variants

Several variants mix coconut milk and fish and can be identified as either curry or asam laksa.

Johor laksa (Malay: *Laksa Johor*), from Johor state in southern Malaysia, resembles Penang laksa only in the kind of fish used but differs in everything else. Johor laksa has coconut milk, use kerisik, dried prawns, lemon grass, galangal and spices akin to curry. The garnishing comprises slices of onion, beansprouts (taugeh), mint leaves, Vietnamese coriander or 'daun kesum', cucumber and pickled white radish. *Sambal belacan* (a kind of chili paste) is placed on the side. Finally, just before eating, freshly squeezed lime juice is sprinkled on the dish. Unique to Johor laksa is its Italian connection – spaghetti is used instead of the normal rice noodles or vermicelli. Johor laksa is traditionally eaten using the hand and the noodles are usually knitted (cetak) into a disk for each serving.

Sarawak laksa (Malay: *Laksa Sarawak*) comes from the Malaysian state Sarawak, on the island of Borneo. It is actually very different from the curry laksa as the soup contains no curry at all. It has a base of *Sambal belacan*, sour tamarind, garlic, galangal, lemon grass and coconut milk, topped with omelette strips, chicken strips, prawns, fresh coriander and optionally lime. Ingredients such as bean sprouts, (sliced) fried tofu or other seafood are not traditional but are sometimes added.

Kelantan laksa (Malay: *Laksa Kelantan*) is the easiest laksa recipe that is famous among peoples from the town of Kota Bharu of the Kelantan state, located at the east coast of Peninsular Malaysia. The main ingredient of Kelantan Laksa's sauce is 'ikan kembong' or round scad mackerel that are boiled and minced. The minced fish are fried with onions, garlic, ginger, datil pepper, belacan, 'kantan' flower, Vietnamese coriander or 'daun kesum', lemon grass and dried tamarind slice. Coconut milk will then be added as the final ingredient and stirred until it is all mixed up and becomes thick. Kelantan Laksa is served just like the Italian spaghetti by adding 'ulam' (raw vegetables) and blended chili on the side. Another variable of Kelantan Laksa is 'Laksam'. The sauce's recipe are exactly the same but the noodles are a bit bigger and flat.

Bogor Laksa (Indonesian: *Laksa Bogor*) probably is the most famous Laksa variant in Indonesia from Bogor town, West Java. The thick yellowish coconut milk based soup is a mixture of shallot, garlic, *kemiri* (candlenut), *kunyit* (turmeric), *ketumbar* (coriander), *sereh* (lemongrass), and salt. The hot soup runs, drained, and filled several times into the bowl contains bihun (rice vermicelli), ketupat (glutinous rice cake), smashed oncom (similar to tempe but different fungi), *tauge* (bean sprout), kemangi (basil leafes), cooked shredded chicken and prawn, boiled egg, until all the ingredients is soft and cooked. Usually Laksa Bogor is served with sambal cuka (grinded chilli in vinegar).

Betawi laksa with "emping" (melinjo cracker)

Betawi Laksa (Indonesian: *Laksa Betawi*) is a Laksa variant from Jakarta, Indonesia. The thick yellowish coconut milk based soup is a mixture of shallot, garlic, *kunyit* (turmeric), *lengkuas* (galangal), *sereh* (lemongrass), *salam* leaf and kaffir lime leaf, ginger, pepper, and contains *rebon* (dried small shrimp) to gave the unique taste. The dish contains ketupat (compressed rice cake wrapped in young coconut leaf), *tauge* (bean sprout), *kemangi* (Indonesian basil leaf), and boiled egg.

Palembang Laksan (Indonesian: *Laksan Palembang*): often referred as pempek served in laksa soup, it is a specialty of Palembang, South Sumatra. It is a pempek based fishcake soup, sliced pempek served in coconut milk based soup, shrimp broth and spices, sprinkled with fried shallots.

Palembang Lakso (Indonesian: *Lakso Palembang*): The Palembang style laksa. Unlike laksan that uses slices of pempek, laksan uses noodle-like steamed sago paste served in coconut milk soup with mixture spices: of palm sugar, black pepper, turmeric, coriander and candlenut, sprinkled with fried shallots.

Banjar Laksa (Indonesian: *Laksa Banjar*): The Banjarmasin style laksa that has snakehead as one of its ingredients.

Summary table

The general differences between *curry laksa*, *asam laksa* and *Sarawak laksa* are as follows:

Curry Laksa	Asam Laksa	Sarawak Laksa
Coconut milk is used	No coconut milk used	Coconut milk is used
Curry-like soup (*includes curry as one of its ingredients*)	Fish paste soup, tastes sour due to tamarind (*asam*)	Red curry-like soup (*does not use curry*)
Except for bean sprouts, no other vegetable is used	Pineapple, shredded cucumber, raw onions may be used	Except for bean sprouts and fresh coriander as garnish, no other vegetable is used.
Bean Curd puff is used	No Bean Curd puff used	No Bean Curd puff used
Served with thick or thin rice vermicelli (usually thick). Occasionally served with *yellow mee*.	Served with thick or thin rice vermicelli (usually thick)	Served with thin rice vermicelli only
Hard-boiled egg may be added	No hard-boiled egg added	Sliced omelette is used
Slices of fish cake and either prawns or chicken is used	Fish, normally *kembung* fish, is used	Whole prawns and serrated chickens are used
Variants Laksa lemak Katong laksa Nyonya laksa Johor laksa	Variants Asam Laksa Penang laksa	Variants (none)

Laksa is simply referred to or ordered at a restaurant as laksa (curry laksa) or asam laksa. By default, laksa means the standard curry laksa while asam laksa refers to the standard Penang version. If a restaurant serves a non-standard version, the restaurant will qualify the laksa by the version being sold. For example, a restaurant serving Katong laksa will list Katong laksa on the menu.

Similar dishes

Mohinga, a Burmese fish noodle soup
Ohn no khao swè, Burmese version of coconut chicken noodle soup
Khao soi, a northern Thai noodle dish
Khow suey, a noodle dish originally from the Shan state in Burma

Laksa products

Laksa paste to cook laksa can be purchased from supermarkets. Laksa flavoured instant noodles are also available at supermarkets.

Source http://en.wikipedia.org/wiki/Laksa

Candied fruit for sale in streets of Tianjin, China

Street food packaged in plastic bags in Bangkok, Thailand

Nikuman in Japan

This is a **list of street foods** from around the world, arranged by country.

Street food is ready-to-eat food or drink sold in a street or other public place, such as a market or fair, by a hawker or vendor, often from a portable stall.

Street food vending is found around the world, but has variations within both regions and cultures. For example, Dorling Kindersley describes the street food of Viet Nam as being "fresh and lighter than many of the cuisines in the area" and "draw[ing] heavily on herbs, chile peppers and lime", while street food of Thailand is "fiery" and "pungent with shrimp paste ... and fish sauce" with New York City's signature street food being the hot dog, although the offerings in New York also range from "spicy Middle Eastern falafel or Jamaican jerk chicken to Belgian waffles" In Hawaii, the local street food tradition of "Plate Lunch" (rice, macaroni salad and a portion of meat) was inspired by the *bento* of the Japanese who had been brought to Hawaii as plantation workers.

Africa

Ethiopia

This meal, consisting of *injera* and several kinds of *wat* or *tsebhi* (stew), is typical of Ethiopian and Eritrean cuisine.

Injera bread is the method of eating several types of street foods. Tibs Wat, a spicy stew is placed on a plate with a folded piece of injera and fried Neeka stalks.

Ghana

Street food in Ghana is mainly based upon local cuisine. Street food is available from travelling pedestrian vendors, street stalls, and ubiquitous "chop bars". Street breakfasts across the country consist of different assortments of porridges, as well as omelettes and bread served with tea. Traditional African dishes, such as fufu, kenkey, banku, fried yams, and bushmeat are popular across the country; regional varieties use local foods, such as tilapia in Ashanti Region, fresh seafood along the coastline and fried cheese in the Northern regions. Rice dishes are also common, consisting of rice served with noodles, baked beans, and can be garnished as according to the customer by extra toppings of egg, chicken, fish, gari, and vegetables. Fruits are also popular street food, ranging from Coconuts and bananas to seasonal oranges and mangoes. Kebabs made from beef and pepper are also widely available from travelling vendors. A wide variety of local snacks are also available, and can differ dramatically from region to region.

Beverages are often sold by food vendors. The most common street beverages, purchased from separate drinks vendors, are small plastic bags filled with purified water. Carbonated drinks in West Africa are usually available from permanent shops instead of temporary vendors, where the drinks are sold in glass bottles which must be returned to the shop for recycling and refilling. Local drinks are also sold throughout the day, such as iced kenkey, lemonade, and a cold ginger drink. As is the case in many members of the Commonwealth of Nations, Ghanaian law prohibits the sale of alcoholic beverages except within licensed establishments, and as such alcoholic drinks are not sold by street vendors except in smaller villages, where pito, the local wine is served in calabashes.

Morocco

Typical street food includes: grilled corn on the cob, merguez, and snails.

Nigeria

Chin chin is a popular dish in Nigeria, and west Africa. Other popular Nigerian street foods include Suya (barbecued meat), (Boli) Roasted plantain, Fried Yam and Fish, Roasted corn, Akara and Moi-Moi (fried or steamed bean cakes respectively). 'Pure Water' (sachet water) is also very popular. It is not uncommon to see 'pure water' sellers (mostly children) run up to vehicles in traffic jams with their wares.

South Africa

A Gatsby sandwich

In South Africa, boerewors and other braai food are available in the street. In townships, ethnic foods are available.

In Cape Town, a popular street food is the Gatsby, a baguette filled with meat (often bologna sausage), salad, cheese and chips. It is said to have originated from a single restaurant, and has become popular throughout Cape Town.

Another popular food is bunny chow. It is a scooped out loaf with fufu or atchar inside and with the scooped out bread placed on top.

Tunisia

Sweet pastries are the most common street food, as well as the ubiquitous tuna baguette.

Asia

Bangladesh

Like other mega cities, Dhaka is populated with many vendors of street food of many different kinds including pitha, chotpoti, puchka, jhalmuri, badam and various fried items. Street food shops are very small, so vendors or hawkers can easily set their shop anywhere. In front of every school, university, office, footpath these shops are available, and they are very popular. These foods are very cheap so anyone can buy them.
Pitha – In the winter season vapa pitha is a very common street food item in Dhaka. Vapa pitha vendor or hawkers are normally women. In the evening they prepare vapa pitha and sell them. Vapa pitha is a very popular evening breakfast menu.
Chotpoti and puchka – Chotpoti and puchka are very popular among young citizens of Dhaka. Chotpoti and puchka shops are available anywhere in Dhaka city.
Jhal Muri – Jhalmuri is widely available and a favorite among children. It is normally served in cone shaped paper.
Badam vaja – Badam vaja (fried peanuts) is a time pass food item and very popular.
Others – Other popular street food items are puri, somucha, singara, beguni, chop etc. these are fried items and very cheap. People eat them as snacks.

China

Signs by the country road near Wuhan, Hubei, invite motorists to try dishes from three other provinces - Lanzhou (Gansu) halal beef noodles, Chongqing (Sichuan) mala bunch (麻辣燙), and Xi'an (Shaanxi) cold noodles (凉面)

Street vendors of snack foods (*xiaochi*) are becoming less common as local governments cut down on the practice, citing safety and traffic congestion as problems. Many vendors have also moved towards opening small restaurants and shops, and "street food" is now commonly eaten indoors at established locations.

The variety of snack foods available varies from region to region. In Sichuan, a variety of such as grilled rice balls and pan-fried noodles are sold. Beijing's Wangfujing Night Market is dedicated to street food vendors that feature many of the more unusual items one might purchase, like a large assortment of insects, as well as more typical foods like *chuanr* (kebabs).

Bing, a flatbread made of flour and fried in oil, were once a Northeastern street food that can also be found in many areas around the country. They can be served plain or stuffed with meat or eggs, or seasoned with scallions, sauces, or other flavours. One variety originating in Shandong and now found throughout China, *jianbing guozi* (煎饼果子), is made more akin to a crepe than its fried cousins, with the batter poured directly onto an iron skillet and evened out into a thin pancake. An egg is cracked on top, then various seasnoings are added. In the end, like a crepe, it is rolled for portability.

Tang hu lu are skewers of fruit, usually Chinese hawthorn, coated by a hardened sugar syrup. Root vegetables such as the potato, taro, and sweet potato are sometimes also used.

Hong Kong

In Hong Kong notable foods include skewered beef, curry fish balls, stuffed peppers and mushrooms, and dim sum. Street side food vendors are called *gaai bin dong* (Chinese: 街邊檔; literally "street side stalls"). Street food in Hong Kong can grow into a substantial business with the stalls only barely "mobile" in the traditional street food sense (see dai pai dong).

India

Dosa in Ongole, Andhra Pradesh

The quintessential Indian street food is Chaat—a generic name for a tangy and spicy mix, whose ingredients can be quite varied. The tangy flavor is usually imparted by the use of lemon, pomegranate seeds, Kala Namak (black salt), tamarind, and various chutneys. Chaat can be prepared with fruit, with popular ones including guava, banana, apple, melon, etc. It could instead be made using small crisp pancakes made from fried flour, called "paapri", along with yogurt. Potatoes sauteed with black cumin powder constitute another variant. In Indian cities, street vendors also sell drinks including Lassi (yogurt drink sold plain/salty, sweet, or fruit flavored), Sherbet and Jaljeera. Additionally, hole-in-the-wall kebab shops can be found in major cities.

Chaat stall in Mussoorie, India

Pani Puri (also known as *gol gappa*s or *phuchka*s) and Bhelpuri. Panipuri are hollow crisp balls made from dough, and filled as-you-eat with a spicy concoction of water and potatoes, topped by a choice of sweet or spicy chutney.
Aloo Tikki These are patties made up of mashed potatoes and masala deep fried in oil. They are served typically with a curry called Chholey (chick peas). They are popular in winter in North India.
Chaap is a version of potato patties dipped in flour batter and deep fried. They are served along with onion and beet slices. They are referred to by this name in the Eastern part of the country. One can obtain chaap on local trains travelling to and from Kolkatta. The word "chaap" is probably a corruption of "chop".
Poori-Subzie (or Bhaajee) This is available mostly in North India, especially in Uttar Pradesh. The curry (subzie) consists usually of potatoes in gravy. Sometimes, especially in the southern part of the country the potatoes do not have gravy and the poories are exclusively made up of refined flour (maida).
Chai-faen This term refers to tea with a roasted biscuit called "faen", possibly a corruption of "fan" which the shape of the biscuit resembles. The biscuit is also called "khaaree biscuit" in other parts of the country. This is available in North India, especially in Uttar Pradesh in cities like Agra and Mathura.
Vada pav is an example of West Indian street food. Masala chai, a spiced tea, is also for sale. A syrup-covered deep-fried sweet is sold in the North as jalebi and the South as jangiri. It is generally cheap and available throughout India.
Thattu Dosa is a variation of Dosa served in Southern India.
Bajji (deep fried vegetables in a gram flor dough), Bonda (deep fried potato balls in gram flour) and vadai (deep fried lentil dough) are snacks available in the street stalls.
Putu mayam, a cold coconut and rice-noodle concoction, is eaten for breakfast or a snack.

Regional variations

India being a big country is rich with regional variations in street food.
There are many street offerings in the state of Maharashtra. Pune's street food culture includes "Vada paav, sabudana vada, Panipuri, ragda raav, kutchi daabeli, Sevpuri, Dahipuri, pav bhaji, egg bhurji, chanachur, buddhi ke baal and gola." Mumbai, Maharashtra, is the place where Vada pav originated. Pav bhaji, is another popular dish. It acquired the status of restaurant food but had humble beginnings as street food. It has retained its original roadside availability despite this. Another concoction is pav-sample which is found at several places in Maharashtra. The "sample" refers usually to Sambar and the dish is simply pav (white bread) to be had with the curry called Sambar which is well known in India. Sambar being widely used for several other dishes as well, it was perhaps used in experimentation with pav. An extra dish of sambar is referred to as "sample". Although widely used in Maharashtra in roadside eateries, sambar is not native to the local culture. "Sample" could also mean a plate of curry called "Usal", which is a water based preparation of cooked sprouted lentils. Occasionally the term "sample" could mean anything that goes conveniently with pav (usually implying a liquid nature). Some more popular variants include the Kanda Bhajji (Crispy Onion Fritters) which are eaten as is or with Pav. Samosas and Kachori are quite common at the railway stalls in Mumbai which are served with the sweet and sour tamarind chutney & Spicy Mint Chutney. Kacchi dabeli has found its way into the heart of Maharashtrians which has its origins in Gujarat. One should not leave Mumbai/Pune without biting into the Bun Maska and Khari at the Irani Joints. Some more to join the list would be Poha, Batata Bhajji, Palak Bhajji, Upma, Sheera, Sabudana Kichadi, Dhokla(Origins in Gujarat), Thalipith, Kharwas. Off late, you can also see Hot Dogs being sold on carts in some places in Mumbai.

Pakora

Calcutta street food includes *phuchka*, *jhal mudi*, rolls (mainly egg, also chicken and mutton), mixed vegetable and potato chops (distinct from the Mumbai vada, see above), groundnuts, popcorn, and fritters. Fritters are commonly eaten with *mudi* (puffed rice). Common varieties of fritters include *beguni* (eggplants fried in chickpea batter), *phuluri* (fried chickpea batter), and *pakodas* (various vegetables fried in chickpea batter). Calcutta is also known for street-side eateries called rice hotels, serving meals centred on rice.
Kerala, in South India, has "thattukadas:

a covered cart or van with stoves and utensils, popularly found in almost all cities and towns of the state. The thattukadas operate only from evenings and goes on serving till early morning. They offer "Thattu dosa"—a light rice-flour crepe (dosa) fried in coconut oil and served with coconut chutney. The popular menu at a thattukada includes omelettes served as a side to thattudosas, spicy pork fry, crispy fried chicken, quail egg fries and parottas (like naan, but beaten and mixed with oil). The thattukada also famous for its evening snacks, mainly fried chilly bajji (deep fried big chilly marinated in spicy mix), onion rings, Kerala's famous banana fry etc and Paripuvada (deep fried balls made of lentils).

Tamil Nadu has its "thalluvandis similar to Kerala's "thattukada"s and popularly referred to as "Kaiyendhi Bhavans", a play on famous hotels like Saravana Bhavan. Traditional street food varieties include 'bajji' (deep fried vegetables in a gram flour batter), 'bonda' (deep fried vegetable balls in gram flour batter), 'vadai' (deep fried lentil dough), and the numerous varieties of dosais and idlis all served with traditional sambar and coconut chutney. Barotta, kothu parrotta, Kuska with Chicken and Mutton Gravy are other food varieties served on these thalluvandis. Tea Shops are also common street eateries in Tamil Nadu, where you can get Breads, Snacks, Bajjis with getti chutneys. Vegetable soup stalls are also now making an appearance on the street food scene in Tamil Nadu and are gaining popularity soon.

Indonesia

Street food in Indonesia seems to be everywhere. A lot of times the street food is better than restaurant food, especially in tourist areas where the meals are over charged and the quality is usually poor. The cost can range from 10,000 Rp. - 100,000 Rp. depending how much food you take and how hungry you are. Street foods are sold by hawkers peddling their goods on bicycles or carts, known as *pedagang kaki lima* or *makanan*. The food being sold varies from mixed rice, fried rice, soups

A satay stall in Indonesia

(such as soto ayam), satay, fried chicken, cakes, tempeh or beverages, such as *Es kacang hijau*, *Es cendol*, or *Es cincau*.

Japan

In Japan, udon, soba, and ramen noodles are ubiquitous, as highlighted in the film *Tampopo*. Takoyaki (octopus dumplings), nikuman and Castella (a kind of sponge cake) are also famous as street food in Japan. Sweet cakes such as taiyaki and imagawayaki are also popular. Yakitori is also popular. A yatai is a small, mobile food stall typically selling ramen or other hot food.

Korea (South)

Boiled snail and silk worm larva on Insadong in Seoul, South Korea.

Tteokbokki, sundae, oden, mandu, gimbap, boiled silkworm pupa and river snail, fried squid, fried shrimp, and chicken skewers are among common street foods found in foodstalls throughout South Korea. Most street vendors will fire up their woks or large pots of frying oil in the evenings in anticipation of pedestrian traffic. For breakfast, Korean-style toast sandwiches are still very popular in Seoul and other large cities. Other commonly eaten snacks are sweet-filled pastries such as hotteok and bungeoppang.

Sometimes original street food concepts become full-fledged franchises, as seen in the case of Isaac Toast followed by Sukbong Toast and Toastoa, which are all large Korean toast and sandwich franchise chains.

Pakistan

Pakistan shares a lot of culinary parallels with India. Popular street food in Pakistan includes Dahi Bardhay or Vadas, which is essentially fried lentil dumplings soaked in salted water, drained and served with a spicy tangy yoghurt mixed with boiled potatoes and herbs. Then there is Pani Puri, which is fried semolina puffs with a tamarind based dip. Spiced fruit salad Chaat is a common street food too. Other common items which are available all over Pakistan are Bun Kebab (Karachi) or the Pappu Burger (Lahore) served with halal shami kebab, mash potato Kebab and omellete and condiments, also Gunnay ka Rus with lemon and ginger(sugar cane juice). Other foods are Paratha roll which is either beef or chicken stuffed in a shallow fried flat bread made with plain flour; onions, tomato, and raita (mint & cilantro yogurt) are also added. Jalebi is a popular sweet dish served throughout Pakistan.

Roasted or slow baked Corn or chick peas are sold all over the city by moving vendors. They are dry roasted in very a hot sand/salt mixture and then sifted through before serving. In winters especially in northern parts of Pakistan, Chicken corn soup with or without eggs, and Yakhni plain chicken stock (referred to as pathan soup in Karachi) (traditionally made with free range chicken with its skin and feet) are the regular delicacies. In Gujranwala Punjab Chiras Accentor are the local delicacy, which are wild birds char grilled on charcoal fire and eaten whole.

Philippines

Street foods in Manila, Philippines.

The most common Philippine street foods include fried squidballs, fishballs, *kikiam*—a type of processed chicken and pork, which is served on a stick, with a variety of dipping sauces.

Roadside stands also serve barbecued pork, chicken and offal, such as pig's blood or dried chicken blood (colloquially, *Betamax* after its rectangular shape resembling the Betamax tape), chicken heads (*helmet*), chicken feet (*adidas*), pig's ears (*tenga*) and chicken intestines (*isaw*). Among more esoteric foods are *balut* and *penoy* (duck eggs; with fetus and without, respectively), *tokneneng* and *kwek-kwek* (battered, deep-fried chicken and quail eggs similar to Tempura) and deep-fried day-old-chick.

Taho, a type of soft beancurd served with syrup and tapioca balls is another snack, as are other offerings, such as burgers, hot dogs and cotton candy.

Palamig (literally, coolers) are sold, such as traditional offerings like *halo-halo* to fruit juices. *Sorbetes* (or, colloquially, "dirty ice cream" locally-produced usually with coconut milk as popularly called Pinoy sorbetes ice cream in flavors such as mango, cheese and yam) and Halo-Halo - a Filipino cold treat made up of crushed ice with fruits (na-ta de coco, kaong or palm fruit, jackfruit meat, sweet beans, mung beans, yam, macapuno - gelatinuous coconut meat, tapioca, and jelly, with skim milk and toppings - usually rice crispies, leche flan, and ice cream that brings nostalgia to Filipinos.

Calamares (battered squid pieces deep-fried in cooking oil ([a lot cheaper than the traditionally available])) is also widely consumed throughout the country. It is gaining its popularity because of its cheap price.

Taiwan

Oyster omelette, a type of street food commonly sold at Taiwan's Night Markets

Taiwan's street food sold at night markets is well known in Asia, especially that from the city of Tainan.

Influences include the Hoklo (Min Nan) flavor brought by the emigrants during the Ming loyalist rule era and Japanese tastes in the Japanese colonial period, to 1949, when the Nationalist retreated to the island with people from every other province of the mainland.

Bubble/Boba Milk Tea originated on the streets of Taiwan.

Taiwanese street food includes fried stinky tofu, oyster omelette, Zongzi (especially in Tainan), fried meatball, sugarcane juice (Taiwanese sugarcane was sweet famous with Cuba), fish ball soup, Baozi and water fried Baozi, rice cakes made with pork blood, and rice and noodle dishes.

Thailand

Street food in Thailand includes noodle dishes, among them are Pad Thai, Rad Naa, flat noodles with beef, pork, or

A vendor barbecuing along the streets of Bangkok, Thailand

chicken and vegetables, topped with a light gravy, and Rad Naa's twin, Pad See Iw, the same flat noodles dry-fried(no gravy) with a dark soy sauce, vegetables, meat, and chili. Other dishes include Tom Yum Kung (a soup), Khao Pad (fried rice), various kinds of satay, various curries. Japanese chikuwa and German sausages have also appeared in Bangkok. Canal food has been sold from boats on Thailand's rivers and canals for over two centuries, but since the early 20th century King Rama V's modernizations have caused a shift towards land-based stalls. In Bangkok parlance, a housewife who feeds her family from a street food vendor is known as a "plastic-bag housewife", which originated from streets vendors packaging the food in plastic bags.

Many Thai people will eat four or five meals a day, and often these will be taken with friends or family at streetside dining carts. In some areas of Thailand, an inconspicuous car-park or roadside area may be empty by day, but turn into a bustling food district as the sun goes down, when local street vendors arrive with their carts. This is the case in most provincial capitals.

Middle East

Shawarma is popular and is usually made of chicken or lamb. Ful, a dish made from fava beans, is common in many Arab countries. In Syria and Lebanon, pastries made with a soft dough are sold, either open like a mini-pizza or filled, and are termed *fatayir*, *man'oushe*, or *basbouse* depending on the type. Toppings or fillings include zaatar, chili, spinach, meat, sausage meat, cheese, and olives. Fruit juice counters in Syria and Egypt provide fresh juice from all seasonal fruit as well as sugar-cane.

Sweets such as knafeh, made from cheese and pastry, and madlu'e, made from sweet cheese curds on a rich biscuit dough, are also sold from counters, drenched in syrup, and eaten on the street in Palestine, Syria, Jordan and Israel. "Cheese sweets" are a specialty of Hama in central Syria.

Israel
In Israel, street eaters enjoy sabikh, a pita stuffed with hard-boiled egg, eggplant, tahini, and a mango pickle similar in taste to chutney or atchar. It was introduced by Iraqi Jews. Bourekas are common, being sold out of carts in front of bakeries.

Syria
In springtime in Syria, whole green almonds are sold from carts on the street. In summer, prickly pears and whole fresh pistachios are sold. Pavement vendors, as well as drink sellers in traditional costume with their goods in a pot strapped to their back, sell mulberry and liquorice juice. Falafel and Shawarma are the most common Syrian street food.

Europe
There are many national street foods in Europe, but some foods have transcended borders. A good example of this is shawarma, brought to Europe by Arab and Turkish immigrants. The Quartier Latin in Paris is packed with shawarma vendors.

Balkans
Street food in the Balkans, like the rest of Balkan cuisine, is heavily influenced by the cuisine of the Ottoman Empire. Variations of the burek, a filled flaky pastry, are common throughout the Turkey and the Balkans. Ćevapi, a sort of kebab, is popular throughout the region comprised by the former Yugoslavia, and Romania where it is called Mititei.

Buregdžinica in Zagreb

Benelux
In the Netherlands and Belgium, french fries are served with sauces such as mayonnaise, ketchup, curry or tartar sauce (the latter mainly in Belgium). The combination mayonnaise, ketchup or curry and chopped onions is called "speciaal" (special) and mayonnaise mixed with peanut sauce is called "oorlog" (war).

Belgium

A *Frituur*, a French fries street vendor in Brussels.

In Belgium, a thicker variety of fries is used, called "frieten". They are mainly sold by street vendors (see picture), known as a *frituur*. In Belgium, french fries are traditionally fried in suet (beef fat).

In Belgium, Liège-style waffles (Dutch: "Wafel" or French: "Gaufre") are served warm as a street snack, similar to what is known in other countries as "Belgian Waffles". The pancake is also popular here, being sold fluffier than the French crêpe or the Russian blin.

Netherlands
In the Netherlands, the French fries are thinner and generally referred to as "patat" (the word for 'potato' in the south of the Netherlands and in Flanders) or "friet" (from the French verb 'frire' meaning 'deep-frying') or "patat friet". Some shops in the Netherlands also sell "Vlaamse friet" (Flemish fries, similar to the type sold in Belgium) but this is less common than the thinner variant. In the Netherlands, French fries are traditionally fried in vegetable oil.

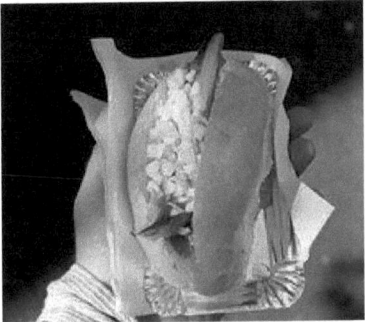

A "broodje haring met ui": a soft bun with raw herring and chopped onions

In the Netherlands, street foods are usually sold by a small store which is a mix of a cafe/bar and a fast-food restaurant, known as a *snackbar* or *cafetaria*. These stores may also contain the typically Dutch vending machine called an "automatiek". While "patat friet" forms the main portion of the foods sold, many other items are also on offer including different types of deep-fried snack meats such as "kroketten" and "frikandellen", and cheese snacks such as the "kaassouffle" (cheese deep fried inside a crispy bread crumb crust). Often, the product range includes other foods such as hamburgers, ice cream, bread rolls with different fillings, and occasionally pizza, falafel, doner kebab and shoarma. Deep fried Vietnamese spring rolls and other, originally Asian and/or Surinamese snacks such as "bapao" (a baozi filled with minced meat) and "barra" (a kind of deep fried savoury doughnut), have become increasingly popular since the 1980s.

In addition to the snackbars, one can also find street stalls selling different fried, smoked and raw fish products called a "viskraam" or "haringkar" (Dutch for fish stall or herring cart). Besides the popular raw herring served with chopped onions (bread rolls and pickled cucumber are optional), these stalls also sell fish products such as smoked mackerel, smoked eel and "kibbeling" (deep fried cod nuggets).

At festivals, markets and especially on New Year's Eve, street stalls around the country sell a type of beignets called oliebollen (literally 'oil balls'). In addition they might have other sweet pastries such as waffles and apple beignets.

Czech Republic

The most common and traditional Czech street food is Smažený sýr, which is a soft piece of cheese deep-fried and served on a hamburger bun. It is typically served with tartar sauce, but some prefer ketchup.

Finland

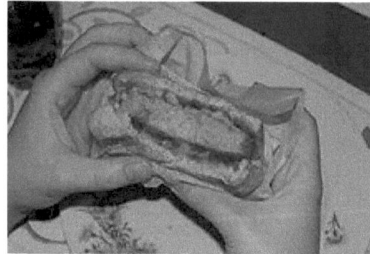

A *porilainen* sandwich

In Finland, street food can mostly be found at market squares and kiosks, although hamburger chains Hesburger and McDonald's are also available. A variety of savoury pastries such as *lihapiirakka* and *karjalanpiirakka* and sweet pastries such as *pulla*, usually served with coffee, are very common. Fish stands at the market squares also serve cured salmon (*graavilohi*) on rye bread as an open sandwich or *loimulohi*. Regional specialties sold at the market squares include *sultsina* and *kalakukko*.

In addition to hamburgers and hot dogs, Finnish meat pastries with sausages are available at kiosks, especially a sausage sandwich called a *porilainen*. Condiments include ketchup, Finnish mustard, pickle relish, mayonnaise and mustard relish as well as lettuce, tomato and onion. Another common late night street food fare found at kiosks is Finnish meatballs (*lihapulla*) and french fries with condiments. Doner kebabs are readily available at both kiosks and kebab restaurants and extremely popular.

France

In France, sandwiches are a common street food. Most of them are baguette bread sandwiches with different kinds of fillings such as "Jambon/Beurre" (ham / butter), "Jambon/Fromage" (Ham with cheese) or "Poulet/Crudités" (Chicken with vegetables). In France, crêpes are another street food. A crêpe complète containing ham, shredded cheese, and an egg provides a filling lunch. Sweet crêpe or Waffle, containing Nutella and banana or Grand Marnier and sugar are also popular snacks.

Other street foods include slices of pizza, "kebab" (actually Gyros) type sandwiches and panini, a grilled and pressed sandwich.

During the winter, roasted chestnuts can be bought.

Germany

Bratwurst and Glühwein in Garmisch

Germany, with its high Turkish population, has a number of Turkish street foods beyond the pan-European shawarma. Döner is similar to shawarma and available everywhere, especially in Berlin Kreuzberg. More traditionally, there is the Bavarian Fleischkäse (also called Leberkäse), which is similar to meatloaf, sliced to the thickness of a finger and generally served with either hot mustard or sweet mustard in a roll. Germany is also known for its various types of sausage, as well as the recent hybrid curry-sausage, Currywurst. French fries ("Pommes" in German, derived from French but pronounced according to German orthographic rules) are popular, served with ketchup and/or mayonnaise, and sometimes with sausage. Beer is sold at all sidewalk snack stands, which usually feature beers and small bottles of whiskey, schnapps, or vodka.

There are an increasing number of North African stalls that sell shawarma, falafel and halumi.

Hungary

Street food is not particularly common in Hungary, although gyros shops are becoming more common. Rétes (strudel) is fairly common, and lángos (a deep fried bread) is usually available at markets and during celebrations. In general, Hungarians looking for quick food will stop to sit down and eat, even if only at a Chinese buffet or a *főzelékfaló* (vegetable purée bar).

Italy

Pizza al taglio shop in Rome

The most notable Italian street food is pizza, sold in take-aways and bakeries. Take-away pizza (or "Pizza al taglio") is quite different from pizzeria pizza. Unlike the round pizza normally found in restaurants, which originated in Naples as a street food itself, it is generally baked on large square trays, and square or rectangular portions are sold. It usually has quite a thick base, again unlike the traditional Italian restaurant pizza.

Toppings include margherita, mushrooms, Italian sausage, ham, and vegetables.

Other street foods are the Genoese Focaccia di Recco, a double layer of thin dough filled with quark cheese and baked, Farinata, a thin, baked chickpea-flour batter, topped with salt, pepper and olive oil, often served with focaccia (a thin bread, also with salt and olive oil), Florentine trippa and lampredotto, ox stomach cooked in a seasoned broth and served in a bread roll, Roman "supplì", rice balls filled with cheese and/or various fillings, covered in egg and breadcrumbs and deep fried, similar to Sicilian arancini, where the usual filling is a meat sauce with green peas.

Pani ca meusa served in a rotisserie in Palermo

Piadina's kiosk in Macerone, Cesena

In Palermo, a street food would be "Pani ca meusa" (bread rolls with sliced, cooked pork spleen), and "Panelle", deep-fried chickpea flour batter. In central Italy "porchetta" is common, a spicy roasted pork meat (from the whole, boned animal), usually served in a panino (bread roll).

In Naples, fried food stalls, known as *friggitorie*, sell filled, deep-fried pastries and other foods. A street food made of offals, commonly found in fairs and religious festivals in Naples and in the whole Campania, is the *'O pere e 'o musso* (*The paw and the muzzle*), calves heads and pork paw boiled: sliced and chopped at the moment, they are seasoned with salt and lemon juice before being served. Locally, it is also named also *Musso re puorco* (*pork muzzle*) although only calf heads are normally used.

Vendors sell watermelons during the summer months, as well as roasted chestnuts ("caldarroste") stalls during the winter, and especially before Christmas.

Rosticcerie, while most often selling food to be eaten at home, also sometimes have a counter for immediate consumption of their goods, the most common of which are roast chicken, roast potatoes, fried polenta and other accompaniments.

Substantial immigration from Turkey and the Middle East has also gained Shawarma (best known in Italy as kebab), as well as other middle-eastern traditional dishes an increasing popularity.

Gelato (ice cream) is commonly available.

In Romagna subregion, and especially in Forlì-Cesena province, a flatbread called *Piadina* is available. It is sold in kiosks, usually as sandwich filled with mixed cold cut meats, cheese and/or vegetables. A widely used variant is the *Crescione*, a Piadina cooked like a turnover; in this version the most common filling are "tomato sauce - mozzarella" and "pumpkin - boiled potato - sausage".

Malta

Pastizzi are small, ricotta cheese or pea-paste filled puff-pastry squares that can be bought from vendors in practically every village in Malta. Ricotta pastizzi (Pastizzi tal-irkotta) are diamond shaped with a hole in the middle where the ricotta stuffing can be seen whilst pea pastizzi (Pastizzi tal-pizelli) are of the same shape but are more like an envelope of puff pastry with no holes.

The shops selling these pastries are called "Pastizzeriji". They also sell items such as pies, pizza al taglio, sausage rolls, baked rice, baked maccaroni (timpana) and sometimes arancini.

Another local street food found in such pastizzerias is the "Qassatat". This is a ball-shaped pie crust with an open top, filled with the same two basic fillings of ricotta or peas, and sometimes a tuna and spinach mixture.

Imqaret are deep fried pastries filled with a mashed date mixture.

Hamburgers, hot dogs and other such products being sold from vans, replace perennial Maltese favorites such as Ħobż biż-żejt, bigilla and timpana.

However Ħobż biż-żejt is another street food, usually bought from the inside of shops rather than stalls. This is the local sandwich, a local flat-bun called a "ftira" or a rounder one called "hbejza" are filled with various ingredients available at the counter displays. The basic Ħobż biż-żejt recipe consists of filling the bread with oil and kunserva (tomato paste), tuna-fish, pickles and other delicacies which vary from shop to shop. These shops usually serve tea with milk in small glasses to their regulars.

Occasionally a street vendor will sell Sinizza, deep fried ball of fish, batter and other ingredients.

Poland

A *zapiekanki*

Popular street snacks in Poland include: *zapiekanki*, essentially Polish-style French-bread pizzas with a variety of toppings—the *obwarzanki* of Kraków, which are like bagels (only with bigger holes); and *precle* (or pretzels). The most common street food in Poland, however, seems to be *lody*, or ice cream. Long lines outside ice cream shops, and scores of pedestrians toting cones, are a regular fixture of Polish streetscapes.

Hot dogs, hamburgers and french fries are also very popular, often sold in the same shops and kiosks as zapiekanki.

Romania
In Romania there is a fair amount of street food. The most commonly available during the day are covrigi, hot pretzels covered in sesame or poppy seeds, and "plăcinte". "Plăcinte" can refer to sweet or savory pies with various fillings or to large pieces of fried dough eaten with garlic sauce, sour cream, cheese, or jam similar to Hungarian lángos. In the south and along the Black Sea, "plăcintă dobrogeană" is available. This type of plăcintă is more like the burek encountered in other parts of the Balkans. Doughnuts called gogoși are also commonly available. At fairs and in winter time kürtős kalács (tulnic in Romanian) with nuts or cinnoman is very popular. Mititei or "mici", small grilled skinless sausages, are often available in the summer in marketplaces and at fairs. Other street foods include popcorn, steamed ears of corn, roasted chestnuts in winter, and ice cream in summer.

Russia
Traditional Eastern European items such as blini, pirozhki and sausages are widely available.

The cuisine of Russia's Turkic minority is popular, with dishes like shawerma, rotisserie chicken, shashlik, chebureki and *plov* (pilaf).

Kvas, a small beer made (usually) from bread, with honey being a frequent additive (*myodniy kvass*), is sold out of tanks or barrels on the street.

In areas with Chinese immigrant pop-

Kvass vendor in Kiev, Ukraine

ulations, Chinese dishes are sold.

Ice cream is enjoyed even on the coldest of Moscow days. Pizza is also available.

Kiosks sell candy, snacks, produce, beer and other beverages, in addition to cigarettes and household products.

Slovakia
In Slovakia street offerings include steamed sweetcorn cobs, fried flat bread loaves with garlic and salt or other condiments (*langos*), fried buns with poppy seed, jam or cream cheese filling (*pirozky*); seasonally, ice-cream is eaten in summer and roasted chestnuts in autumn. *Ciganska pecienka* (gypsy-style roasted pork), roasted sausage and more are sold at Saturday markets. Crepes and fresh sandwiches are available.

Spain
The concept of eating in the street is very rooted in the Spanish culture, even though in the last few decades the law has forbidden the sale of food in the streets due to hygiene concerns. The most common way to eat is still inside a bar with friends (tapeo), however, in winter, roast chestnuts can be bought in the street, especially in the north, and during fiestas, churros are also sold. Additionally, the typical bocadillo is the most common snack all around Spain for school children and workers. Bocadillos can be filled with various foodstuffs typical of the province (anchovies, sweet peppers, tortilla de patatas, tuna, ham, meat, cheese, Empanada Gallega, etc.) and are very convenient as "food on the go". Some major cities will have vendors selling ice cream, nuts and snacks from kiosks.

During summer in Málaga (and many small towns nearby), the fruit of the higo chumbo (a local cactus) is often sold.

Switzerland
Street foods available in Switzerland are sandwich-like, either the typical grilled panini, but also pretzels, grilled chicken, hot dogs or the traditional Bratwurst served with a slice of bread and sometimes mustard. Sweet foods include ice cream and crêpes. Stalls will typically be motorized trucks, rather than smaller wheeled carts.

Turkey
In Turkey, street foods show considerable change from region to region. Here is a comprehensive list of most of the typical street foods that can be found around large Turkish metropolises:

Istanbul

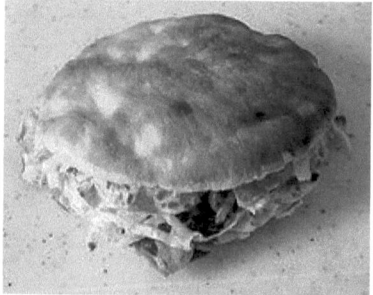
Döner served in a "*tombik pide*" ("fatty" pita) also called in (Turkish: *gobit*)

Döner served either in:
Dürüm - the "Kaşarlı Dürüm" variation of Taksim is extremely popular, that consists of a toasted dürüm with kaşar cheese added to the döner meat
Tombik i.e. "*fat bread*"
Balik-Ekmek - freshly cooked fish served inside a bun of bread. This is typically served on the Eminonu square straight from the boat on which it is prepared.
Pilav - steamed rice with chicken and chickpeas, mostly sold in steam carts at night
Midye - mussels, that come in two forms:
Midye Dolma - stuffed mussels with rice, pine nuts and raisins, eaten cold with lemon and olive oil

Midye Tava - mussels on a skewer, that are fried in oil, and eaten with a garlic sauce

Kokoreç - the Istanbul version is typically cooked on a pan rather than on charcoal, and can be spicy

Uykuluk - sweetbread and other soft glands of lamb, grilled on charcoal, and especially popular in the European Side

Patsos - a sandwich composed of fried french fries and sausage topped with kaşar, more than popular in the Asian Side

Dilli Kaşarlı - a tiny toast comprising thin sliced smoked tongue with kaşar, a fine delicacy of Etiler

Adana Kebabı - served in a dürüm

Sucuk Ekmek - sucuk served in fresh crusty bread as a sandwich

Islak Hamburger - another specialty of the Taksim neighbourhood, consisting of a garlic meatball in a tiny bun, that is dipped in a pepper sauce and reheated

Kumpir - a baked potato filled to the maximum with a variety of toppings, popular around Ortaköy

Boza - a fermented drink, drunk in winter nights

İzmir

Boyoz

Kokoreç made exclusively from milk fed lamb, grilled on hot charcoal, served barely cleaved inside of a grilled bread quarter, with very little spice, often accompanied with cold beer

Çöp Şiş - a kebab consisting of very small milk fed lamb cuts mounted on tiny skewers (made of dried squash) grilled on charcoal and served in very large numbers, around 15 at a time

Kelle Söğüş - different parts, including cheek, tongue brain and eyes from a boiled sheep head, that are cooled and marinated in olive oil, then all chopped together and served wrapped in a lavaş with a slice of tomato and a hint of spice. It is considered to be a local delicacy of İzmir by excellence

Közde Sandviç - Literally "*Sandwich on Charcoal*", that is bread toasted on a charcoal grill, alongside the meat and cheese that are grilled on charcoal to be then added to the toast. Comes in two main variations:

Kumru - *lit "the Dove"*, that consists of a lemon-shaped bread and has mostly a cheese filling

Yengen - *lit. "Your Aunt"* that has a round and crusty bread with a meatier filling, with mayonnaise

Midye - mussels, that come in two forms:

Midye Dolma - stuffed mussels, different from the Istanbul version in that they are tiny, and are sold by the dozen

Midye Tava - fried mussels, different from the Istanbul version as they are fried in olive oil and do not come with skewers

Sardalya Tava - small sardines fried in olive oil

Boyoz - hot, greasy and flaky pastry typical of İzmir, baked in a masonry oven and served with a hard-boiled egg

Gevrek - the İzmir version of the Simit

Turşu Suyu - sour brine that is left from pickling, consumed cold, somewhat of an acquired taste

Lokma - a sweet summer specialty, sold on carts

Ankara

Ankara is a rather poor city when it comes to local cuisine in general, but a few street specialties are still to be counted:

Simit in its Ankara variant, that is thinner, and baked exclusively in masonry ovens after being brushed with pekmez, making it crustier

Köfte Ekmek - spicy meatballs grilled on charcoal and served inside crusty bread or grilled bazlama generally consumed with Ayran

Tavuk Döner - Döner made with marinated chicken that is generally preferred in Ankara to the meat Döner

Kumpir - a baked potato filled to the maximum with a variety of toppings, popular in Çankaya

Gözleme - savoury hand made and hand rolled pastry, with a selection of fillings, grilled on a sac top

Adana-Mersin

A street mangal cart serving Kıyma Kebabı in Adana

Kıyma Kebabı - a particularly delicious kebab, consisting of roasting a huge skewer of hand-minced ram meat mixed with tail-fat and red pepper on an open mangal, called "*Adana Kebabı*" in the rest of Turkey, eaten in its street version as a dürüm wrapped in lavaş

Ciğer Dürüm - liver that has been roasted on a mangal, alternatively with pieces of tail-fat, wrapped with onions, parsley and pomegranate syrup in a dürüm that takes a "V" shape

Tantuni a spicy lavaş wrap consisting of julienned lamb stir-fried on a sac on a hint of cotton oil, a specialty of Mersin

Şırdan - boiled sheep rumen filled with rice, and eaten with cumin, considered to be an Adana delicacy

Bici Bici - a very popular ice dessert, consisting of sweetened peeled ice put on top of diced haytalya pieces (sweet semolina jelly) swimming in rose syrup. The peeled ice is then lightly soaked with different natural syrups, coloring it. This particular dessert is nowhere to be found outside of Adana-Mersin, and until very recently, could be only bought from street vendors

Şalgam - a beverage made of fermented red and black carrots, very sour, that comes in mild and hot versions. Both Adana and Mersin compete for the best Şalgam

Antep

Beyran - a dish made of a small amount

of rice topped with the soft meat and neck fat of lamb in a small copper plate that is left to burn on a potent fire for some time. considered to be an Antep delicacy

Nohut Dürüm - a very interesting dürüm made out of chickpeas steamed in a spicy sauce, that are served crushed and wrapped in a thick lavaş. This may be Turkey's only entirely vegetarian dürüm.

Cağırtlak - liver, fat, and other offal (mostly heart and kidney) are impaled on skewers and grilled on a mangal to be served in a lavaş, a favorite late-night dish of Eastern Turkey

Fıstıklı Kebap - lit. "Kebab with Pistachio" is basically a Kıyma Kebabı less the spice and plus the ground pistachios that are added in the mixture. The street version is served as a dürüm.

Urmu Dutu - the juice of freshly squeezed sour blackberries (a variety endemic to the region) that is typically only sold in the street carts, where the blackberries are cooled on a block of ice

Urfa

Turkish Lahmacun with salad

Lahmacun - ubiquitous to the city, with the street version being substantially smaller than the regular one, and sold by higher quantity

Çiğ Köfte Dürüm - as the name says it consists of Çiğ Köfte that has been wrapped with a lettuce leaf inside a dürüm

Haşhaş Kebabı - a local variation of the Kıyma Kebabı, very popular in Aleppo as well, that is made by hand-mincing the meat in a thinner manner than the classic recipe, and by adding crushed garlic into the mixture.

Ciğer dürüm - sold everywhere in the streets of the city and even eaten for breakfast, it consists of 8 skewers of charcoal grilled lamb liver and tail fat, marinated with Urfa pepper wrapped in a dürüm with cumin, sumac and onions.

Yürek dürüm - the same wrap as the Ciğer dürüm, but with lamb heart instead of the liver, eaten the same way, slightly seasoned with paprika.

Böbrek dürüm - 8 skewers of unseasoned lamb kidneys, wrapped with onions and sumac.

United Kingdom

Converted vans sell kebabs, jacket potato, hamburgers and chips, especially at night. At fairs, stalls sell candy floss and doughnuts. In Lancashire, hot parched peas (black peas) are bought from stalls, especially in the colder months. During winter there are stalls selling hot chestnuts.

Ice cream vans are considered one of the signs of summer, and they usually play well-known tunes such as Greensleeves or Teddy Bears' Picnic through a PA system. Street carts can be seen in some cities selling products such as roast nuts and hot dogs, especially in places frequented by tourists.

North America

Barbados

In Barbados, fishcakes are a common street food. Fishcakes are made with bits of saltfish, seasoned and mixed with flour and then deep fried. Fishcakes are sold at community events such as school fairs and concerts and can also be found at fish fries such as those in Baxter's Road in the capital city of Bridgetown or the Friday evening event in the southern fishing town of Oistins. Fishcakes are commonly eaten with saltbread, a thick, round bread; the sandwich is called a "bread-and-two" and can be found at most village shops throughout the island.

Canada

While most major cities in Canada offer a variety of street food, regional "specialties" are notable. While poutine (french fries with gravy and cheese curds) is available in most of the country. Similarly, hot dog stands can be found across Canada, but are far more common in Ontario (often sold from mobile canteen trucks, usually referred to as "chip wagons") than in Vancouver or Victoria (where the "Mr. Tube Steak" franchise is notable). Montreal offers a number of specialties including Shish taouk, the Montreal hot dog, two-dollar chow mein on St. Laurent and dollar falafels. Although falafel is widespread in Vancouver, 99 cent pizza slices are much more popular. Shawarma is quite prevalent in Ottawa, while Halifax offers its own unique version of the Doner kebab called the Donair, which features a sauce, made from condensed milk, sugar, and vinegar. Ice cream trucks can be seen (and often heard) nationwide during the summer months. Corn on the Cob is found, often grilled.

Dominican Republic

Fried foods are common in the Dominican Republic. Empanadas are a very typical snack, made of fried flour, though empanadas made out of cassava flour, called *catibias*, are also common. Fillings include cheese, chicken, beef, and vegetables, or a combination of these. *Yaniqueques* are sold at many empanada stands. *Yaniqueques* (from Jonnycake) are essentially round flour shaped cakes which are fried and usually eaten with salt and/or ketchup. Other vendors sell plantain fritters and fried or boiled salami.

Hamburgers are sold at stands called *chimis*, which also offer sandwiches called *chimichurris*, though these bear little to no resemblance to the South American sauce of the same name. *Chimis* occasionally also offer hot dogs and other sandwich varieties.

Corn on the cob can be bought on the street, usually sold by traveling vendors who move around on a tricycle. Sweets vendors who sell treats such as candied coconut and *dulce de leche* sell their goods at major intersections in cities and sometimes have their own stands.

Haiti

In Haiti street vendors sell dishes such as fried plantains, griot (deep-fried pork or beef), frescos (fruit soda drink), cassava bread, and Haitian patties (pastry filled with choice of chicken, fish, beef, or pork).

Jamaica

A plate of jerk chicken, with rice, plantains, carrots and green beans

The most common Jamaican street food is jerk chicken or pork and can be found everywhere on the island. Jerk is marinade that is a blended primarily from a combination of scotch bonnet peppers, onions, scallions, thyme and allspice. Once marinated, it is often barbecued on converted steel drum or whatever else locals can construct as a grill/smoker. It is often accompanied with breadfruit and/or festival, a sweetened fried dough.

Meat patties in a sweet bread called "coco bread" are the most popular street food. Bun and cheese is also eaten.

Mexico

A street food vendor in Mexico City selling crepes

In Mexico, there is a great variety of antojitos Mexicanos that are found at street food vendors, at any time of night or day: tacos, tortas (traditional Mexican sandwiches), tostadas, picadas, quesadillas, guaraches, panuchos, sopes, gorditas, tamales, atole, aguas frescas, and cemitas.

Puerto Rico

Puerto Rico is well known for its street foods (referred to collectively as *cuchifritos* in New York City) and is popular both in the Caribbean and in mainland North America. Typical Bastreet foods include *pinchos* (a kebob of skewered pork, seafood or chicken, usually spicy and topped with barbecue sauce on bread; often fried whole).

Empanadas are very popular. Fried flour or yuca flour pastries stuffed with chicken, ground meat, potatoes, corn, fruit, cheese, or seafood. There are also combinations such as cheese with meat, cheese with fruit, potatoes with meat, even pigeon peas with coconut and pizza empanadas.

There's the *papa rellena*, fried potato balls stuffed with meat or cheese.

The alcapurria, a ground *malanga* croquette filled with meat or ground yuca filled with seafood. The malanga can have a combination of potatoes, plantains, green bananas, and/or calabazas (tropical pumpkins). Picadillo is the typical stuffing.

There are also arepas stuffed with fried meat, seafood salad or usually seafood cooked in coconut milk if one likes.

Dishes based on plantains or green bananas are popular as street food throughout Puerto Rico. Pasteles are a combination of mashed tubers, plantains, or bananas filled with pork and wrapped in banana leaves and then boiled. Piononos a sliver or ripe plantain sliced down the middle, fried and then stuffed with ground meat, cheese, raisins, capers, and olives. Plátano relleno similar to papa rellena but with ripe plantains rather than potatoes.

Bacalaítos are a fried pancake-like dough that are served with salted codfish. These foods can be found on the side of just about any busy street, but also typically in kiosks, often near the beach.

Sorullos a fried cornmeal batter shaped like fat fingers; they can be sweet or savory. Sorullos are stuffed with Puerto Rican white cheese, Cheddar or mozzarella and is served with Russian dressing. Sweet sorullos contain sugar and are filled with Puerto Rican white cheese and fruit paste such as goiabada.

Trinidad and Tobago

In Trinidad and Tobago there are roti and shark & bake stands that provide quick foods like roti, dhal puri, fried bake, and the most popular, Doubles. Roti is a thin flat bread originating from India that is fluffy on the inside and crispy and flaky on the outside. It is cooked on a flat iron plate called a tawah (< Hindi tawa) or platain and served with curried chicken, pork or beef. Dahl puri is similar to the roti but is softer and pliable and has crushed dahl lentils cooked with saffron and placed in the centre of the dough before it is rolled out and cooked. This is also served with either curried chicken, pork or beef.

Fried bake is made by frying flattened balls of dough that becomes fluffy and increases in height as it is fried. It can be served with fried ripe plantains, meat or gravy. At the shark & bake stands fried bakes filled with well-seasoned shark fillets and dressed with many different condiments including pepper, garlic and chadon beni can also be found.

Doubles is made with two flat breads called baras (from Hindi bara, "big") that are filled with channa (from Hindi "chick peas") and topped with pepper, cucumber chutney, mango chutney, coconut chutney or bandania/chadon beni. It can be eaten either wrapped up as an easy to eat sandwich, or open it up and eat each bara separately.

United States

Street food vendor in New York City.

Street food vendor in Los Angeles serving a bacon-wrapped hot dog

In the United States, hot dogs and their many variations (corn dogs, chili dogs) are perhaps the most common street food, particularly in major metropolitan areas such as New York City (the Easy-Bake Oven was said to have been inspired by New York City carts roasting chestnuts). Roasted nuts and gyros are often sold in the cities. Cheesesteaks, breakfast sandwiches, and pretzels are common in Philadelphia. Throughout the US, ice cream is sold out of trucks. Tacos and Tortas are sold from open food stalls. Pizza and egg rolls are available from window counters.

Some vendors operate out of food trucks and food carts, which offer a low overhead for entrepreneurs and often serve a huge variety of cuisines. Like restaurants, they are regulated and subject to inspections by the local municipal or county health departments.

Diversity and the lack of a strictly defined national cuisine means that, in most urban areas in the US and Canada, vendors sell hot dogs, pizza, falafel, gyros, kebobs, tortilla-based snacks such as tacos and burritos, panini, crêpes, french fries, egg rolls, and other various dishes.

Virgin Islands

Popular street foods in the Virgin Islands include *patés*, fried fish, fried chicken leg and *johnnycake* (fried dough). Pates, similar to the empanadas of Puerto Rico and the Dominican Republic, consist of fried flour filled with various meats, including conch, saltfish, beef, chicken and lobster.

Oceania

A pie floater

An ice cream van at Batemans Bay, New South Wales, Australia

Australia

The most common street food in Australia is the *sausage sizzle*, usually consisting of a thin sausage or sandwich steak cooked on a barbecue and served on a slice of bread with optional fried onions, cheese, mustard and tomato or barbecue sauce. The stalls are usually run by local sporting or charity groups as fundraiser.

A pie floater is a meal served at pie carts in Adelaide and elsewhere in South Australia. It was once more widely available in other parts of Australia, but its popularity waned. It consists of an Australian meat pie covered with tomato sauce, sitting in a plate of green pea soup.

People can buy soft serve and other ice creams from vans which drive around the streets. The vans alert potential customers with a tinkling tune, for example *Greensleeves* or *The Entertainer*.

In Melbourne and Sydney, kebabs and souvlakis have taken over as the main street food due to the high percentage of Greek and Lebanese people in both cities, and is popular as a late night snack, especially after a few beers. They are known to curb late night drunken violence as punters gather around and enjoy a meal together and share stories of their night.

New Zealand

Vans selling burgers, New Zealand hotdogs (a battered sausage on a stick), toasted sandwiches and chips are the most common type of street food in New Zealand. *The White Lady* food van in downtown Auckland is a well-known icon of the city. There are many coffee carts and coffee vans operating the streets, both independent ones as well as vans operating as part of a franchise system such as *The Coffee Guy*.

Like Australia, ice cream vans and sausage sizzles are also common in New Zealand. The most well known ice cream franchise is *Mr Whippy*, a franchise that originally came from England, and also operates in Australia. *Mr Whippy* softserve icecream is an iconic symbol of a New Zealand summer to many Kiwi.

South America

Argentina

In Argentina, vendors sell Choripan, a barbequeued sausage served wrapped in French bread, or morcipan, using a blood sausage (morcilla) instead.

Pizza is very popular, in part due to the country's heavy Italian immigration in the early 20th century. Local versions include the fugazzeta, a pizza made with mozzarella cheese and onions, and the fainá: a pizza made with garbanzo bean flour with no toppings, generally served as a side dish to regular pizza.

The empanada, which in gourmet versions is baked, is usually deep-fried in this case. Empanadas can be made with beef, fish, ham & cheese, neapolitan (using the same toppings as that pizza) or vegetarian.

Sandwiches are usually served hot, like the Tostado or the Lomito, the latter having a great number of versions, with food courts offering all kinds of ingredients and combinations.

Other local street food includes local versions of the hotdog called pancho, and the hamburger or hamburguesa. Despite being very popular in the past, these have been displaced by a number of reasons, mainly a local perception that American-style foods are unhealthy and of low quality.

Sweets and desserts usually found in Argentine streets include caramel apple (manzana acaramelada), cotton candy (algodon de azucar), sweet popcorn (pochoclo) and a local snack called garrapiñada, which is made of peanuts, vanilla and sugar caramel, and sold in small bags in the shape of tubes.

Brazil

Cheese buns

Pão de queijo, which can be translated as "cheese bread", is a street snack in the southeast of Brazil and, increasingly, the rest of the country. Hot dogs, cooked in a tomato-based sauce with bell peppers and onions, are often sold with grated cheese, ketchup, mayonnaise, green peas, corn kernels, fried potato sticks (batata palha), potato salad or mashed potatoes as choice of toppings. Hamburgers are also offered with an assortment of toppings, such as mozzarella cheese, bacon, fried eggs, lettuce, tomato, mayonnaise, ketchup and mustard, the popular "X-Tudo" (or cheese-all, a souped up cheeseburger). Calabresa (Pepperoni) sausage sandwiches are also popular.

Rio de Janeiro beach vendors sell *Mate Gelado* (erva mate iced-tea), *biscoitos de polvilho* (sour manioc flour puffs), roasted peanuts and *queijo coalho* (grilled cheese on sticks, barbecued on the spot) as well as popsicles, cold beer and home-made sandwiches (*sanduiche natural*). In the northeastern state of Bahia, the region's African heritage is reflected in the iconic *acarajé* (deep fried black eyed pea bun filled with *caruru*, made from salted dried shrimp, and *vatapá*, a creamy combination of coconut milk, palm oil and cashew nuts) or sweets like *cocada* (candied coconut) and *pé-de-moleque* (peanut brittle). All over the country, popcorn is always offered in push carts both savory or sweet (with sugar and cocoa powder). *Churros* push carts (sausage shaped deep fried dough filled with a choice of *doce-de-leite* caramel or chocolate sauce) are also found on any major city street.

Chile

In Chile, sopaipillas, a deep fried dough made out of flour and pumpkin, Anticucho, completo, calzones rotos, fresh fruit juices, soft drink, French fries, pizza, churros, empanadas, sweets and sweets are sold by street vendors.

Colombia

Empanadas

In Colombia, the empanada, a deep-fried meat-filled patty, is sold. It is also a very popular side dish. Various types of arepa are also a common street food. Also popular is the chuzo (meat skeewer), consisting of pork or chicken speared shish-kebab style on a thin wooden stake (hence the name *chuzo*, from *chuzar* meaning to "to pierce or spear") and cooked over charcoal on a pushcart. Most chuzos are garnished with a small arepa at the top and a small roasted potato at the bottom. Morcilla, various sausages, and chinchuria are also sold by street vendors.

Buñuelos and natilla are popular especially during the Christmas season.

In the Paisa region pan de bono, pan de yuca, pan de queso, pastries and wine cake are sold at street stalls. Ice cream treats and paletas are also popular at street vendors. Fruit salad with condensed milk, granizado shakes, salpicon, and fresh fruit are also sold in the land of "eternal spring". Carimañolas are sold in coastal regions.

Peru

In Peru, anticuchos, a type of kebab, are often sold by street vendors called *anticucheras*. Also, cuy, a species of Guinea Pig is served as a delicacy on religious holidays.

Venezuela

In Venezuela, the arepa is a common fast-food meal. It consists of a flattened cornmeal bun, about the size and shape of an English muffin, split open and usually stuffed with soft cheese. Other fillings include shredded chicken salad with mayonnaise and avocado (reina pepiada), shredded brisket cooked with onions, red bell peppers and tomatoes (carne mechada) and pickled octopus. Also popular are cachapas, flat cakes made from fresh corn, rather than corn flour. Empanadas are also eaten in Venezuela, and are made out of corn flour, rather than wheat flour, as in the rest of the continent. They are filled with the same ingredients as arepas.

Source http://en.wikipedia.org/wiki/List_of_street_food

Malatang

Malatang (simplified Chinese: 麻辣烫; traditional Chinese: 麻辣燙; pinyin: *málàtàng*) is a common type of Chinese street food, especially popular in Beijing. It originated in Sichuan, but it differs mainly from the Sichuanese version

Malatang in Sanlitun, Beijing

in that the Sichuanese version is more similar to what in northern China would be described as hot pot.

Procedure

Typically a table with a big and flat saucepan is set up on the street, with a large number of ingredients in skewers being cooked in a mildly spicy broth. Customers sit around the table picking up whatever they want to eat. Given the large number of ingredients available, normally not all ingredients are in the saucepan at the same time, and customers may suggest what is missing and should be added.

All skewers normally cost the same. Currently in Beijing (as of June 2012) they cost one RMB each. Customers keep the used wooden sticks by their plates, and when a customer finishes eating, the price to pay is determined by counting the number of empty sticks.

Common ingredients

Some of the common ingredientes include:

bean curd
beef (chunks)
dumplings
fish balls
lettuce
lotus root
mushrooms
noodles
pork liver
pork lung
potato
quail eggs
sausages
shanyao
sheep bowels
tofu

Source http://en.wikipedia.org/wiki/Malatang

Maruya (food)

A serving of maruya.

Maruya are a type of fritters from the Philippines usually made from bananas. It is prepared by coating thinly sliced and 'fanned' bananas in batter and deep frying them. They are then sprinkled with sugar and served with slices of jackfruit preserved in syrup.

Maruya traditionally use a type of banana in the Philippines called *Saba* (A cooking banana also known as the Cardaba Banana). Other types of *maruya* use dessert bananas which are usually mashed before mixing them with batter. They can also be made from sweet potatoes.

Maruya are commonly sold as street food though they are also popular as home-made merienda snacks among Filipinos.

Source http://en.wikipedia.org/wiki/Maruya_(food)

Meat pie (Australia and New Zealand)

A typical meat pie with tomato sauce

Origin
Place of origin   Australia and New Zealand
Details
Type   Meat pie

Main ingredient(s)   Diced or minced meat, gravy

A vegan faux-meat pie, containing soy protein and mushrooms, from an Australian bakery.

An **Australian or New Zealand meat pie** is a hand-sized meat pie containing largely diced or minced meat and gravy, sometimes with onion, mushrooms, or cheese and often consumed as a take-away food snack. The pie itself is similar to the United Kingdom's steak pie.

It is considered iconic in Australia and New Zealand. It was described by former New South Wales Premier Bob Carr in 2003 as Australia's "national dish". New Zealanders regard the meat pie as a part of New Zealand cuisine, and it forms part of the New Zealand national identity.

The popular brand Four'N'Twenty produces 50,000 pies per hour and Australians consume an average of 12 meat pies each per year. The average consumption of meat pies in New Zealand is 15 per person per year. The meat pie is heavily associated with Australian rules football as one of the most popular consumed food items whilst watching a game.

Commercial production

Manufacturers of pies in Australia tend to be state-based, reflecting the long distances involved with interstate transport and lack of refrigeration capabilities in the early years of pie production. Many pies sold ready-to-eat at smaller outlets are sold unbranded and may be locally produced, produced by a brand-name vendor, or even imported, frozen pies heated prior to serving.

The Australian meat pie manufacturer Four'N'Twenty says that its pie was invented in 1947 by L. T. McClure in a small Bendigo bakery, to become the brand Four'N'Twenty. Due to its relationship with Australian rules football, Four'N'Twenty has iconic status in Victoria and high popularity outside the state.

Other manufacturers predate this, and the pie manufacturer Sargent can trace their pie making back to 1906.

In South Australia, Balfours has been making pies since the early 1900s and remains (with Vili's) one of two major pie manufacturers in the state. Both of these pie makers supply pies to various venues hosting Australian Rules Football games.

Produced in Western Australia, Mrs Mac's Pies are now sold nationwide, found mostly in service stations and corner stores, competing with other brands in the contested takeaway hotbox market on the basis of quality and fillings other than the normal fare.

In Victoria, some of the well known and famous pie makers are Pie in the Sky from Olinda, Clarke's Pies from Mortlake, Kings Pies from Hamilton, Gillies from Bendigo, Beaumont's Pies from Geelong and Patties Pies from Bairnsdale.

In Tasmania, the main manufacturer of pies is National Pies. National Pies make typical beef mince pies, as well as "Cottage Pies", which are topped with mashed potato. National Pies' mince pies are rectangular in shape, as opposed to most other brands, which are round.

Australian Meat Pies were introduced into the United States in 1994 by Mark Allen, of Boort, Victoria, when he and his wife, Wendy, began operation of Pacific Products, Inc. in Marietta, Georgia.Stutchbury, Michael (20 June 1995). "Pies de resistance in the Land of the Feed". *The Australian Financial Review*. Almer, Sean (3 June 1996). "Aussie strives to put meat pies into diets of Yankee sports fans". *Business Sydney*. Pacific Products was a wholesale only business, selling their pies to chain retailers throughout the United States. Although Pacific Products is no longer in business, Mark Allen and his Partner Neville Steele opened the Australian Bakery Cafe in Marietta Georgia, a retail bakery which also ships its products throughout the USA.

In 1977, during the time that American fast food restaurants moved into New Zealand, Progressive Enterprises created Georgie Pie, a fast food restaurant with a menu based on meat pies. The pies were batch made and frozen at Progressive's Mangere plant. The first Georgie Pie restaurant opened in Kelston, Auckland, and at its peak in the mid-1990s had become a chain of 32 restaurants across New Zealand. However, after a major expansion, Georgie Pie became uneconomic to run and was eventually sold to McDonald's New Zealand in 1996. The last restaurant at Mission Bay, Auckland, closed in 1998.

Nutritional value

Former New South Wales Premier Bob Carr launched a childhood obesity summit in 2002 where he told participants that feeding children a diet of meat pies, sausage rolls and chiko rolls was akin to child cruelty.

In April 2002, the Australian Consumers Association conducted a study of 22 frozen meat pies available in supermarkets. They found three brands did not meet the minimum 25 per cent meat content requirement set by Food Standards Australia New Zealand (FSANZ), they also found that the fat content ranged from 15 to 35 grams of fat per pie. The ACA study was of a select group of frozen meat pies in supermarkets, thus the study does not account for freshly baked meat pies of which the meat content and nutritional value varies from bakery to bakery. Another study by ACA in 2006 found 5 of the 23 pie products tested had less than the minimum 25% meat required.

In 2006, The ACA awarded pie manufacturer Black and Gold *"The CHOICE Shonky Award for UnAustralian Content"* for their pies found to contain just 17% meat.

The meats allowed by FSANZ in a meat pie are beef, buffalo, camel, cattle, deer, goat, hare, pig, poultry, rabbit and sheep. Kangaroo meat, a leaner alternative, is also sometimes used. However, most pie manufacturers specify 'beef' in their ingredients list; typically, those using other types of meat will simply put 'meat' in the list instead. FSANZ's definition of meat includes snouts, ears, tongue roots, tendons and blood vessels. Only offal (such as brain, heart, kidney, liver, tongue, tripe) must be specified on the label. Wild animals ("slaughtered ... in the wild state") may not be used.

Awards

The Great Aussie Meat Pie Contest

Started in 1990 and held annually since, the Great Aussie Pie Contest was created to find the best everyday commercially produced meat pie produced in Australia, to promote the higher quality pie production as well as attempting to increase media attention upon the foodstuff, the iconic meat pie often dwarfed by the omnipresent advertising of fast food chains.

The contest attracts various pie makers Australia wide; the pies for the contest are judged anonymously to avoid bias towards or against specific bakeries or states. Run in parallel to the main contest is one for gourmet pies, with categories for such fillings as chicken, seafood and even vegetarian pies. As well as the main prize, certificates of excellence are awarded for entries that reach set quality standards. The main award is highly coveted due to the greatly increased sales it generates, with many people travelling interstate to sample the winning pie.

Bakels New Zealand Supreme Pie Awards

In New Zealand an annual pie competition is held since 1997, the Bakels New Zealand Supreme Pie Awards aims to recognise the best pie manufacturers in New Zealand and assisting them in producing award-winning pies and continuing to help foster and encourage developments within this category of baking.

They were entered in 11 categories – mince and gravy; chicken and vegetables; gourmet meat; bacon and egg; gourmet fruit; steak, vegetable and gravy; steak and cheese; vegetarian; mince and cheese; seafood and commercial wholesale pies. The pies were judged on presentation, the pastry on the top and bottom, the filling and the profile.

Celebrity judges included New Zealand food writers Julie Biuso and Richard Till.

Other cultural references

In the 1970s meat pies were mentioned in an advertising jingle for General Motors Holden Australia. The jingle — *football, meat pies, kangaroos and Holden cars, they go together underneath the Southern Stars* — was an adaptation of an American jingle for the General Motors Chevrolet brand.

Fair-Go Dibbler, citizen of Fourecks (*The Last Continent*) in Terry Pratchett's *Discworld* series, is famous for selling the archetypal pie floaters to his unsuspecting customers.

In 2007, Domino's Australia and Domino's New Zealand both released a meat pie pizza, consisting of minced beef, peas, diced fresh tomato, onions, gravy, thick pastry and tomato sauce.

Source http://en.wikipedia.org/wiki/Meat_pie_(Australia_and_New_Zealand)

Pad Thai

Pad Thai in Bangkok

Pad Thai or **Phat Thai** (Thai: ผัดไทย, RTGS: Phat Thai, ISO phadịthy, [pʰàt tʰāj], "fried Thai style"; Vietnamese: "Phở Xào") is a dish of stir-fried pho noodles, a type of rice noodle, with eggs, fish sauce (Thai: น้ำปลา), tamarind juice, red chili pepper, plus any combination of bean sprouts, shrimp, chicken, hot dogs, or tofu, garnished with crushed peanuts, coriander and lime, the juice of which can be added along with Thai condiments (crushed peanuts, garlic, tomato, chives, pickled turnip, coriander, lime, spicy chili oil, chili powder, vinegar, fish sauce, sugar). It is usually served with scallions and pieces of raw banana flower.

It is listed at number 5 on *World's 50 most delicious foods* readers' poll compiled by CNN Go *in 2011.*

History

Pad Thai is of Vietnamese origin, which uses pho noodles (*Bánh Phở* in Vietnamese) and Chinese ingredients. In Vietnam, it is called "phở xào" or "bánh phở xào sa tế," meaning "stir-fried pho," a popular street food, with sate (garlic, peanuts, and chiles), mung bean sprouts, meat of some sort, scallions, and fish sauce, often served with pickled vegetables. The dish was said to be imported to the ancient Thai capital city of Ayuthaya by Viet traders, and was then altered to reflect the Thai flavor profile and assigned a name reflecting its newly acquired Thai character. The dish was made popular in Thailand by Luang Phibunsongkhram, the prime minister during the late 1930s and 1940s, and renamed to pad Thai as part of his campaign to promote Thai nationalism and centralization, seeking to reduce domestic rice consumption. The Thai economy was heavily dependent on rice exports, and the prime minister hoped to increase the amount for available to export by encouraging Thais to make and sell rice noodles from street carts and in small restaurants. Pad Thai has since become one of Thailand's national dishes.

Pop culture

The Thai film *Jao saao Pad Thai* uses pad Thai as a plot device as the protagonist claims she will marry whoever eats her pad Thai for 100 days in a row.

In 2008, in an episode of *Throwdown! with Bobby Flay*, Bobby Flay was defeated by Chef Nongkran Daks at her restaurant, Thai Basil, in Chantilly, Virginia.

Source http://en.wikipedia.org/wiki/Pad_Thai

Panipuri

Panipuri

Origin	
Alternative names(s)	Pani Ke Patashe, Puchka, Gu Chup, Paani Poori, Pani ke Bataashe, Pakodi, Gol Gappa
Place of origin	Indian subcontinent
Region or state	India, Pakistan, Nepal, Bangladesh
Details	
Type	Snack
Main ingredient(s)	Flour, spiced water, onions, potatoes, chickpeas

The **golgappa** (also known as **panipuri** पानीपूरी, *pānīpūrī*, **pani ke bataashe**, Marathi: पाणीपुरी *pāṇīpurī*, Urdu: گول گپے, Gujarati: પાણી પુરી, term used in Western India, **puchka** (Bengali: ফুচকা, or **gup chup** (Oriya: ଗୁପଚୁପ)) is a popular street snack in India, Pakistan, Bangladesh, Sri Lanka and Nepal. It consists of a round, hollow puri, fried crisp and filled with a mixture of flavored water ("pani"), tamarind chutney, chili, chaat masala, potato, onion and chickpeas. It is generally small enough to fit completely into one's mouth. It is a popular street food dish in Mumbai, Delhi, Karachi, Lahore, Dhaka, Kolkata and Kathmandu.

The name gol gappa refers to the crisp sphere (gol) that is placed in the mouth and eaten (gappa) one at a time. *Pani* comes from the Hindi word for water and *puri* (or *poori*) is the name of an Indian bread made by deep frying in oil. It is known as *bataasha* in the Western region of Uttar Pradesh. Bataasha is something which gets smashed with application of a slight pressure; the bataasha gets smashed as soon as it is placed inside the mouth. It is known as *Puchka* in Eastern Indian states like Bihar, Jharkhand and West Bengal, also in Bangladesh. Because of the bursting sound in the mouth when it is eaten, called *gup chup* in Odisha and South Jharkhand. Gol-Gappa or Pani Pataase in Madhya Pradesh, Gup-Chup or Gol-Gappa or Panipuri in Chhattisgarh. In several parts of Gujarat and Kutch. It is commonly known as *pakodi* (પકોડી), not to be confused with *pakoda*.

History

The puritan originated from the Magadh region of India, present day South Bihar where it is also known as phoolki. The English meaning of golgappa is "watery bread" or "crisp sphere eaten." The literal meaning suggests that it may have originated from Banares. In West Bengal and specifically Kolkata, *Puchka* is considered to be **the** king of this variety of snacks, compared to its cousins like golgappas or panipuris. The filling is made by lightly mashing boiled potatoes with black salt, salt, some spices, a generous portion of tamarind pulp (made by mashing ripe tamarind in tamarind water), chilli (powder/chopped/boiled & pasted). The tamarind water *Tetul Jol* is made by mixing tamarind and spices/ salt and making a light and tart liquid with water. At some places like Deshpriya Park, a very famous variety is made with sour curd, and called *Dahi (curd) Puchka*.

Names

Its popular names and the area where it is known by this name are:

Name	Region
Pani Ke Patashe	Haryana
Gol gappa, Water balls	New Delhi, Punjab, Haryana, Jharkhand, Bihar, Madhya Pradesh, Pakistan
Pani ke bataashe / Patashi	Rajasthan, Uttar Pradesh
Panipuri	Hilly part in Nepal, Maharashtra(Mumbai and all the parts of Maharashtra), Madhya Pradesh, Gujarat, Andhra Pradesh, Karnataka, Tamil Nadu
Puchka	Bangladesh, West Bengal (India)
Gup chup	Odisha, South Jharkhand, Chhatisgarh
Pakodi	Gujarat (some parts)
Phulki	Terai Part in Nepal, Madhya Pradesh
gol gappa	Himachal pardesh

Presentation

Panipuri

Home made Panipuri.

Panipuri stall

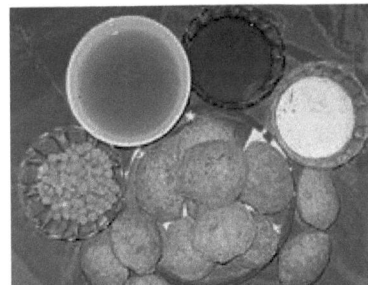

A plate of Pakistani gol gappas (centre) accompanied with other foods

Typically, 4–8 panipuris are served over a portion on a triangular plate made from dry sal leaves. Some places offer panipuris prepared on a whole plate, but the popular way for them to be served is one-at-a-time from a roadside vendor. Customers hold a small plate or bowl (*katori*) and stand around the vendors cart. The server then starts making one panipuri at a time and gives one to each individual. Panipuri servers have to remember each customer's preferences such as sweetened pani, more filling or extra onions, for example. The server must keep count of how many panipuris each person has had.

Traditionally, panipuris are eaten by placing the entire puri into the mouth in one go and biting into it. This releases a barrage of tastes and textures. Panipuris may be finished off with a cup of the pani, sweetened or made tarter to taste.

Variations

While many regions in India have their own variations of the panipuri, the most famous ones are from Kolkata, called 'Puchka'.

In Lucknow, this dish is known as "Pani ke bataashe", which means a crispy round dish having spicy water inside. A hole is made using a thumb in the "Bataasha" and a small amount of boiled peas is filled inside it and then the "Bataasha" is dipped in the spicy water or "Pani". In the Lucknow region the Pani is prepared using mint, tamarind, asafoetida (hing), black pepper, red chili powder and salt. At Hazaratganj in Lucknow you can savour *Paanch Swaad Ke bataashe* which means the bataashe are served with five differently tasting Pani one after another.

In most parts of India, a panipuri is made with flavoured water. Some examples are *imli ka pani* (tamarind in water), *nimbu ka pani* (lemon juice in water), *pudine ka pani* (mint in water) and *khajur ka pani* (dates mixed in water). In West Bengal, Odisha, Mithilanchal part of Bihar and the southern part of Jharkhand, many people enjoy panipuris containing no sweet but with tamarind juice and spicy mashed potato.

In parts of Bihar, however it is also served along with *"patta chat"* comprising **khesiya** dried channa Black gram (*Kala Chana*) or dried yellow peas coated with hot freshly grinded green masalas recipe for which is basically dried black, yellow or green Bengal gram that is soaked in water for a minute and then washed in running water immediately and put in a frying pan/kardahi with shallow filled with mustard oil reaching smoky point preferably cooked in Chinese wok style, and the moment it starts giving/releasing pleasant sweet smell/scent/aroma/odour/fragrance/parfumes then add the dry green masalas comprising onion, garlic, ginger, green chilli, black & red pepper powder {curry leaves & a pinch of asfoetida optional} grounded/pounded in the puree/paste form in the rough style once the spices are evenly mixed remove it from flame let it cool, this can be stored as snacks too for up to a month. Alternatively, this at times is replaced with *Ghugaeni alias Ghoogini*. It is then served with *muri* (*sometimes spelled mouri*)(*mur-mure/kurmura/churmura* or *Muhdhi*), and at times with hot onion pakoda/bonda or Uggani/Goli Baje/Wadaieyan Batata vada/*ambode/Maddur vade/*Sabudana vada style bhajiya *Fritter* of dried chick peas dumplings made up with onion slices/julienned with grated green chilli & potato or garlic. Make small balls with this mixture (a little smaller than a golf ball), flatten them a bit, and set aside. Fry these flattened pieces in the smoky hot oil, until they turn golden brown. Then, put it in diluted watery gravy in garam masala seasoning and cooked in cverd lid just ot make them tender for a while, in the traditional eastern Indian style & thereafter, **kachalou** is prepared with par-boiled blanch-cooked peeled potatoes are cut in slices, cubes or crumbled with sour hung/thick curd and mixed with chat masala & jeera namak (grounded black rock salt along with roasted cumin seeds, white & red pepper powder apportioned and mixed in 3:2:1 ratio) in a very pungent manner and then diluted with (dried mango powder)amchoor/tamarind & pudina/dhaniya water as per own taste bud. These all go very well as a filling in the Pani Puri.

In Jamshedpur, a mixture of hot "chole" made of yellow peas, boiled smashed potato, lots of fresh onion pieces, green chillies, tamarind juice and spices are mixed to make stuffing for golgappe. There are two types of golguppe: with tamarind water (a.k.a. phulki) or dry (aka; papadi).

One needs to break open the golgappe and stuff the mixture into it and put tamarind water in it. Papadi are those golgappe which are mostly flat. All the stuffing goes on the top of the papadi.

In Maharashtra, by contrast, the recipe is usually spicier and contains boondi or sprouts in addition to other ingredients. Panipuris are also eaten with curd and different types of masalas such as onion, *sev* (a type of besan vermicelli without any spices & seasoning)|(a fried snack shaped like thin noodles made from besan flour), and mixture (a mix of different types of fried snacks mixed together) or Bhujia along with available seasonal nuts, as the base of the snack. As we go down south India pani puri has taken its own variations in many regions. Hyderabad is famous for panipuri in Andhra Pradesh. Here the road side stalls serve pani puris with Boiled Chickpeas filled accompanied by spicy pani. At times the boiled chick peas is again warmed upon the tava with the addition of few more spices to this and is filled into the puris. These are lighter when compared to the potato stuffing. The Gulbarga town of Karnataka state is also considered famous for panipuri. The serving style is different in Gulbarga when compared with other place. Here a wooded slab is fixed over the cart for serving pani puris. The plates are placed on this slab and are filled with a mixture of boiled green peas, potatoes and rawo onions. Then the puris filled with pani are served into this plate. The stall keepers server at a very faster pace when compared to other parts of the country. In Bangalore the puchka version of panipuris are served on streets with raw onions added.

The panipuri is also an off-beat recent entrant delicacy in northeastern as well in southern part of India popularized by Bollywood movies and the heavy influence following of neighbouring Northern Indian states traditions of cuisine culutural pot-pourrie. It is blamed for an increase on stomach ache there.

Cultural references

A monthly children's magazine, *Golgappa*, was published from 1970 in Delhi.

Nutritional information

Golgappas are generally considered to be a popular low calorie snack (typical serving size being 4 golgappas). The nutritional information per typical unstuffed suji golgappa is (approximately 12g)

Nutrient	Weight
Fats	3 g
Carbohydrates	4 g
Protein	1 g

Calorie information for the golgappa (12g unstuffed) would be:

Calories from Fats	27 Kcal
Calories from Carbohydrates	16 Kcal
Calories from Protein	04 Kcal

Also see : Nutrition facts

Source http://en.wikipedia.org/wiki/Panipuri

Pani ca meusa

Pane ca meusa served in a rotisserie in Palermo

Pani ca meusa (Sicilian: *U pani ca meusa*) is a Sicilian example of street food. Literally, its name means *bread with spleen*; the italians call it *panino con la milza*. It is a dish typical exclusively from Palermo and it consists of a soft bread (locally called *vastedda* or *vastella*) flavoured with sesame stuffed with chopped veal's lung and spleen that had been boiled and after fried in the lard. On request it could be added also caciocavallo or ricotta, in this case the pani ca meusa is said (sicilian) *maritatu* (married), if served without is said (sicilian)*schettu* (single). It is sold mainly by peddlers (specifically indicated locally as *meusari*) in Palermo's main markets as the Vucciria and the Ballarò.

Source http://en.wikipedia.org/wiki/Pani_ca_meusa

Panzarotti

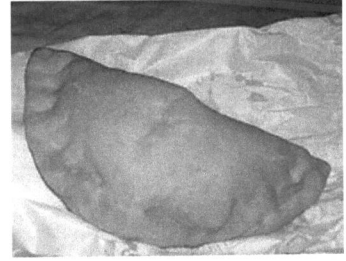

Origin	
Alternative name(s)	Panzerotti
Place of origin	Italy
Region or state	Apulia
Details	
Type	Savoury pie
Main ingredient(s)	Tomato, mozzarella

Panzarotti or **panzerotti** are filled, savory pastries, different forms of which are popular in Italy, Canada, and the United States.

Italy

Panzerotti originated in central and southern Italy, especially in Apulia. They are small versions of the *calzone* or closed pizza, but produced with a softer dough. The most common fillings are tomato and mozzarella, but spinach, mushrooms, baby corn, and ham are often used. Another filling is onions stir fried in olive oil and seasoned with salted anchovies and capers, a seasoning that, mixed with bread, is also used in Apulia for stuffed bell peppers.

In the city of Molfetta located in the Bari province of the Puglia region, frittelle (sometimes spelt frittelli) is used as another name for panzerotti.

Giuseppina Luini brought panzerotti to the northern Italian city of Milan in the late 1940s, setting up a shop near the city's Gothic cathedral. Panificio Figli Luini's proximity to the Duomo, the Galleria, and the via Dante pedestrian zone has made the panzerotti widely known among both Milanese and tourists. Luini has gone on to open a London café, since renamed "Sfizio".

The analogous word, *pansoti*, is used in the Genoa area for stuffed pasta similar to tortellini.

United States

In America the word has come to be spelled "panzarotti", and is regarded as singular (with the plural being "panzarotties" or "panzarotti"). They can come in various sizes from 4" to 12", and are most commonly semi-circular shaped.

It consists of a pocket of dough filled with varying amounts of melted mozzarella cheese, tomato sauce, and any reasonable number of fillings, which is then wrapped, salted, and deep-fried. The panzarotti rises during this process, creating a pocket containing a considerable amount of steam which should be partially released prior to eating.

Panzarottis are available in much if not most of the United States, but they are widely considered to be a specialty of South Jersey.

Canada

Since the mid-1960s, panzarottis have been a popular fast food item in Canada where the singular form is often "panzerotto". Commercialized frozen versions are called Pizza Pockets or Pizza Pops.

Source http://en.wikipedia.org/wiki/Panzarotti

Papri chaat

Bhala *Papri chaat* in dahi with Saunth chutney.

Papri Chaat, **Paapri Chaat** or **Papdi Chaat** is a Pakistani and north Indian fast food. Chaat, an Indo-Aryan word which literally means *lick*, is used to describe a range of snacks and fast food dishes; *papri* refers to crisp fried dough wafers made from refined white flour and oil. In Papri Chaat, the papris are served with boiled potatoes, boiled chick peas, chilis, yogurt and tamarind chutney and topped with chaat masala and 'sev'.

The popular dish is often eaten from travelling food vendor stalls.

Source http://en.wikipedia.org/wiki/Papri_chaat

Papri the key ingredient of Papri Chaat.

Pasty

A Cornish pasty

Origin	
Alternative names(s)	Cornish pasty, pastie, British pasty, oggie, oggy, teddy oggie, tiddy oggin, etc.
Place of origin	United Kingdom
Region or state	Often associated with Cornwall
Details	
Course	Main
Serving temperature	Hot or cold
Main ingredient(s)	A pastry case with variable fillings, usually beef and vegetables

A **pasty** (pron.: /ˈpæsti/, Cornish: *Hogen; Pasti*), (sometimes known in Britain as a **Cornish pasty**, and in the United States as a **pastie** or **British pasty**) is a baked pastry, a traditional variety of which is particularly associated with Cornwall, the westernmost county in England. It is made by placing uncooked filling typically of meat and vegetables, without meat in vegetarian versions, on a flat pastry circle and folding it to wrap the filling, crimping the edge to form a seal. After baking, the result is a raised semicircular comestible.

The traditional Cornish pasty, which has Protected Geographical Indication (PGI) status in Europe, is filled with beef, sliced or diced potato, swede (also known as a yellow turnip or rutabaga – referred to in Cornwall as turnip) and onion, seasoned with salt and pepper, and is baked. Today, the pasty is the food most associated with Cornwall, it is regarded as the national dish, and it accounts for 6% of the Cornish food economy. Pasties with many different fillings are made; some shops specialise in selling all sorts of pasties.

The origins of the pasty are unclear, though there are many references to them throughout historical documents and fiction. The pasty is now popular world-wide due to the spread of Cornish miners, and variations can be found in Australia, the United States, Mexico and elsewhere.

History

Despite the modern pasty's strong association with Cornwall, its exact origins are unclear. The term "pasty" is an English word borrowed from Medieval French (O.Fr. *paste* from V.Lat *pasta*) for a pie, filled with venison, salmon or other meat, vegetables or cheese, baked without a dish. Pasties have been mentioned in cookbooks throughout the ages; for example the earliest version of *Le Viandier* has been dated to around 1300 and contains several pasty recipes. In 1393, *Le Menagier De Paris* contains recipes for *pasté* with venison, veal, beef, or mutton.

An old postcard from Cornwall showing a part-eaten pasty

Other early references to pasties include a 13th century charter which was granted by Henry III (1207–1272) to the town of Great Yarmouth. The town is bound to send to the sheriffs of Norwich every year *one hundred herrings, baked in twenty four pasties*, which the sheriffs are to deliver to the lord of the manor of East Carlton who is then to convey them to the King. Around the same time, 13th century chronicler Matthew Paris wrote of the monks of St Albans Abbey "according to their custom, lived upon pasties of flesh-meat". A total of 5,500 venison pasties were served at the installation feast of George Neville, archbishop of York and chancellor of England in 1465. They were even eaten by royalty, as a letter from a baker to Henry VIII's third wife, Jane Seymour (1508–1537) confirms: "... hope this pasty reaches you in better condition than the last one..." In his diaries written in the mid 17th century, Samuel Pepys makes several references to his consumption of pasties, for instance "dined at Sir W. Pen's ... on a damned venison pasty, that stunk like a devil.", but after this period the use of the word outside Cornwall declined.

In contrast to its earlier place amongst the wealthy, during the 17th and 18th centuries the pasty became popular with working people in Cornwall, where tin miners and others adopted it due to its unique shape, forming a complete meal that could be carried easily and eaten without cutlery. In a mine the pasty's dense, folded pastry could stay warm for several hours, and if it did get cold it could easily be warmed on a shovel over a candle.

Side-crimped pasties gave rise to the suggestion that the miner might have eaten the pasty holding the thick edge of pastry, which was later discarded, thereby ensuring that his dirty fingers (possibly including traces of arsenic) did not touch food or his mouth. However many old photographs show that pasties were wrapped in bags made of paper or muslin and were eaten from end-to-end; according to the earliest Cornish recipe book, published in 1929, this is "the true Cornish way" to eat a pasty. Another theory suggests that pasties were marked at one end with an initial and then eaten from the other end so that if not finished in one go, they could easily be reclaimed by their owners.

In 2006, a researcher in Devon discovered a recipe for a pasty tucked inside an audit book and dated 1510, calculating the cost of the ingredients. This replaced the previous oldest recipe, dated 1746, held by the Cornwall Records Office in Truro, Cornwall. The dish at the time was cooked with venison, in this case from the Mount Edgcumbe estate, as the pasty was then considered a luxury meal. Alongside the ledger, which included the price of the pasty in Plymouth, Devon in 1509, the discovery sparked a controversy between the neighbouring counties of Devon and Cornwall as to the origin of the dish. However, the term pasty appears in much earlier written records from other parts of the country, as mentioned above.

Cornish pasty

The pasty is regarded as the national dish of Cornwall. Following a nine-year campaign by the Cornish Pasty Association, the trade organisation of about 50 pasty makers based in Cornwall, the name "Cornish pasty" was awarded Protected Geographical Indication (PGI) status by the European Commission on 20 July 2011. According to the PGI status a Cornish pasty should be shaped like a 'D' and crimped on one side, not on the top. Its ingredients should include uncooked beef, swede (called turnip in Cornwall), potato and onion, with a light seasoning of salt and pepper, keeping a chunky texture. The pastry should be golden and retain its shape when cooked and cooled. The PGI status also means that Cornish pasties must be prepared in Cornwall. They do not have to be baked in Cornwall, nor do the ingredients have to come from the county, though the Cornish Pasty Association noted that there are strong links between pasty production and local suppliers of the ingredients. Packaging for pasties which conform to the requirements will be stamped with an authentication logo.

Producers outside Cornwall have objected to the PGI award, with one saying "[EU bureaucrats could] go to hell", and another that it was "protectionism for some big pasty companies to churn out a pastiche of the real iconic product". Major UK supermarkets Asda and Morrisons both stated they would be affected by the change, as did nationwide bakery chain Greggs, though Greggs is one of seven companies allowed to continue to use the name "Cornish pasty" during a three-year transitional period.

Members of the Cornish Pasty Association (CPA) made about 87 million pasties in 2008, amounting to sales of £60 million (about 6% of the food economy of Cornwall). Over 1,800 permanent staff are employed by members of the CPA and some 13,000 other jobs benefit from the trade. Recent surveys by the South West tourism board show that one of the top three reasons people visit Cornwall is the food and that the Cornish pasty is the food most associated with Cornwall.

Recipes and ingredients

The recipe for a Cornish pasty, as defined by its protected status, includes diced or minced beef, onion, potato and swede in rough chunks along with some

A traditional Cornish pasty filled with steak and vegetables

"light peppery" seasoning. The cut of beef used is generally skirt steak. Swede is sometimes called turnip in Cornwall but the recipe requires use of actual swede, not turnip. Pasty ingredients are usually seasoned with salt and pepper, depending on individual taste. The use of carrot in a traditional Cornish pasty is frowned upon, though it does appear regularly in recipes.

The type of pastry used is not defined, as long as it is golden in colour and will not crack during the cooking or cooling, although modern pasties almost always use a shortcrust pastry. There is a humorous belief that the pastry on a good pasty should be strong enough to withstand a drop down a mine shaft, and indeed the barley flour that was usually used does make hard dense pastry.

Variations

Although the official pasty has a specific ingredients list, old Cornish cookery books show that pasties were generally made from whatever food was available. Indeed, the earliest recorded pasty recipes include venison, not beef. "Pasty" has always been a generic name for the shape and can contain a variety of fillings, including stilton, vegetarian and even chicken tikka. Pork and apple pasties are readily available in shops throughout Cornwall and Devon, with the ingredients including an apple flavoured sauce, mixed together throughout the pasty, as well as sweet pasties with ingredients such as apple and fig or chocolate and banana, which are common in some areas of Cornwall.

A part-savoury, part-sweet pasty (similar to the Bedfordshire clanger) was eaten by miners in the 19th century, in the copper mines on Parys Mountain, Anglesey. The technician who did the research and discovered the recipe claimed that the recipe was probably taken to Anglesey by Cornish miners travelling to the area looking for work. No two-course pasties are commercially produced in Cornwall today, but are usually the product of amateur cooks. They are, however, commercially available in the British supermarket chain Morrisons (under the name 'Tin Miner Pasty').

A pasty is known as a "tiddy oggy" when steak is replaced with an extra potato, "tiddy" meaning potato and "oggy" meaning pasty.

Shape

Whilst the PGI rules state that a Cornish pasty must be a "D" shape, with crimping along the curve (i.e., side-crimped), crimping is variable within Cornwall, with some advocating a side crimp while others maintain that a top crimp is more authentic.

Some sources state that the difference between a Devon and Cornish pasty is that a Devon pasty has a top-crimp and is oval in shape, whereas the Cornish pasty is semicircular and side-crimped along the curve. However, pasties with a top crimp have been made in Cornwall for generations, yet those Cornish bakers who favour this method now find that they cannot legally call their pasties "Cornish".

In other regions

A "Cousin Jack's" pasty shop in Grass Valley, California

Migrating Cornish miners (colloquially known as Cousin Jacks in the US) helped to spread pasties into the rest of the world during the 19th century. As tin mining in Cornwall began to fail, miners brought their expertise and traditions to new mining regions around the world. As a result, pasties can be found in many regions, including:

Many parts of Australia, including the Yorke Peninsula, the site of an annual pasty festival since 1973, which claims to be the world's largest. A clarification of the Protected Geographical Status ruling has confirmed that pasties made in Australia are still allowed to be called "Cornish Pasties".

The Upper Peninsula of Michigan. In some areas, pasties are a significant tourist attraction, including an annual Pasty Fest in Calumet, Michigan in late June. Pasties in the Upper Peninsula of Michigan have a particularly unusual history, as a small influx of Finnish immigrants followed the Cornish miners in 1864. These Finns (and many other ethnic groups) adopted the pasty for use in the Copper Country copper mines. About 30 years later, a much larger flood of Finnish immigrants found their countrymen baking pasties. The pasty has become strongly associated with Finnish culture in this area, and in the culturally similar Iron Range in northern Minnesota.

Mineral Point, Wisconsin was the site of the first mineral rush in the USA during the 1830s. After lead was discovered in Mineral Point many of the early miners migrated to this south-western Wisconsin area from Cornwall. Those Cornish miners brought their skills working in the deep underground tin mines of Cornwall. They also brought their recipe and appetite for the pasty.

A similar local history about the arrival of the pasty in the area with an influx of Welsh and Cornish miners, and its preservation as a local delicacy, is found in Butte, Montana.

The Anthracite regions of northeastern Pennsylvania including the cities of Wilkes-Barre, Scranton, and Hazleton, had an influx of miners to the area in the 1800s and with them brought the pasty. To this day pasties are still a local favourite. In 1981, a Pennsylvania entrepreneur started marketing pasties under the brand name Mr. Pastie.

The Mexican state of Hidalgo, and the twin silver mining cities of Pachuca and Real del Monte (Mineral del Monte), have notable Cornish influences from the Cornish miners who settled there with pasties being considered typical local cuisine. In Mexican Spanish, they are referred to as *pastes*.

They are also popular in South Africa and New Zealand.

In culture
The Merry Ballad of the Cornish Pasty – Robert Morton Nance, 1898
Source http://en.wikipedia.org/wiki/Pasty

Pav Bhaji

Pav Bhaji

Origin	
Alternative name(s)	Bhaji-pav
Place of origin	India
Region or state	Maharashtra
Details	
Course	Snack
Main ingredient(s)	Bread, potatoes, onions, mixed vegetables

Pav bhaji (Marathi: पाव भाजी) is a Maharashtrian fast food dish that originated in Mumbai cuisine. It is native to Mumbai and has now become popular in most metropolitan areas in India, especially in those of central and western Indian states such as Gujarat and Karnataka. *Pav* originates from the Portuguese *Pao*, which means bread. *Bhaji* in Marathi means vegetable dish. Pav bhaji consists of bhaji (a thick potato-based curry) garnished with coriander, chopped onion, and a dash of lemon and lightly toasted pav. The pav is usually buttered on all sides.

History
The origin of this dish is traced to textile mill workers in Mumbai in the 1850s.

The mill workers used to have lunch breaks too short for a full meal, and a light lunch was preferred to a heavy one, as the employees had to return to strenuous physical labor after lunch. A vendor created this dish using items or parts of other dishes available on the menu. Roti or rice was replaced with pav and the curries that usually go with Indian bread or rice were amalgamated into just one spicy concoction, the 'bhaji'. Initially, it remained the food of the mill-workers. With time the dish found its way into restaurants and spread over Central Mumbai and other parts of the city via the Udipi restaurants.

Such is the popularity of this dish, that it is common to find it on the menu of most Indian restaurants serving fast food in Asia (especially Singapore, Hong Kong), America, UK (London), Switzerland and elsewhere. It has also come to become the staple dish in many Indian diets, due to its simplicity and delicacy.

Preparation

A Pav Bhaji stand at Chandni Chowk, Delhi.

The recipe for Pav Bhaji varies greatly as it is essentially a fast food dish to be prepared quickly. The general procedure for making the bhaji remains the same. Potatoes are mashed on a flat griddle (tava), and made into a thick gravy after adding diced tomatoes, finely chopped onion, green peas and chopped capsicum (green bell pepper). Other assorted vegetables such as cauliflower and carrots are mashed and added. Garlic too is added at times to spice it up. A special blend of spices simply called the *pav bhaji masala* is added to this thick gravy giving pav bhaji its authentic slightly orange brown color. The gravy is then allowed to simmer on the pan for a few minutes and is served hot in a flat dish with a tablespoon of butter on top.

Pav Bhaji being prepared on an iron tava

The pav is heated on the griddle and buttered generously. The Bhaji is garnished with coriander and diced onions.

In restaurants some more varieties are available including;
Cheese Pav Bhaji, in which the *bhaji*

had an additional garnishing of cheese
Paneer Pav Bhaji, Prepared with *paneer*(cottage cheese) as one of the ingredients in the bhaji along with the vegetables.
Mushroom Pav Bhaji, with mushrooms as one of the ingredients in the bhaji along with the vegetables.
Khada Pav Bhaji, ('खडा'). Vegetables are not mashed, but small pieces cooked with masala gravy.
Jain Pav Bhaji, replacing the potatoes with plantain, as the Jains do not eat potatoes. Onion and Garlic is not added either.
Kathyawadi Pav Bhaji with buttermilk, eaten particularly in the Kathiyawad.
Dryfruit Pav Bhaji with added dry fruits.

Versatility

It can be eaten as a snack or as a meal in itself. It is often eaten as an evening snack between lunch and dinner, particularly in western India. In this part, Pav bhaji is available on hand carts and at kiosks. It is also available in hotels and eateries serving fast food. In recent years, Pav bhaji is also consumed as a light evening meal, and is also a party favorite.

In popular culture

Sanjay Dutt played the role of a pav bhaji vendor in the Hindi movie *Vaastav.*
In the Telugu film *Dubai Seenu*, Ravi Teja and his friends opened a pav bhaji stand on the road in Mumbai, India.
In RK Laxman's comics, Bhavesh, Ramesh and DVD opened a Pav-Bhaji stall as a side business
In *Ghulam*, Rani Mukherjee's character, who is from a high class family enjoys streetside pav-bhaji.
Source http://en.wikipedia.org/wiki/Pav_Bhaji

Pho

"Saigon-style" pho

Origin

Place of origin	Vietnam
Region or state	Hanoi, Nam Dinh

Details

Type	Noodle soup
Main ingredient(s)	Noodles (rice flour), beef or chicken
Variations	Beef pho, Chicken pho, *phở tái* (Pho topped with sliced raw beef)
Approximate calories per serving	varies by recipe

Pho (/fʌ/; Vietnamese: *phở* pronounced [fəː˧˩] (listen)) is a Vietnamese dish consisting of broth, noodles made from rice, a few herbs, and meat. It is a popular street dish, and the specialty of several restaurant chains. The two main varieties are chicken pho and beef pho. There is also Saigon-style pho (sweetened) and Hanoi-style pho (no sugar). The word "pho" may be derived from French *pot-au-feu* (beef stew).

History

Pho originated in the early 20th century in northern Vietnam, apparently southeast of Hanoi in Nam Định province, then a substantial textile market. At first, it was sold by vendors from large boxes. Pho restaurants opened in Hanoi in the 1920s.

The word "pho" may be derived from French *pot-au-feu* (beef stew), or from Cantonese rice vermicelli, referred to in Vietnamese as *hà in* (河) or *phấn* (粉).

Nguyen Tung, an anthropologist based in Paris who has researched Vietnamese food suggests that pho derived from the Cantonese pronunciation of "粉" (rice noodles).

Tung agreed with Georges Dumoutier, an earlier writer, that pho did not exist in 1907.

Tung went on to suggest that pho derived from the Cantonese pronunciation of "fun" (noodle), and thus the source of pho probably came from the Chinese refugees flowing into Vietnam in the late 19th Century and bringing with them a number of dishes which later were adopted by the Vietnamese: hu tieu, hoanh thanh, lap xuong, xa xiu, xi dau, pha lau, lau, ta pin lu, etc.

The variations in meat, broth and additional garnishes, such as lime, bean sprouts, *ngò gai* (culantro), *húng quế* (Thai/Asian basil), and *tương* (bean sauce/hoisin sauce) appear to be innovations introduced in the south. Pho did not become popular in South Vietnam until 1954.

Possibly the earliest reference to pho in English was in the book *Recipes of All Nations*, edited by Countess Morphy in 1935. In the book, pho is described as "an Annamese soup held in high esteem ... made with beef, a veal bone, onions, a bayleaf, salt, and pepper, and a small teaspoon of *nuoc-mam*."

With the Vietnam war and the victory of the North Vietnamese, pho was brought to many countries by Vietnamese refugees fleeing Vietnam from the 1970s onwards. It is especially popular in large cities with substantial Vietnamese populations and enclaves such as Paris, major cities in Canada, the United States, and Australia. Pho is listed at number 28 on "World's 50 most delicious foods" compiled by *CNN Go* in 2011. Pho is listed as the number 1 Vietnamese food in Vancouver according to the Vancouver Sun newspaper.

Ingredients and preparation

Pho is served in a bowl with a specific cut of white rice noodles in clear beef broth, with slim cuts of beef (steak, fatty flank, lean flank, brisket). Variations feature tendon, tripe, or meatballs in

A typical pho spice packet, sold at many Oriental food markets, containing a soaking bag plus various necessary dry spices. The exact amount differs with each bag.

southern Vietnam. Chicken pho is made using the same spices as beef, but the broth is made using only chicken bones and meat, as well as some internal organs of the chicken, such as the heart, the undeveloped eggs and the gizzard.

Broth

The broth for beef pho is generally made by simmering beef bones, oxtails, flank steak, charred onion, charred ginger and spices. For a more intense flavor, the bones may still have beef on them. Chicken bones also work and produce a similar broth. Seasonings can include Saigon cinnamon or other kinds of cinnamon as alternatives (may use stick or powder), star anise, roasted ginger, roasted onion, black cardamom, coriander seed, fennel seed, and clove. The broth takes several hours to make. For chicken pho, only the meat and bones of the chicken are used in place of beef and beef bone. The remaining spices remain the same, but the charred ginger can be omitted, since its function in beef pho is to get rid of the "cow's smell".

The spices, often wrapped in cheesecloth or soaking bag to prevent them from floating all over the pot, usually contain: clove, star anise, coriander seed, fennel, cinnamon, black cardamom, ginger and onion.

Careful cooks often roast ginger and onion over an open fire for about a minute before adding them to the stock, to bring out their full flavor. They also skim off all the impurities that float to the top while cooking; this is the key to a clear broth. Salt, or preferably *nước mắm* (fish sauce) is added toward the end.

Garnishes

Typical garnishes for *phở Sài Gòn*, clockwise from top left are: onions, chili peppers, culantro, lime, bean sprouts, and Thai basil.

Vietnamese dishes are meals typically served with lots of greens, herbs, vegetables, and various other accompaniments, such as dipping sauces, hot and spicy pastes, and a squeeze of lime or lemon juice; it may also be served with hoisin sauce. The dish is garnished with ingredients such as green onions, white onions, Thai basil (not to be confused with sweet basil), fresh Thai chili peppers, lemon or lime wedges, bean sprouts and coriander or culantro. Fish sauce, hoisin sauce and chili sauce may be added to taste as accompaniments.

Several ingredients not generally served with pho may be ordered by request. Extra-fatty broth (*nước béo*) can be ordered and comes with scallions to sweeten it. A popular side dish ordered upon request is *hành dấm*, or vinegared white onions.

Regional variants

The several regional variants of pho in Vietnam, particularly divided between northern (Hanoi, are called *phở bắc* or

Chicken pho at a typical street stall in Hanoi - note the lack of side garnishes, typical of northern Vietnamese-style cooking

"northern pho"), and southern pho (Saigon, called *phở Sài Gòn*). Northern pho tends to use somewhat wider noodles and much more green onion, and garnishes offered generally include only vinegar, fish sauce and chili sauce. On the other hand, southern Vietnamese pho broth is slightly sweeter and has bean sprouts and a greater variety of fresh herbs. The variations in meat, broth, and additional garnishes such as lime, bean sprouts, *ngò gai* (*Eryngium foetidum*), *húng quế* (Thai/Asian basil), and *tương đen* (bean sauce/hoisin sauce), *tương ớt* (hot chili garlic sauce, e.g., Rooster Sauce) appear to be innovations made by or introduced to the south, also called **Pho SaiGon** ("Saigon Style" Pho).

International variants include pho made using tofu and vegetable broth for vegetarians, and a larger variety of vegetables, such as carrots and broccoli.

In recent years, several chains have commercialized the soup, most notably Pho 24 in Vietnam and Pho Mi 99 in Canada. The word "pho" was added to the *Shorter Oxford English Dictionary* in 2007.

Gallery

Pho alla Saigon

Pho served both rare and well-done beef brisket
Pho with chicken
Pho Vietnamese Restaurant in Hong Kong
Pho Vietnamese Restaurant in Paris
Pho Vietnamese Restaurant in California

Source http://en.wikipedia.org/wiki/Pho

Picarones

File:Picaron.jpg
Picarones

Origin
Place of origin — Peru
Details
Type — Doughnut
Main ingredient(s) — Squash, sweet potatoes, chancaca syrup

Picarones is a Peruvian dessert originated in the colonial period. Its principal ingredients are squash and sweet potato. It is served in a doughnut form and covered with syrup, made from chancaca (solidified molasses). It is tra-

Picarones mix.

ditional to serve picarones when people prepare anticuchos, another traditional Peruvian dish. Picarones were created during the colonial period to replace Buñuelos as buñuelos were too expensive to make. People started replacing traditional ingredients with squash and sweet potato. Accidentally, they created a new dessert that rapidly increased in popularity throughout the country.

Picarones are also mentioned in the book of a famous Peruvian writer, Ricardo Palma. In his book, *Tradiciones Peruanas*, (lit. Peruvian traditions) he mentions this dessert. Picarones is also featured in traditional Peruvian music and poetry.

Recently a company has produced a Picarones mix.

External

Source http://en.wikipedia.org/wiki/Picarones

Pilgrim (sandwich)

Origin
Alternative name(s) — Puritan
Place of origin — United States
Details
Type — Sandwich
Main ingredient(s) — Bread slices or bap

A *Pilgrim* or **Puritan** is a sandwich which has connotations with the American Pilgrim Fathers and Thanksgiving Day. It was a traditional a way of using up leftover food from Thanksgiving Day and thus is composed essentially of bread slices or a bap, into which are placed sliced roast turkey, cranberries or cranberry sauce and cheddar cheese. There is an enormous variation in its composition with a huge range of ingredients being employed in some sandwiches and a great variation of ingredients between recipes. At its most basic it can be two slices of bread with slices of turkey, herb stuffing, cranberry sauce and some gravy.

More sophisticated versions of the Pilgrim sandwich include store-bought corn muffins, crusty hoagie, French bread, ciabatta rolls, extra virgin olive oil, butter, chopped apple, chopped onion, celery, flat leaf parsley, Thousand Island dressing and sliced/chopped pickled gherkins for topping.

A well known international magazine poll reported it to be one of America's favourite sandwiches, the version illustrated included Muenster cheese and lettuce in addition to turkey, stuffing and cranberry chutney.

Paul Simon mentions pilgrims (and

po' boys) in his song Graceland from his 1986 Graceland album.

Source http://en.wikipedia.org/wiki/Pilgrim_(sandwich)

Pizza al taglio

Origin
Alternative name(s)	Pizza al trancio
Place of origin	Rome, Italy

Details
Type	Pizza
Main ingredient(s)	Pizza dough, sauce, cheese, toppings

Pizza al taglio or **pizza al trancio** (Italian for pizza by the slice — literally "by the cut") is a variety of pizza baked in large rectangular trays, and generally sold in rectangular or square slices by weight, with prices marked per kilogram or per 100 grams. This type of pizza was invented in Rome, Italy, and is common throughout Italy. Many variations and styles of Pizza al taglio exist, and the dish is available in other areas of the world in addition to Italy.

Preparation

In the most traditional Italian pizza al taglio 'parlours' or outlets, such as *pizzerie* and bakeries, the pizza is often cooked in a wood-fired oven. In today's establishments, electric ovens are also often used. The concept is similar to what is known as fast food in Western cultures. The main emphasis may not be upon the visual aspect of the pizza. Rather, the taste of the product and convenience of the process may be a priority. The rectangular pizza shape makes it easier to cut and divide the pizza to the buyer's desire, which is often distinguished by weight.

Varieties

The simplest varieties include *pizza Margherita* (tomato sauce and cheese), *pizza bianca* (olive oil, rosemary and garlic), and *pizza rossa* (tomato sauce only). Other typical toppings include artichokes, asparagus, eggplant, ground meat and onions, potatoes, prosciutto, salami, sausage, ground truffles, zucchini, olive oil sundried tomatoes, rocket, gorgonzola, anchovies, and black olives.

By region

Pizza al taglio was invented in Rome, Italy. It's a popular casual food in Italy and Malta, where for many years it has been a common way for people to grab a quick snack or meal. The dish is often eaten as a takeaway dish that is eaten outside of restaurants where it is served, such as in a piazza. It has started to catch on in many other countries with differences in the styles of crusts, and toppings, suiting their own cultures.

Source http://en.wikipedia.org/wiki/Pizza_al_taglio

Pojangmacha

Pojangmacha

Pojangmacha food stall

Korean name
Hangul	포장마차
Revised Romanization	pojangmacha
McCune–Reischauer	p'ochangmach'a

Pojangmacha refers to small tented restaurants on wheels, or street stalls in South Korea which sell a variety of popular street foods as such *hotteok, gimbap, tteokbokki, sundae, odeng,* and *anju* (dishes accompanied with drinking). It literally means "covered wagon" in Korean. In the evening, many of these establishments serve alcoholic beverages such as soju and anju.

Pojangmacha is a popular place to have a snack or drink late into the night. The food sold in these places can usually be eaten quickly while standing or taken away. Some offer cheap chairs or benches for customers to sit, especially the ones serving late night customers who come to drink soju.

As of 2012, there were approximately 3,100 in Seoul. This number has declined since city officials sought to shut them down, as they are considered by them to be eyesores, illegal and unsanitary.

Source http://en.wikipedia.org/wiki/Pojangmacha

Poutine

Poutine	
Origin	
Place of origin	Canada
Region or state	Quebec (late 1950s)
Creator(s)	Multiple claims
Details	
Course	Main dish or side dish
Serving temperature	Hot
Main ingredient(s)	French fries, thin brown gravy, cheese curds
Variations	Multiple

Poutine (pron.: /puːˈtiːn/; French: [putin], Quebec French:[put͡sɪn] (listen)) is a typical Canadian dish (originally from Quebec), made with french fries, topped with brown gravy and cheese curds. Sometimes additional ingredients are added.

Poutine is a fast food dish that can now be found across Canada (and is also found in some places in the northern United States). It is sold by national and international fast food chains, in small "greasy spoon" type diners (commonly known as "cantines" or "casse-croûtes" in Quebec) and pubs, as well as by roadside chip wagons (commonly known as "cabanes à patates", literally meaning "potato shacks"). International chains like McDonald's, A&W, KFC, and Burger King also sell mass-produced poutine in Canada. Poutine may also contain other ingredients such as beef, pulled pork, lamb, lobster meat, shrimp, rabbit confit, caviar, and truffles.

Origins

The dish originated in rural Quebec, Canada, in the late 1950s. Several Québécois communities claim to be the birthplace of poutine, including Drummondville (by Jean-Paul Roy in 1964), Saint-Jean-sur-Richelieu, and Victoriaville. One often-cited tale is that of Fernand Lachance, from Warwick, Quebec, which claims that poutine was invented there in 1957; Lachance is said to have exclaimed, "*ça va faire une maudite poutine*" ("it will make a damn mess") when asked to put a bunch of curds on some french fries, hence the name. The sauce was allegedly added later, to keep the fries warm longer. Over time the dish's popularity spread mainly across the province (and later throughout Canada), often served in small town restaurants, bars, as well as being quite popular in ski resorts.

Etymology

The *Dictionnaire historique du français québécois* lists 15 different meanings of *poutine* in Quebec and Acadian French, most of which are for kinds of food; the word *poutine* in the meaning "fries with cheese and gravy" is dated to 1978. Other definitions of the word have been in use at least since 1810.

While the exact provenance of the word *"poutine"* is uncertain, some of its meanings undoubtedly result at least in part from the influence of the English word *pudding*. Among its various culinary senses, that of "a dessert made from flour or bread crumbs" most clearly shows this influence; the word *pouding*, borrowed from the English *pudding*, is in fact a synonym in this sense. The pejorative meaning "fat person" of *poutine* (used especially in speaking of a woman) is believed to derive from the English *pudding* "a person or thing resembling a pudding" or "stout, thick-set person".

In other meanings of *poutine*, the existence of a relation to the English word *pudding* is uncertain. One of these additional meanings — the one from which the name of the dish with fries is thought to derive — is "unappetizing mixture of various foods, usually leftovers." This sense may also have given rise to the meaning "complicated business, complex organization; set of operations whose management is difficult or problematic."

The *Dictionnaire historique* mentions the possibility that the form *poutine* is simply a gallicization of the word *pudding*. However, it considers it more likely that it was inherited from regional languages spoken in France, and that some of its meanings resulted from the later influence of the similar-sounding English word *pudding*. It cites the Provençal forms *poutingo* "bad stew" and *poutité* "hodgepodge" or "crushed fruit or foods"; *poutringo* "mixture of various things" in Languedocien; and *poutringue*, *potringa* "bad stew" in Franche-Comté as possibly related to *poutine*. The meaning "fries with cheese and gravy" of *poutine* is among those held as probably unrelated to *pudding* provided the latter view is correct.

Recipe

La Banquise in Montreal serves twenty-five different varieties of Quebec style poutine.

In the basic recipe for poutine, French fries are covered with fresh cheese curds, and topped with brown gravy. In a Quebec poutine:

Fries: Usually of medium thickness, and fried (sometimes doubly) so that the inside stays soft, while the outside is crispy.

Cheese curds: Fresh cheese curds are used to give the desired texture. The curd size may vary but is usually slightly smaller than bite-sized.

Gravy: Generally a light and thin chicken, veal, or turkey gravy, mildly spiced with a hint of pepper, or a *sauce brune* which is a combination of beef and chicken stock, a variant originating in Quebec. The gravy should be thin enough to easily filter down into the mass of fries and cheese curds. These sauces typically also contain vinegar or a sour flavouring to balance the richness of the cheese and fries. Traditional poutine sauces (*mélange à sauce poutine*) are sold in Quebec, Ontario, and Maritime grocery stores in jars or cans and in powdered mix packets.

Heavy beef or pork-based brown gravies are rarely used. To maintain the texture of the fries, the cheese curd and gravy are added immediately prior to serving the dish. The hot gravy is usually poured over the cold cheese curds, so that the cheese is warmed without completely melting. It is important to control the temperature, timing and the order in which the ingredients are added, so as to obtain the right food textures which is an essential part of the experience of eating poutine.

Variations

Poutine made with thick beef gravy on French fried potatoes with fresh cheese curds. A style commonly found outside Quebec.

There are many variations of poutine. Some restaurants offer poutine with such additions as chicken, bacon, or Montreal-style smoked meat. Some such restaurants even boast a dozen or more variations of poutine. For instance, more upscale poutine with three-pepper sauce, Merguez sausage, foie gras or even caviar and truffle can be found. Some variations eliminate the cheese, but most francophone Quebecers would call such a dish a "frite sauce" ("french fries with sauce") rather than poutine. Shawinigan and some other regions have Patate-sauce-choux where shredded raw cabbage replaces cheese. Fast food combination meals in Canada often have the option of getting french fries "poutinized" by adding cheese curds (or shredded cheese in the Prairies and Western Canada) and gravy.

Outside Canada, poutine is found in northern border regions of the United States such as New England, the Pacific Northwest and the Upper Midwest. These regions offer further variations of the basic dish. Cheeses other than fresh curds are commonly used (most commonly mozzarella cheese), along with beef, brown or turkey gravy. In the county culture especially, a mixed fry can also come with cooked ground beef on top and is referred to as a hamburger mix, though this is less popular than a regular mix.

Name	Fries	Cheese	Gravy
Italian poutine			Bologn sauce
Greek poutine	Shoestring fries	Feta cheese	Medite vinaigr and gra
Poutine Dulton			
Doner or gyro poutine			
Poutine persillade	Persillade potatoes		
Poutine Galvaude			
Poutine à l'etranger		Sometimes with Grated cheese	Thick g
New Jersey Poutine		Mozzarella	

Similar dishes

Chips and Gravy ("chips" being the British term for thicker French fries) is a staple of the cheaper bistro style menus, in such places as Royal Canadian Legion and Workers Clubs.

Carne asada fries, also known as "Mexican poutine".

In Newfoundland and Labrador, most non-national chain restaurants serve a traditional dish called chips, dressing and gravy (a.k.a. "Newfie fries"). "Dressing" is a mixture of mainly white bread crumbs and savoury and is often referred to as "stuffing" outside of Atlantic Canada. Chips, dressing and gravy is served much like poutine, except for the dressing substituting for the cheese. While loved by Newfoundlanders and Labradorians, the dish is not very widely known of outside the Canadian province, and within pockets of NL exiles.

On Prince Edward Island, a common dish is "Fries with the Works" which is fries with ground beef and onions, topped with thick beef gravy and fresh green peas.

Disco Fries, also known as "Elvis Fries," served in New Jersey and select New York City diners, are made with brown gravy, mozzarella, and heavier steak fries. Elsewhere in the greater New York City area and Long Island, diners serve "cheese fries," using either American (processed) cheese or mozzarella. Diners in New York, New Jersey, and Connecticut serve "gravy-cheese-fries" or even "french fries with cheese and gravy"; these are most commonly steak fries, brown gravy, and American cheese.

"Chili Cheese Fries" are served in Coney Island restaurants around Detroit, Michigan. Shoestring French Fries are covered with the hot dog sauce ("chili" sauce) unique to the Detroit area, then covered with shredded cheddar cheese. (See Coney Island (restaurant))

In-N-Out's Animal Fries

The American fast food diner chain Waffle House offers hashbrowns *Covered* in processed American cheese, *Topped* with chili, or *Country* with sausage gravy amongst other topping options. The chain operates throughout the United States.

Cheese fries are also served in many diners in the American Southwest; in Texas, for example, they usually include at least one variety of grated Cheddar cheese, and are commonly served with ranch dressing and, sometimes, bacon, jalapenos and chives, whereas in New Mexico, the fries are typically served with green chili and cheese, creating a dish that combines two Southwest favorites, french fries and chile con queso. The secret menu at In-N-Out Burger includes "animal fries," a dish consisting of cheese, grilled onions, and the chain's "secret sauce" over fries. Around Chicago in Northern Illinois, up though Wisconsin and into Minnesota, cheese fries are often made using a natural cheddar spread such as Merkt's brand, which has an intense flavor and distinctive texture. Chili cheese fries are a common variation.

European variations

In the United Kingdom (particularly the Isle of Man, the north of England and Scotland), the dish is simply named *Chips, Cheese and Gravy*. The dish is common in chip shops, and other small, local fast food stores and consists of thick-cut chips, shredded cheddar cheese (and sometimes a 50/50 mix of cheddar and mozzarella cheese), topped with thick gravy. A variant is sometimes made with curry sauce instead of gravy. The dish is believed to have developed independently of poutine..

In the Netherlands, a dish named "kapsalon" (hair salon) consists of french fries, shawarma meats or doner kebab, and grilled gouda cheese, topped with salad, garlic sauce and sambal. The dish was invented in Rotterdam by a kebab shop owner who served it to employees of a local hair salon. It gained popularity and is now widely available across the Netherlands.

Cultural aspect

A cultural marker, poutine has long been Canada's 'embarrassing but adored' junk food. In 2007 the CBC declared the outcome of a viewer survey on the greatest Canadian inventions of all time. Poutine arrived at No. 10, beating, among other items, the electron microscope, the BlackBerry, and the paint roller.

However, poutine has since made inroads into proper culinary circles, challenging its junk food status. Thus in 2011, well-known chef Chuck Hughes won on *Iron Chef America* (episode 4 of season 9) by beating out his heavyweight competitor with a plate of lobster poutine.

Poutine in politics

In a *Talking to Americans* segment on the Canadian mock television news show *This Hour Has 22 Minutes* during the 2000 American election, comedian Rick Mercer posed as a reporter and asked several people (including then-Texas governor George W. Bush) what they thought of "Prime Minister Jean Poutine" and his endorsement of Bush for president. (The Prime Minister of Canada at the time was Jean Chrétien). None of the interviewees noticed the insertion of "Poutine." A few years later when Bush made his first official visit to Canada as President, he joked during a speech, "I told [Prime Minister] Paul [Martin] that I really have only one regret about this visit to Canada. There's a prominent citizen who endorsed me in the 2000 election, and I wanted a chance to finally thank him for that endorsement. I was hoping to meet Jean Poutine." The remark was met with laughter and applause.

The name of the President of Russia, Vladimir Putin is coincidentally transliterated as Vladimir *Poutine* in French.

Source http://en.wikipedia.org/wiki/Poutine

Pretzel

An assortment of pretzels

Origin
Place of origin   Germany
Type   Bread, Pastry

A **pretzel** (known as *Brezel* in German, sometimes also *Brezn* or *Breze*) is a type of baked food made from dough in soft and hard varieties and savory or sweet flavors in a unique knot-like shape, originating in Europe. The pretzel shape is a distinctive symmetrical looped form, with the ends of a long strip of dough intertwine brought together and then twisted back onto itself in a certain way ("a pretzel loop"). Pretzels in stick form may also be called pretzels in the English-speaking context. For seasoning and decoration various glazes, salt crystals, sugar and various seeds or nuts can be used. The size varies from large enough for one to be a sufficient serving, to much smaller.

A bread pretzel popular in southern Germany and adjoining German-speaking areas, as well as in some areas of

An illustration from the 12th century *Hortus deliciarum* from Alsace may be the earliest depiction of a pretzel, shown at a banquet with Queen Esther and King Ahasuerus

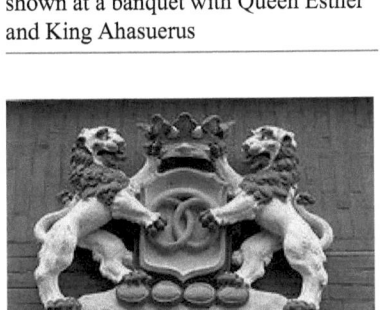

Emblem of the Baker's Guild in Germany

Variety of Southern German lye breads (*Laugengebäck*)

New Year's pretzel in a Stuttgart bakery (Swabia)

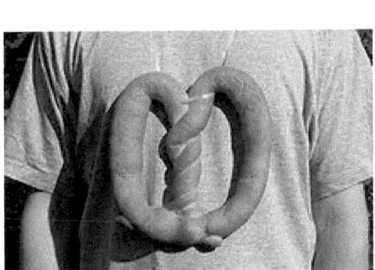

Pretzel from Burg, typically carried around the neck

Fountain in Speyer with pretzel boy statue

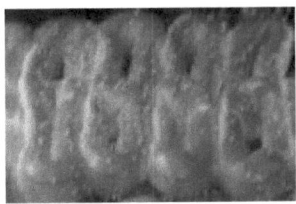

USA Philadelphia PA style soft pretzel

Pretzel sticks and varieties

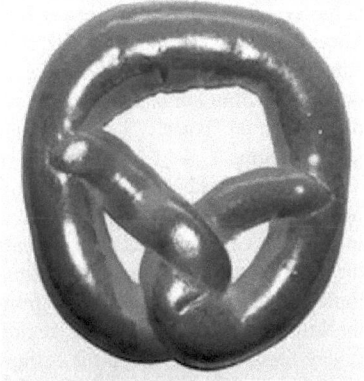

Viipurinrinkeli, a pretzel from Vyborg (Finnish: Viipuri), Russia

the United States, is made from wheat flour, water and yeast, usually sprinkled with coarse salt, hand-sized and made for consumption on the same day. It is relatively soft, rather than brittle. To avoid confusion with any other kind of pretzel, German speakers call this variety "Laugenbrezel" (lye pretzel) because it is dipped in lye solution (NaOH) before baking. Sweet pastry pretzels with many textures, toppings and coatings, are made. Crisp hard pretzels, e.g. pretzel sticks and a variety of shapes basically made from the same ingredients, have evolved from the lye pretzel by baking out excess moisture, thereby increasing shelf life and crispness.

History

There are numerous accounts on the origin of pretzels, as well as the origin of the name; most agree that they have Christian backgrounds and were invented by monks. According to *The History of Science and Technology*, by Bryan Bunch and Alexander Hellemans, in 610 AD "...an Italian monk invents pretzels as a reward to children who learn their prayers. He calls the strips of baked dough, folded to resemble arms crossing the chest, 'pretiola' ("little rewards")". However, no source is cited to back up these details. Another source locates the invention in a monastery in southern France. The looped pretzel may also be related to a Greek ring bread, derived from communion bread used in monasteries a thousand years ago. In Germany there are stories that pretzels were the invention of desperate bakers held hostage by local Dignatories. *Meyers Konversations-Lexikon* from 1905 suspects the origin of pretzels in a ban of heathen baking traditions, such as in the form of a sun cross, at the Synod of Estinnes in the year 743. The pretzel may have emerged as a substitute. The German name "*Brezel*" may derive also from Latin *bracellus* (a medieval term for "bracelet"), or *bracchiola* ("little arms").

The pretzel has been in use as an emblem of bakers and formerly their guilds in southern German areas since at least the 12th century. A 12th-century illustration in the *Hortus deliciarum* from the southwest German Alsace region (today France) may contain the earliest depiction of a pretzel.

Within the Catholic Church, pretzels were regarded as having religious significance for both ingredients and shape. Pretzels made with a simple recipe using only flour and water could be eaten during Lent, when Christians were forbidden to eat eggs, lard, or dairy products such as milk and butter. As time passed, pretzels became associated with both Lent and Easter. Pretzels were hidden on Easter morning just as eggs are hidden today, and are particularly associated with Lent, fasting, and prayers before Easter.

Like the holes in the hubs of round Swedish flat bread (which let them be hung on strings), the loops in pretzels may have served a practical purpose: bakers could hang them on sticks, for instance, projecting upwards from a central column, as shown in a painting by Job Berckheyde (1630–93) from around 1681.

Upper-German-speaking countries
Pretzel baking has most firmly taken root in southern Germany and adjoining Upper German-speaking areas, and pretzels have been an integral part of German baking traditions for centuries.

Lye pretzels are popular in southern Germany, Alsace, Austria and German-speaking Switzerland as a variety of bread, a side dish or a snack, and come in many local varieties. Almost every region and even city has its own way of baking them. Examples for pretzel names in various Upper-German dialects are *Brezn*, *Bretzel*, *Brezzl*, *Brezgen*, *Bretzga*, *Bretzet*, *Bretschl*, *Kringel*, *Silserli* and *Sülzerli*. Baked for consumption on the same day, they are sold in every bakery and in special booths or stands in downtown streets. Often, they are sliced horizontally, buttered, and sold as *Butterbrezel*, or come with slices of cold meats or cheese. Sesame, poppy, sunflower, pumpkin or caraway seeds, melted cheese and bacon bits are other popular toppings. Some bakeries offer pretzels made of different flours, such as whole wheat, rye or spelt. In Bavaria, lye pretzels accompany a main dish such as Weisswurst sausage. The same dough and baking procedure with lye and salt is used to make other kinds of "lye pastry" (*Laugengebäck*): lye rolls, buns, croissants and even loaves (*Laugenbrötchen*, *Laugenstangen*, *Laugencroissants*, *Laugenbrot*). Yet, in some parts of Bavaria, especially in lower Bavaria, unglazed "white" pretzels, sprinkled with salt and caraway seeds are still popular. Basically with the same ingredients, lye pretzels come in numerous local varieties. Sizes are usually similar; the main differences are the thickness of the dough, the content of fat and the degree of baking. Typical Swabian pretzels, for example, have very thin "arms" and a "fat belly" with a split, and a higher fat content. The thicker part makes it easier to slice them for the use of sandwiches. In Bavarian pretzels, the arms are left thicker so they do not bake to a crisp and contain very little fat.

The pretzel shape is used for a variety of sweet pastries made of different types of dough (flaky, brittle, soft, crispy) with a variety of toppings (icing, nuts, seeds, cinnamon). Around Christmas they can be made of soft gingerbread ("Lebkuchen") with chocolate coating.

In southern Germany and adjoining German-speaking areas, pretzels have retained their original religious meanings and are still used in various traditions and festivals.

In some areas, on January 1, people give each other lightly sweetened yeast pretzels for good luck and good fortune. These "New-Years pretzels" are made in different sizes and can have a width of 50 centimetres (20 in) and more. Sometimes children visit their godparents to fetch their New Years pretzel. On May 1, love-struck boys used to paint a pretzel on the doors of the adored. On the other hand, an upside-down pretzel would have been a sign of disgrace. Especially Catholic areas, such as Austria, Bavaria or some parts of Swabia, the "Palm pretzel" is made for Palm Sunday celebrations. Sizes can range from 30 cm (1 ft) up to 1 m (3 ft 3 in) and they can weigh up to 2.5 kg (6 lbs). An old tradition on Palm Sunday dating back to 1533 is the outdoor pretzel market (*Brezgenmarkt*) in the Hungerbrunnen Valley near Heldenfingen.

In the Rhineland region, sweet pretzels are made with pudding-filled loops (pudding pretzels).

On Laetare Sunday in Luxembourg, the fourth Sunday in Lent, there is a festival called "Pretzel Sunday". Boys give their girlfriends pretzels or cakes in pretzel form. The size symbolizes how much he likes her. In return, if a girl wants to increase his attention, she will give him a decorated egg on Easter. The pretzel custom is reversed on Pretzel Sunday during leap years. This custom also still exists in some areas of the Swabian Alb.

On the same occasion in Rhenish Hesse and the Palatinate, people have parades carrying big pretzels mounted on colourful decorated poles.

Popular during Lent in Biberach are "Lent pretzels", which are shortly boiled in water before baking and afterwards sprinkled with salt.

Schloss Burg is renowned for a 200-year-old speciality, the "Burger pretzel". Its texture and flavour resembles rusk or zwieback. A local story says that the recipe came from a grateful Napoleonic soldier in 1795, whose wounds were treated by a baker's family in the little town of Burg. The cultural importance of the pretzel for Burg is expressed by a monument in honour of the pretzel bakers, and by an 18-km hiking trail nearby called "Pretzel Hiking Trail".

A variety typical for Upper Franconia is the "anise pretzel". The town of Weidenberg celebrates the "Pretzel weeks" during the carnival season, when anise flavored pretzels are served with special dishes such as cooked meat with horseradish or roast. In the city of Lübeck, the 500-year old guild of boatmen on the Stecknitz Canal call their annual meetings in January *Kringelhöge* (Pretzelfun). The elaborate affair, with about 200 participants, is celebrated as a breakfast with beer, and includes Mass in the Lübeck Cathedral and a presentation of songs by a children's choir. In earlier times, the children were very poor, coming from an orphanage, and each received a *Kringel* (pretzel) as a reward. Hence, the name "Pretzelfun" was adopted, because this gift was considered a highlight. Today, the children come from schools, but they still get the pretzels.

The city of Osnabrück celebrates the anniversary of the Peace of Westphalia (1648) and organizes an annual hobby horse race for grade-four children. On finishing the race, they are presented with a sweet pretzel.

The lye pretzel is the theme for a number of festivals in Germany. The city of Speyer prides itself to be the "pretzel town", and around the second weekend of July, from Friday to Tuesday, it holds an annual funfair and festival called "*Brezelfest*", which is the largest beer festival in the Upper Rhine region, and attracts around 300,000 visitors. The festival includes a parade with over 100 bands, floats and clubs participating from the whole region, and 22,000 pretzels are thrown among the crowds. On the market square of Speyer, there is a fountain with a statue of a boy selling pretzels. The pretzel booths on the main street are permanently installed and were specially designed when the whole downtown area was redone for the 2000th anniversary. One-day pretzel fests and markets in other German towns are in Kirchhellen, a borough of Bottrop, or in Kornwestheim.

In 2003 and 2004, "Peace Pretzels" were baked for a UNICEF charity event and other charity purposes in Munich. Instead of the typical pretzel loop, they were made in the similar shape of a peace symbol.

United States

In the 19th century, southern German and Swiss German immigrants introduced the pretzel to North America. The immigrants became known as the Pennsylvania Dutch, and in time, many handmade pretzel bakeries populated the central Pennsylvania countryside, and the pretzel's popularity spread.

In the 20th century, soft pretzels became extremely popular in other regions of the United States. Cities like Philadelphia, Chicago, and New York became renowned for their soft pretzels. The key to success was the introduction of the new mass production methods of the industrialized age, which increased the availability and quantity, and the opening up of multiple points of distribution at schools, convenience and grocery stores, and entertainment venues such as movie theaters, arenas, concert halls, and sport stadiums. Prior to that, street vendors used to sell pretzels on street corners in wooden glass-enclosed cases.

In particular, it became iconic with Philadelphia and was established as a cuisine of Philadelphia for snacking at school, work, or home, and considered by most to be a quick meal. The average Philadelphian today consumes about twelve times as many pretzels as the national average.

Pennsylvania today is the center of American pretzel production for both the hard crispy and the soft bread types of pretzels. Southeastern Pennsylvania, with its large population of German background, is considered the birthplace of the American pretzel industry, and many pretzel bakers are still located in the area. Pennsylvania produces 80% of the nation's pretzels.

The annual United States pretzel industry is worth over $550 million. The average American consumes about 1.5 pounds (0.7 kg) of pretzels per year.

The privately run "Pretzel Museum" opened in Philadelphia in 1993. In 2003, Pennsylvania Governor Ed Rendell declared April 26 "National Pretzel Day" to acknowledge the importance of the pretzel to the state's history and economy. Philly Pretzel Factory stores offer a free pretzel to each customer on this day.

In Tell City, Indiana, the Tell City Pretzels originated over 100 years ago. In 1858 Casper Gloor, a baker from Switzerland settled in Tell City, Indiana. Gloor was a member of the Swiss Colonization Society. He soon became known for the pretzels that he baked from a recipe brought from Switzerland. Today, the recipe remains in use.

Hard pretzels originated in the United States, where, in 1850, the Sturgis bakery in Lititz, Pennsylvania, became the first commercial hard pretzel bakery. Snack food hard pretzels were shaped as sticks (around 3 millimetres (0.12 in) thick and 12 centimetres (4.7 in) long), loops, braids, letters or little pretzels; they have become a popular snack in many countries around the world. A thicker variety of sticks can be 1 centimetre (0.39 in) thick; in the U. S. these are called Bavarian pretzels. Unlike the soft pretzels, these were durable when kept in an airtight environment and marketable in a variety of convenience stores. In Europe, snack food pretzels are usually sprinkled with salt, but also with sesame seed, poppy seed or cheese. In the U.S., they come in many varieties of flavors and coatings, such as yogurt, chocolate, strawberry, mustard, cheese and others, and chocolate-covered hard pretzels are popular around Christmas time and given as gifts. The variety of shapes and sizes became contest of imagination in the marketing of the pretzels taste. During the 1900s, people in Philadelphia would use the small slender pretzel stick as a common accompaniment to ice cream or would crumble pretzels as a topping. This combination of cold sweet and salty taste was very popular for many years. Eventually this led to the development of an ice cream cone tasting like a pretzel. More recently Mars, Incorporated manufactures M&M's with a small spherical pretzel covered in milk chocolate and candy coated in all of the standard M&Ms colors, called "Pretzel M&M's".

Pennsylvania milestones
1800s
Southern German and Swiss German immigrants who became known as the Pennsylvania Dutch introduced soft pretzels and pretzel bakery businesses.
1861
Sturgis Pretzel House in Lititz, Pennsylvania becomes the first commercial hard pretzel bakery in the United States.
1889
The Anderson Pretzel Factory in Lancaster, Pennsylvania is founded. Today it calls itself the world's largest, producing 65 tons of hard pretzels daily.
1935
The Reading Pretzel Machinery Company in Reading, Pennsylvania introduced the first automatic hard pretzel twisting machine.
1963
The largest soft pretzel of its time, weighing 40 pounds and measuring 5 feet across, is baked by Joseph Nacchio of the Federal Pretzel Baking Company. for film "It's a Mad Mad Mad World."
1978
The first machine-produced stamped cut soft pretzel was innovated at Federal Pretzel Baking Company.
1993
The first Pretzel Museum of soft pretzels is opened in Philadelphia. Designed and operated by the Nacchio family. A short 7 minute film, demonstration of championship hand twisting at 57 per minute and tasting were highlights.
2003
Pennsylvania Governor Ed Rendell declares April 26 National Pretzel Day to acknowledge the importance of the pretzel to the state's history and economy.

Other countries
Although not as popular as among German speakers and Americans, the looped pretzel is known in other European countries and in other countries around the world. In the Czech Republic, the pretzel is known as *preclík*, in Finland as *viipurinrinkeli*. The Spanish, French and Italians call it *pretzel*, *bretzel* or *brezel*, the Dutch favor sweet variants called *krakeling*, Norwegian and Danish call it a *kringle*, in Polish it is *precel*, in Serbian it is *pereca*, and in Hungarian it is *perec*. In Romania the pretzel is known as *covrigi* and it's a very popular fast food in urban areas and also as a holiday gift.

In popular culture
The pretzel has become an element in popular culture, both as a food staple and its unique knotted twist shape which has inspired ideas, perspectives, attitudes, memes, images and other phenomena. Although historically, the pretzel has influenced culture it has recently been heavily influenced by mass media. Landscape architecture and sculpture memorialized the strong identity that the City of Philadelphia had with pretzel cuisine of local bakers and popularity in Philadelphia. The Philadelphia Recreation Department renamed in 2004 a facility formerly identified as Manayunk Park, located on the 4300 block of Silverwood Street as "Pretzel Park." The re-designed park includes pretzel like looped pathways and a public art statue in the shape of a pretzel sculpted by Warren C. Holzman.
Municipal government adopts pretzel logo as trademark by the City of Freeport, Illinois, also known as "Pretzel City USA".
Dance steps developed in swing dancing became the "pretzel dance move", which dates back to the 1920s.
Furniture Design inspired Pretzel Chair designed in 1952 by George Nelson.
Amusement ride of the Pretzel Loop design in Roller coaster elements maximizes the g-forces on riders, increasing the "thrill element" of riding a roller coaster. On a pretzel loop, riders are upside down at the beginning, and on their backs and going backwards at the bottom.
Fashion inspired sling bikini is a pretzel bathing suit design emerged in the early 1990s, as a new fashion product of Spandex. It is a bikini variant, haltered maillot that criss-crosses the front and fastens to the waistline. With the advent of the 1990s fabric known as Lycra, these bikinis first emerged and became most popular on the beaches of Europe, including Saint Tropez, Marabella, Mykonos and Ibiza.
"Pretzel Logic" is the name of a single released by the pop music group Steely Dan from their album *Pretzel Logic*, originally released in 1974. *Pretzel Nugget* is a 1994 EP by the Beastie Boys, released on the Grand Royal records label.
Slang "Pretzelphyte" meaning a follower loyal to soft pretzels; or a soft pretzel aficionado.
Ecosystem ecology The "SolVin-Pretzel" because of its shape was the name given to the inflatable United Nations Global Canopy Programme's light weight research platform which is placed on top of the canopy of rainforests to study the ecology below.
Viral Media President George W. Bush faints in January 2002 after choking on a pretzel. He tells a press conference, "When you're eating pretzels, chew before you swallow. Listen to your mother."
Source   http://en.wikipedia.org/wiki/Pretzel

Proben

Proben (sometimes also "Chicken proben", or spelled "*Proven*") is a type of street food popular in some regions

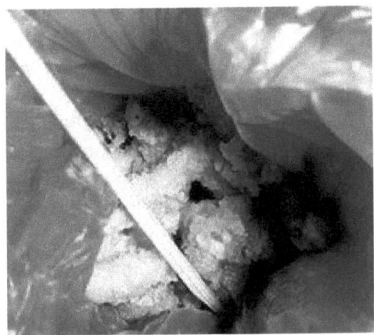

Proven from Los Baños, Laguna, Philippines

of the Philippines. It consists essentially of the proventriculus of a chicken, dipped in cornstarch, and deep-fried. It is served either in a small bagful of vinegar, or skewered on bamboo sticks to be dipped in the vinegar just before it is eaten.

Proven is particularly favored among towns in Laguna, and by students of the University of the Philippines Los Baños, where enjoying a taste of the snack in the afternoon has become a popular part of campus culture, similar to the iconic status given to Isaw at the University of the Philippines Diliman.

Nutritional value

A nutritional study conducted by UPLB noted that, as with most street foods, the microbial quality of the proben is a concern. However, the study noted that the pathogenic food-borne microbes in proben are mostly destroyed when it is cooked. The microbes only return if the proben is stored at ambient temperature after having been cooked. The study concluded that the risk of contamination can be reduced simply "*through practice of personal hygiene employing standard cooking temperature (171-185 deg C) and time (10-15 min)*" and by making sure that the proben is cooked just before it is eaten.

The same study showed that the nutrient content of newly cooked proben was "*crude fat(31%), fiber (131%), carbohydrates (21%), caloric contents (935%), crude protein (26%), calcium (21%), phosphorus (4%), iron(44%), ash (32%) and moisture (56%).*"

Source http://en.wikipedia.org/wiki/Proben

Quail eggs

Potato galettes, served with quail eggs.

Quail eggs are considered a delicacy in many countries, including western Europe and North America. In Japanese cuisine, they are sometimes used raw or cooked as *tamago* in sushi and often found in *bento* lunches.

In some other countries, quail eggs are considered less exotic. In Colombia and Venezuela, a single hard-boiled quail egg is a common topping on hot

Quail Egg as compared to a chicken egg, duck egg, and human hand

dogs and hamburgers, often fixed into place with a toothpick. In the Philippines, *kwek-kwek* is a popular street food delicacy, which consists of soft-boiled quail eggs dipped in orange-colored batter before being skewered and deep-fried. In Vietnam, bags of boiled quail eggs are sold on street stalls as inexpensive beer snacks. In South Korea, large, inexpensive bags of boiled quail eggs are sold in grocery stores. In Indonesia, small packages of hardboiled quail eggs are often found to be sold by street vendors as snacks.

Quail eggs are often believed to be high in cholesterol, but evidence shows their cholesterol levels are that of chicken eggs.

Source http://en.wikipedia.org/wiki/Quail_eggs

Quesadilla

A *huitlacoche* (corn smut) quesadilla

Origin

Place of origin	Mexico

Details

Main ingredient(s)	Tortillas, cheese, meat, refried beans, avocado or other vegetables

Sorry, your browser either has JavaScript disabled or does not have any supported player.
You can download the clip or download a player to play the clip in your browser.
How to make a cheese quesadilla.

A **quesadilla** (pron.: /ˌkeɪsəˈdiːjə/, Spanish: [kesaˈðiʎa], [kesaˈðiʝa]) is a flour tortilla or a corn tortilla filled with a savory mixture containing cheese, other ingredients, and/or vegetables, (often) then folded in half to form a half-moon shape. This dish originated in Mexico, and the name is derived from tortilla and the Spanish word for cheese *queso*.

History

The specific origin for the quesadilla was in colonial Mexico. The quesadilla as a food changed and evolved over many years as people experimented with different variations of it.

Preparation

A quesadilla is made with a tortilla and is filled primarily with cheese. Other ingredients, such as pork, ham, avocado, or other vegetables may be added. The filled tortilla is then warmed until the cheese is melted. Some variations toast or even fry the quesadilla. Once the quesadilla is cooked it is ready to eat. Sometimes salsa is added. In the USA the term quesadilla usually refers to what in Mexico is called sincronizada de queso and it is usually cut into slices or wedges. In Mexico the sincronizada is usually translated in menus as quesadilla so tourists would know what it is.

Most quesadillas are prepared by just folding and filling a tortilla, but other variations have tortillas specially made for filling. The type of tortilla varies by region. In most of Mexico, Central and South America, corn tortillas are traditionally preferred. In northern regions of Mexico, along the United States border and across the USA, quesadillas are most commonly prepared with flour tortillas. Another variation is deep fried; its preparation resembles more of a pastry than a tortilla. Quesadillas from the San Luis Potosí region are not quesadillas in the traditional sense, but rather are *enchiladas potosinas*. Red or occasionally green salsa is added to the flour, which makes the tortilla red or green. In making these enchiladas, cheese is added, and the tortilla is then folded in half and fried.

Types

Mexican quesadilla

In central and southern regions of Mexico, a quesadilla is a flat circle of cooked corn masa, called a *tortilla*, warmed to soften it enough to be folded in half, and then filled. They are typically filled with Oaxaca cheese (*queso Oaxaca*). Oaxaca cheese is a stringy (*pasta filata*) cheese that comes from Mexico. The quesadilla is then cooked on a *comal* until the cheese has completely melted. They are usually cooked without the addition of any oil. Often the quesadillas are served with green or red salsa, chopped onion, guacamole, and sour cream. While Oaxaca (or string) cheese is the most common filling, other ingredients are also used in addition to or even substituting cheese. These can include cooked vegetables, such as potatoes with *chorizo*, squash blossoms, mushrooms, *epazote*, *huitlacoche*, and different types of cooked meat, such as *chicharron*, *tinga* made of chicken or beef, or cooked pork. In some places, quesadillas are also topped with other ingredients, in addition to the fillings they already have: avocado or guacamole, chopped onion, tomato, serrano chiles and parsley are the most common. Salsas may also be added as a topping.

Mexican quesadillas are traditionally cooked on a comal, which is also used to prepare tortillas. As a variation, the quesadillas can be fried in oil to make *quesadillas fritas*. The main difference is while the traditional ones are prepared just filling the partially cooked tortillas, then continue cooking until the cheese melts, the fried ones are prepared like a pastry, preparing the uncooked masa in small circles, then topping with the filling and finally folding the quesadilla to form the pastry. It is then immersed into hot oil until the exterior looks golden and crispy.

Other variations include the use of wheat flour tortillas instead, especially in northeastern Mexico. Wheat dough is most commonly used in place of corn masa. In this case, the flour tortilla is prepared, folded and filled with cheese, exactly as the corn.

Sometimes cheese and ham are sandwiched between two flour tortillas, then cut into wedges to serve what is commonly known as *sincronizada* (Spanish for "synchronized") in Mexico. Despite appearing almost the same as a quesadilla, it is considered a completely different dish. The *sincronizada* is frequently confused with quesadillas by tourists, because it is typically called a quesadilla in most Mexican restaurants outside of México.

American quesadilla

Quesadillas served at a Friendly's restaurant in New Jersey.

The quesadilla is a regional favorite in

the Southwest, United States where it is analogous to a 'grilled cheese sandwich'. It is prepared in a similar manner except for the inclusion of local ingredients and you can use turkey. A flour tortilla is heated on a griddle, then flipped and sprinkled with a grated, melting cheese (*queso quesadilla*), such as Monterey Jack, Cheddar cheese or Colby Jack. Once the cheese melts, other ingredients; such as shredded meat, peppers, onions or guacamole may be added, and it is then folded and served.

Another preparation involves cheese and other ingredients sandwiched between two flour tortillas, with the whole package grilled on an oiled griddle and flipped so both sides are cooked and the cheese is melted. This version is often cut into wedges to serve. A home appliance (quesadilla maker) is sold to produce this kind of quesadilla, although it does not use oil and cooks both sides at once. This type is similar to the Mexican *sincronizada*; but in the United States, they often also have fajita beef or chicken or other ingredients instead of ham.

There is a lot of regional variation to specific recipes throughout the Southwest.

Variations

Quesadillas have been adapted to many different styles. In the United States, many restaurants serve them as appetizers, after adding their own twist. Some variations are: goat cheese, black beans, spinach, zucchini, or tofu. Even dessert quesadillas are made, using ingredients such as chocolate, butterscotch, caramel, and different fruits.

Source http://en.wikipedia.org/wiki/Quesadilla

Sabich

Sabich

Sabich (Hebrew: סביח [saˈbiχ]) is an Israeli sandwich, consisting of pita stuffed with fried eggplant and hard boiled eggs. Local consumption is said to have stemmed from a tradition among Mizrahi Jews, who ate it on Shabbat morning.

Etymology

One theory is that Sabich comes from the Arabic word صباح [sˤaˈbaːħ], which means "morning", as the ingredients in the sabich are typical for an Iraqi breakfast..

Ingredients

Sabich, served in pita bread, traditionally contains fried eggplant, hard boiled eggs, hummus, tahini, Israeli salad, potato, parsley and amba. Traditionally it is made with haminados eggs, slow-cooked in hamin until they turn brown. Sometimes it is doused with hot sauce and sprinkled with minced onion.

History

Sabich was brought to Israel by Mizrahi Jews who moved in the 1940s and 1950s. On the Sabbath, when no cooking is allowed, Mizarhi Jews ate a cold meal of precooked fried eggplant, cooked potatoes and hard-boiled eggs. In Israel, these ingredients were stuffed in a pita and sold as fast food. In the 1950s and 1960s, vendors began to sell the sandwich in open-air stalls.

Source http://en.wikipedia.org/wiki/Sabich

Sandwich

Salmon cream cheese sandwiches

Details

| Main ingredient(s) | Bread, salad vegetables, meat, cheese, sauce or savoury spread |

A sandwich is handheld and portable, this one is made with salami

A **sandwich** is a food item consisting of two or more slices of bread with one or more fillings between them. Sandwiches are a widely popular type of lunch food, typically taken to work, school, or picnics to be eaten as part of a packed lunch. The bread can be used as it is, or it can be coated with any condiments to enhance flavour and texture. They are also widely sold in restaurants and cafes, served hot or cold.

Thought to be the namesake of John Montagu, 4th Earl of Sandwich, following the claim that he was the eponymous inventor of the sandwich.

History

The ancient Jewish sage Hillel the Elder is said to have wrapped meat from the Paschal lamb and bitter herbs between

English sandwiches, crustless on a plate

Sandwich with fried egg, tomato and cucumber

two pieces of old-fashioned soft matzah, flat, unleavened bread, during Passover in the manner of a modern sandwich wrap made with flatbread. Flat breads of only slightly varying kinds have long been used to scoop or wrap small amounts of food en route from platter to mouth throughout Western Asia and northern Africa. From Morocco to Ethiopia to India, bread is baked in flat rounds, contrasting with the European loaf tradition.

Olive and red Tomato sandwich

During the Middle Ages in Europe, thick slabs of coarse and usually stale bread, called "trenchers", were used as plates. After a meal, the food-soaked trencher was fed to a dog or to beggars at the tables of the wealthy, and eaten by diners in more modest circumstances. Trenchers were the precursors of open-face sandwiches. The immediate culinary precursor with a direct connection to the English sandwich was to be found in the Netherlands of the 17th century, where the naturalist John Ray observed that in the taverns beef hung from the rafters "which they cut into thin slices and eat with bread and butter laying the slices upon the butter"— explanatory specifications that reveal the Dutch *belegde broodje*, open faced sandwich, was as yet unfamiliar in England.

Initially perceived as food men shared while gaming and drinking at night, the sandwich slowly began appearing in polite society as a late-night meal among the aristocracy. The sandwich's popularity in Spain and England increased dramatically during the 19th century, when the rise of an industrial society and the working classes made fast, portable, and inexpensive meals essential.

It was at the same time that the sandwich finally began to appear outside of Europe. In the United States, the sandwich was first promoted as an elaborate meal at supper. By the early 20th century, as bread became a staple of the American diet, the sandwich became the same kind of popular, quick meal as was already widespread in the Mediterranean.

Etymology

The first written usage of the English word appeared in Edward Gibbon's journal, in longhand, referring to "bits of cold meat" as a "Sandwich". It was named after John Montagu, 4th Earl of Sandwich, an 18th-century English aristocrat, although he was neither the inventor nor sustainer of the food. It is said that he ordered his valet to bring him meat tucked between two pieces of bread, and because Montagu also happened to be the Fourth Earl of Sandwich, others began to order *"the same as Sandwich!"* It is said that Lord Sandwich was fond of this form of food because it allowed him to continue playing cards, particularly cribbage, while eating without getting his cards greasy from eating meat with his bare hands.

The rumour in its familiar form appeared in Pierre-Jean Grosley's *Londres* (Neichatel, 1770), translated as *A Tour to London* 1772; Grosley's impressions had been formed during a year in London in 1765. The sober alternative is provided by Sandwich's biographer, N. A. M. Rodger, who suggests Sandwich's commitments to the navy, to politics and the arts mean the first sandwich was more likely to have been consumed at his desk.

Before being known as sandwiches, the food seems to simply have been known as "bread and meat" or "bread and cheese".

Usage

In the United States, a court in Boston, Massachusetts ruled that "sandwich" includes at least two slices of bread. and "under this definition, this court finds that the term "sandwich" is not commonly understood to include burritos, tacos, and quesadillas, which are typically made with a single tortilla and stuffed with a choice filling of meat, rice, and beans." The issue stemmed from the question of whether a restaurant that sold burritos could move into a shopping centre where another restaurant had a no-compete clause in its lease prohibiting other "sandwich" shops.

In Spain, where the word sandwich is borrowed from the English language, it refers to a food item made with English sandwich bread. It is otherwise known as a *bocadillo*.

The verb **to sandwich** has the meaning *to position anything between two other things of a different character, or to place different elements alternately*, and the noun sandwich has related meanings derived from this more general definition. For example, an ice cream sandwich consists of a layer of ice cream between two layers of cake or biscuit. Similarly, Oreos and Custard Creams are described as sandwich biscuits because they consist of a soft filling between layers of biscuit.

The word "butty" is often used in Northern areas of the United Kingdom as a synonym for "sandwich", particularly in the name of certain kinds of sandwiches such as a chip butty, bacon butty, or sausage butty. "Sarnie" is a similar colloquialism, as is the Australian English colloquialism "sanger". Likewise, the words "sanger" and "piece" are used for sandwich in Scottish dialect; regarding the latter, an example of the use of "piece" is "piece and ham", meaning "piece of bread and ham".

Examples of sandwiches

The following represent common varieties of American sandwich.
Peanut butter and jelly sandwich
Club sandwich
Sloppy joe
Reuben
Monte Cristo
Grilled cheese
BLT
Muffuletta
Dagwood
Po' boy
Pilgrim
French dip
Philadelphia cheesesteak
Submarine sandwich
Hamburger

Gallery

Club sandwich
Croque-monsieur, a French ham and cheese hot sandwich
A hamburger, one of the most popular types of hot sandwiches
Peanut butter and jelly sandwich

A Philly cheese steak, a type of submarine sandwich

Reuben sandwich

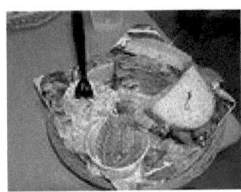

Smoked meat sandwich

French bread sandwich with fries

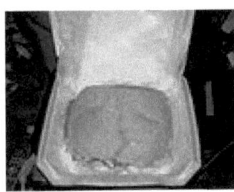

Example of a large sandwich. Weight approx. 2 pounds (1 kg), total.

Sandwich making

Shawarma sandwich

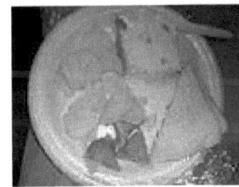

A cucumber sandwich with chips and cake
Source http://en.wikipedia.org/wiki/Sandwich

Sardenara

Details

Origin	
Alternative name(s)	Sardenaira
Place of origin	Italy
Region or state	West Liguria
Course	Snack
Type	Pizza
Main ingredient(s)	Bread dough (flour, yeast, olive oil, milk), cooked tomatoes and onions, capers, garlic, black olives, oregano

Sardenara or Sardenaira is a snack from West Liguria similar to a pizza, baked in very large rectangular baking trays and generally bought from a bakery in small rectangular cut pieces. The light, crispy base is normally approximately 15 mm (0.59 in) and is made from a bread-type dough of wheat flour (the flour is normally of cake quality), sometimes with the addition of potato flour mixed with yeast, olive oil and milk. The tomato topping consists of tomatoes and onions cooked before putting on the base, as opposed to a pizza, where the topping is left uncooked before going into the oven, all finished off with sardine paste (sarde, which give it its name), capers, garlic, local black olives, and oregano, and brushed with olive oil.

Source http://en.wikipedia.org/wiki/Sardenara

Satay

Sate Ponorogo, grilled marinated chicken satay served in peanut sauce, a speciality of Ponorogo, a town in East Java, Indonesia.

Origin	
Alternative name(s)	Sate
Place of origin	Indonesia
Region or state	Nationwide in Indonesia, also popular in Malaysia, Singapore, Brunei, Thailand, and the Netherlands
Creator(s)	Indonesian cuisine
Details	
Course	Entrée or main course
Serving temperature	Hot
Main ingredient(s)	Skewered and grilled meats with various sauces, mainly peanut sauce
Variations	Numerous variations across Southeast Asia

Satay (/ˈsæteɪ/, /ˈsɑːteɪ/ *SAH-tay*), or sate, is a dish of seasoned, skewered and grilled meat, served with a sauce. Satay may consist of diced or sliced chicken, goat, mutton, beef, pork, fish, other meats, or tofu; the more authentic version uses skewers from the midrib of the coconut palm frond, although bamboo skewers are often used. These are grilled or barbecued over a wood or charcoal fire, then served with various spicy seasonings.

Satay originated in Java, Indonesia. Satay is available almost anywhere in Indonesia, where it has become a national dish. It is also popular in many other Southeast Asian countries, including Malaysia, Singapore, Brunei, the Philippines, and Thailand, as well as in the Netherlands, as Indonesia is a former Dutch colony.

Satay is a very popular delicacy in Indonesia; Indonesia's diverse ethnic groups' culinary arts (see Indonesian cuisine) have produced a wide variety of satays. In Indonesia, satay can be obtained from a travelling satay vendor, from a street-side tent-restaurant, in an upper-class restaurant, or during traditional celebration feasts. In Malaysia, satay is a popular dish—especially during celebrations—and can be found throughout the country.

Close analogues are yakitori from Japan, shish kebab from Turkey, shashlik from Caucasus, chuanr from China, and sosatie from South Africa. It is listed at number 14 on *World's 50 most delicious foods* readers' poll complied by CNN Go *in 2011*.

Origin

Satay seller in Java, c. 1870.

Although both Thailand and Malaysia claim it as their own, its Southeast Asian origin was in Java, Indonesia. There satay was developed from the Indian kebab brought by the Muslim traders. Even India cannot claim its origin, for there it was a legacy of Middle Eastern influence.

—Jennifer Brennan (1988), *Kitchen Daily: Satay*

A dish with widespread popularity, the origins of satay are unclear. The word "satay" itself is thought to have been derived from Indonesian: *sate* and Malay: *saté or satai*, both perhaps of Tamil origin. Satay was supposedly invented by Javanese street vendors as an adaptation of Indian kebabs. This theory is based on the fact that satay has become popular in Java after the influx of Muslim Tamil Indian and Arab immigrants to Dutch East Indies in the early 19th century. The satay meats used by Indonesians and Malaysians — mutton and beef — are also favoured by Arabs and are not as popular in China as are pork and chicken.

Another theory states that the word "satay" is derived from the Min Nan words *sa tae bak* (三疊肉), which mean "three pieces of meat". This theory is discounted, however, as traditional satay often consists of four pieces of meat and the fact that four is considered to be an inauspicious number in Chinese culture.

From Java, satay spread through the Malay Archipelago and, as a consequence, numerous variations of the dish have been developed and exist. By the late 19th century, satay has crossed the Strait of Malacca into neighbouring Malaysia, Singapore, and Thailand. In the 19th century, the term migrated, presumably with Malay immigrants from the Dutch East Indies, to South Africa, where it is known as *sosatie*. The Dutch also brought this dish as well as many other Indonesian specialties to the Netherlands, thereby influencing Dutch cuisine even to this day.

Preparation

Turmeric is a necessary ingredient used to marinate satay, which gives the dish its characteristic yellow colour. Meat commonly used includes beef, mutton, pork, venison, fish, shrimp, squid, chicken, rabbit and tripe. Some have also used more exotic varieties of meat, such as turtle, crocodile, horse, lizard, and snake meat.

Satay may be served with a spicy peanut sauce dip, or peanut gravy, slivers of onions, cucumbers, and ketupat (rice cakes). Pork satay can be served in a pineapple-based satay sauce or cucumber relish. An Indonesian version uses a soy-based dip.

Satay variants and outlets of note

Indonesia

Sate Padang with yellow sauce.

A street-side chicken satay seller near Borobudur, Central Java.

Sate Ponorogo being grilled in a food-stall in Surabaya, East Java, Indonesia

Sate buntel, minced goat meat wrapped in membrane, Solo, Central Java

Horse satay, Yogyakarta, Indonesia

Indonesian Chinese version of nasi campur with pork satay

Sate Padang vendor in Batam, Indonesia

Balinese nasi campur with sate lilit.

Quail eggs satay and chicken liver-intestine satay

Known as *sate* in Indonesian (and pronounced similar to the English), Indonesia is the home of satay, and satay is a widely renowned dish in almost all regions of Indonesia and is considered the national dish and one of Indonesia's best dishes. Satays, in particular, are a staple in Indonesian cuisine, served everywhere from street carts to fine dining establishments, as well as in homes and at public gatherings. As a result, many variations have been developed throughout the Indonesian Archipelago. In Indonesia there are some restaurants that specialized on serving various

Goat liver satay

kinds of satay and present it as their specialty, such as Sate Ponorogo Restaurant, Sate Blora Restaurant, and also chains of Sate Khas Senayan restaurants, previously known as Satay House Senayan. In Bandung, the West Java Governor's office is popularly called Gedung Sate (Indonesian: *Satay building*) to refer the satay-like pinnacle on its roof.

Indonesia has the richest variations of satay in the world. The satay variants in Indonesia usually named after the region its originated, the meats, parts or ingredients its uses, also might named after the process or method of cooking.

Sate Madura
Originating on the island of Madura, near Java, is a famous variant among Indonesians. Most often made from mutton or chicken, the recipe's main characteristic is the black sauce made from Indonesian sweet soy sauce/kecap manis mixed with palm sugar (called *gula jawa* or "javanese sugar" in Indonesia), garlic, deep fried shallots, peanut paste, petis (a kind of shrimp paste), candlenut/kemiri, and salt. Chicken Madura satay is usually served in peanut sauce, while the mutton Madura satay is usually served in sweet soy sauce. *Sate Madura* uses thinner chunks of meat than other variants. It is eaten with rice or rice cakes wrapped in banana/coconut leaves (lontong/ketupat). Raw thinly sliced shallot and plain sambal are often served as condiments

Sate Padang
A dish from Padang and the surrounding area in West Sumatra, which is made from cow or goat offal boiled in spicy broth then grilled. Its main characteristic is a yellow sauce made from rice flour mixed with spicy offal broth, turmeric, ginger, garlic, coriander, galangal root, cumin, curry powder and salt. It is further separated into two sub-variants, the Pariaman and the Padang Panjang, which differ in taste and the composition of their yellow sauces.

Sate Ponorogo
A variant of satay originating in Ponorogo, a town in East Java. It is made from sliced marinated chicken meat, and served with a sauce made of peanuts and chilli sauce and Garnished with shredded shallots, sambal (chili paste) and lime juice. This variant is unique for the fact that each skewer contains one large piece of chicken, rather than several small slices. The meat is marinated in spices and sweet soy sauce, in a process called "bacem" and is served with rice or lontong (rice cake). The grill is made from terracotta earthenware with a hole in one side to allow ventilation for the coals. After three months of use, the earthenware grill disintegrates, and must be replaced.

Sate Tegal
A sate of a yearling or five-month-old lamb; the nickname for this dish in Tegal balibul is an acronym of "baru lima bulan" (just 5 months). Each *kodi*, or dish, contains twenty skewers, and each skewer has four chunks — two pieces of meat, one piece of fat and then another piece of meat. It is grilled over wood charcoal until it is cooked between medium and well done; however it is possible to ask for medium rare. Sometimes the fat piece can be replaced with liver or heart or kidney. This is not marinated prior to grilling. On serving, it is accompanied by sweet soya sauce (medium sweetness, slightly thinned with boiled water), sliced fresh chilli, sliced raw shallots (*eschalot*), quartered green tomatoes, and steamed rice, and is sometimes garnished with fried shallots.

Sate Ambal
A satay variant from Ambal, Kebumen, Central Java. This satay uses a native breed of poultry, *ayam kampung*. The sauce is not based on peanuts, but rather ground tempeh, chilli and spices. The chicken meat is marinated for about two hours to make the meat tastier. This satay is accompanied with ketupat.

Sate Blora
A variant originating in Blora, located in Central Java. This variant is made of chicken (meat and skin) pieces that are smaller compared to the other variants. It is normally eaten with peanut sauce, rice, and a traditional soup made of coconut milk and herbs. Sate Blora is grilled in front of buyers as they are eating. The buyers tell the vendor to stop grilling when they are finished with their meal.

Sate Matang
A satay variant from Matang Geulumpang Dua, Bireun, Aceh. This satay is made from beef, usually served with peanut sauce and soto or soup separately.

Sate Banjar
A variant of satay popular in South Kalimantan, especially in the town of Banjarmasin.

Sate Makassar
From a region in Southern Sulawesi, this satay is made from beef and cow offal marinated in sour carambola sauce. It has a unique sour and spicy taste. Unlike most satays, it is served without sauce.

Sate Buntel (Wrapped Satay)
A specialty from Solo or Surakarta, Central Java. It's made from minced beef or goat (especially meats around ribs and belly area). The minced fatty meats are wrapped by thin fat or muscle membrane and wrapped around a bamboo skewer. The size of this satay is quite large, very similar to a middle eastern kebab. After being grilled on charcoal, the meat is separated from the skewer, cut into bite-size chunks, then served in sweet soy sauce and *merica* (pepper).

Sate Lilit
A satay variant from Bali, a famous tourist destination. This satay is made from minced beef, chicken, fish, pork, or even turtle meat, which is then mixed with grated coconut, thick coconut milk, lemon juice, shallots, and pepper. Wound around bamboo, sugar cane or lemon grass sticks, it is then grilled on

charcoal.

Sate Pusut
A delicacy from Lombok, the neighboring island east of Bali. It is made from a mixture of minced meat (beef, chicken, or fish), shredded coconut meat, and spices. The mixture then is wrapped around a skewer and grilled over charcoal.

Sate Ampet
Another Lombok delicacy. It is made from beef, cow's intestines and other cow's internal organs. The sauce for *sate ampet* is hot and spicy, which is no surprise since the island's name, Lombok Merah, means Red chili. The sauce is santan (coconut milk) and spices.

Sate Maranggi
Commonly found in Purwakarta, Cianjur and Bandung, the cities in West Java, this satay is made from beef marinated in a special paste. The two most important elements of the paste are *kecombrang* (*Nicolaia speciosa*) flower buds and *ketan* (sweet rice) flour. Nicola buds bring a unique aroma and a liquorice-like taste. It is served with ketan cake (*jadah*) or plain rice.

Sate Lembut
A rare satay recipe of the Betawi people. It is can be found in Jalan Kebon Kacang, Central Jakarta. The satay is made from minced beef mixed with shredded coconut and spices, wrapped around a flat bamboo skewer. Usually eaten with ketupat laksa betawi (Betawi style Laksa with ketupat glutinous compressed rice).

Sate Manis
Also a speciality from the Betawi people. It is also can be found in Jalan Kebon Kacang, Central Jakarta. The satay is made from slices of *has dalam* (tenderloin) the finest part of beef, marinated with sweet spices. Usually eaten with ketupat laksa betawi.

Sate Kambing (Goat satay)
A variant of satay popular in Java, made with goat, lamb or mutton meat. Different than other satay, sate kambing is not usually pre-seasoned or pre-cooked. Raw lamb is skewered and grilled directly on the charcoal. It is then served with sweet soy sauce, sliced shallots, and cut-up tomatoes. Since the meat is not pre-cooked, it is important to choose a very young lamb. Most famous vendor usually use lamb under three to five months old. Lamb from goat is also more popular than lamb from sheep due to milder flavor.

Sate Kerbau (Water buffalo satay)
A variant of satay popular in Kudus, where most Muslim believed that it is forbidden to eat beef in order to respect the Hindus. This satay is made with water buffalo meat. The meat is cooked first with palm sugar, coriander, cumin, and other seasoning until very tender. Some vendor choose to even grind the meat first in order to make it really tender. It is then grilled on charcoal, and the served with sauce made with coconut milk, palm sugar, and other seasoning. Traditionally, satay kerbau is served on a plate covered with teak wood leaves.

Sate Kelinci (Rabbit meat Satay)
This variant of satay is made from rabbit meat, a delicacy from Java. It is served with sliced fresh shallots (small red onion), peanut sauce, and sweet soy sauce. Rabbit satay usually can be found in mountainous tourist region in Java where locals breed rabbit for its meat, such as Lembang in West Java, Kaliurang in Yogyakarta, Bandungan and Tawangmangu resort in Central Java, also Telaga Sarangan in East Java.

Sate Burung Ayam-ayaman (Bird Satay)
The satay is made from gizzard, liver, and intestines of "Burung Ayam-ayaman" (a migrating sea bird). After being seasoned with mild spices and stuck on a skewer, this bird's internal organs aren't grilled, but are deep fried in cooking oil instead.

Sate Bandeng (Milkfish Satay)
A unique delicacy from Banten. It is a satay made from boneless "Bandeng" (milkfish). The seasoned spicy milkfish meat is separated from the small bones, then placed back into the milkfish skin, clipped by a bamboo stick, and grilled over charcoal.

Sate Belut (Eel Satay)
Another Lombok rare delicacy. It is made from belut, (lit. eel) commonly found in watery rice paddies in Indonesia. A seasoned eel is skewered and wrapped around each skewer, then grilled over charcoal fire, so each skewer contains an individual small eel.

Sate Kuda (Horse meat Satay)
Locally known as "Sate Jaran", this is made from horse meat, a delicacy from Yogyakarta. It is served with sliced fresh shallots (small red onion), pepper, and sweet soy sauce.

Sate Bulus (Turtle Satay)
Another rare delicacy from Yogyakarta. It is a satay made from freshwater "Bulus" (softshell turtle). It is served with sliced fresh shallots (small red onion), pepper, and sweet soy sauce. Bulus meat is also served in soup or tongseng (Javanese style spicy-sweet soup).

Sate Ular (Snake Satay)
A rare and exotic delicacy usually founds in foodstalls specialize on serving exotic meats like snakes and lizards, such as the one founds near Gubeng train station in Surabaya, or near Mangga Besar and Tebet train station in Jakarta. It usually uses ular sedok (cobra) or sanca (python) meat. It is served with sliced fresh shallots (small red onion), pickles, pepper, and sweet soy sauce.

Sate Babi (Pork Satay)
Popular among the Indonesian-Chinese community, most of whom do not share the Muslim prohibition against pork. This dish can be found in Chinatowns in Indonesian cities, especially around Glodok, Pecenongan, and Senen in the Jakarta area. It is also popular in Bali which the majority are Hindus, and also popular in The Netherlands.

Sate Kulit (Skin Satay)
Found in Sumatra, this is a crisp satay made from marinated chicken skin.

Sate Hati (Liver Satay)
There is two types of liver satays, cattle liver (goat or cow) and chicken liver satay. The cattle liver made by diced whole liver, while the chicken liver satay is made from mixture of chicken liver, gizzard, and intestines. Usually gizzard is placed on the bottom, intestine on the center and liver or heart on the top. After seasoning, the internal organs are not fried or grilled, but are boiled instead. It's not treated as a main dish, but

often as a side dish to accompany bubur ayam (chicken rice porridge).

Sate Usus (Chicken Intestine satay)
This mildly marinated satay is usually fried, also as a side-dish to accompany bubur ayam.

Sate Babat (Tripe satay)
Mildly marinated and mostly boiled than grilled, usually served as a side-dish to accompany soto.

Sate Kerang (Shellfish satay)
The most popular variant of sate kerang is from Medan, North Sumatra, it is rich spicy cooked shellfish in skewer an often become *oleh-oleh* (food gift) for visitors visiting Medan. In Java sate kerang it is mildly marinated and boiled, also served as a side-dish to accompany soto.

Sate Telor Puyuh (Quail eggs satay)
Several hard-boiled quail eggs are put into skewers, marinated in sweet soy sauce with spices and boiled further, also served as a side-dish for soto.

Sate Telor Muda (Young egg Satay)
This satay is made from premature chicken egg (*uritan*) obtained upon slaughtering the hens. The immature eggs that has not developed the eggshell yet are boiled and put into skewers to be grilled as satay.

Sate Torpedo (Testicles Satay)
Satay made from goat testicles marinated in soy sauce and grilled. It is eaten with peanut sauce, pickles, and hot white rice.

Sate Susu (Milky Satay)
A tasty dish commonly found in Java and Bali, made from grilled spicy beef brisket with a distinctive milky taste, served with hot chilli sauce.

Sate Kere (Poorman's satay)
A cheap vegetarian satay made from grounded tempe from Solo city, served in peanut sauce and pickles. The word "kere" in the Javanese language means "poor"; it originally was meant to provide the poor people of Java with the taste of satay at an affordable price, since meat was considered a luxury in the past. Today, sate kere also includes intestine, liver and beef satays mixed with tempe ones.

Malaysia
Known as *sate* in Malay (and pro-

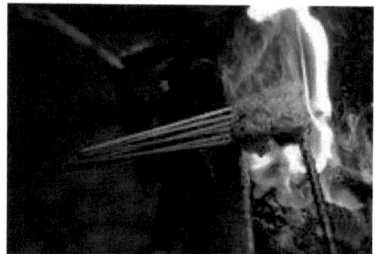
Oil from the satay causes the hot coals to flame

Satay is a popular dish in Malaysia

Woman cooking some satay in Tanjung Aru Beach food stall court, Sabah

nounced similarly to the English), it can be found throughout all the states of Malaysia in restaurants and on the street, with hawkers selling satay in food courts and Pasar malam. While the popular kinds of satay are usually beef and chicken satays, different regions of Malaysia have developed their own unique variations. Sate is often associated with Muslim Malays, but pork sate is also available at non-halal Chinese eating establishments, demonstrating the melding of cultures in this diverse society.

There are a number of well-known satay outlets in Kajang, Selangor which is dubbed the Sate City in the country. *Sate Kajang* is a generic name for a style of sate where the meat chunks are bigger than normal, and the sweet peanut sauce served along with a portion of fried chilli paste. Given its popularity, sate Kajang is now found throughout Malaysia. Stalls and restaurants around Kajang offer not only the more traditional chicken or beef satay, but also more exotic meats such as venison, rabbit or fish, as well as gizzard, liver, and a number of other variations.

Another type of meat satay is the *sate lok-lok* from Penang and *sate celup* (dip satay) from Malacca. Both are Malaysian Chinese fusions of the hotpot and the Malay satay. Pieces of raw meat, tofu, century eggs, quail eggs, fish cake, offal or vegetables are skewered on bamboo sticks. These are cooked by being dipped in boiling water or stock. The satay is then eaten with a sweet, dark sauce, sometimes with chilli sauce as an accompaniment. If the satay is eaten with satay sauce, it is called sate loklok. If the satay is cooked with boiling satay peanut sauce, it is called sate celup. Both dishes are available from street vendors or in certain restaurants, and the majority are not halal. Customers use a common container containing boiling stock to personally cook their satay. Sauces are either served in common containers or individually. There are usually no tables near street vendors, and customers thus tend to gather around the food cart.

Singapore

Singapore satay served with peanut sauce, cucumber and onion

Satay is one of the earliest foods to be associated with Singapore; it has been associated with the city since the 1940s. Previously sold on makeshift roadside stalls and pushcarts, concerns over public health and the rapid development of the city led to a major consolidation of satay stalls at Beach Road in the 1950s, which came to be collectively called the *Satay Club*. They were moved to the Esplanade Park in the 1960s, where they grew to the point of being constantly listed in tourism guides.

Open only after dark with an "al fresco" concept, the Satay Club defined how satay is served in Singapore since then, although they are also found across the island in most hawker stalls, modern food courts, and upscale restaurants at any time of the day. Moved several times around Esplanade Park due to development and land reclamation, the outlets finally left the area permanently to Clarke Quay in the late 1990s to make way for the building of the Esplanade - Theatres on the Bay.

Several competing satay hotspots have since emerged, with no one being able to lay claim to the reputation the Satay Club had at the Esplanade. While the name has been transferred to the Clarke Quay site, several stalls from the original Satay club have moved to Sembawang in the north of the city. The satay stalls which opened at Lau Pa Sat are popular with tourists. Served only at night when Boon Tat Street is closed to vehicular traffic and the stalls and tables occupy the street, it mimics the open-air dining style of previous establishments.

Other notable outlets include the ones at Newton Food Centre, East Coast Park Seafood Centre and Toa Payoh Central.

The common types of satay sold in Singapore include *Satay Ayam* (chicken satay), *Satay Lembu* (beef satay), *Satay Kambing* (mutton satay), *Satay Perut* (beef intestine), and *Satay Babat* (beef tripe).

Singapore's national carrier, Singapore Airlines, also serves satay to its First and Raffles Class passengers as an appetizer.

Thailand

Satay (Thai pronunciation: [sā.téʔ]) is a

Thai pork satay

popular dish in Thailand. Usually served in peanut sauce, Thai satay have various recipes, such as chicken, beef, pork to vegetarian variants that employs soy protein strips or tofu. Satay can easily found in virtually any Thai restaurant worldwide. Because Thai cuisine is heavily marketed internationally and has attracted world culinary attention earlier than Indonesian cuisine, despite its Indonesian origin, there is widespread misconception abroad that satay is originated from Thailand. As the result it is most frequently associated with Thai food.

The Netherlands

Chicken satay in the Netherlands with peanut sauce, French fries, prawn crackers, and mayonnaise; as served in a pub in Amsterdam

Known as saté or sateh it is fully adapted in Dutch everyday cuisine. Pork- and chicken satays, almost solely served with spicy peanut sauce, are readily available in snackbars and supermarkets. The version with goat-meat (sateh kambing) and sweet soy sauce is available in Indonesian restaurants and takeaways. Pork or chicken satay in peanut sauce, with salad and French-fries is popular in pubs or *eetcafes*.

Another favourite in Dutch snackbars is the *satékroket*, a croquette made with a peanut sauce and shredded meat ragout.

Fusion satay

Another popular misconception, the term "satay" is often mistakenly identified as peanut sauce. Traditionally, satay referred to any grilled skewered meats with various sauces, it is not necessarily served solely in peanut sauce. However, since the most popular variant of satay is chicken satay in peanut sauce (*Sate Madura* in Indonesia, *Sate Kajang* in Malaysia, and Thai chicken use peanut sauce); in modern fusion cuisine the term "satay" has shifted to satay style peanut sauce instead.

For example, the fusion "satay burger" refers to beef hamburger served with so-called "satay sauce", which is mainly a kind of sweet and spicy peanut sauce or often replaced with gloppy peanut butter. The Singapore satay bee hoon is actually rice vermicelli served in peanut sauce. The Thai fusion fish fillet in satay sauce also demonstrates the same trend. The fusion French cuisine *Cuisses de Grenouilles Poelees au Satay, Chou-fleur Croquant* is actually frog legs in peanut sauce. The Indomie instant noodle is also available in satay flavour, which is only the addition of peanut sauce in its packet.

Source http://en.wikipedia.org/wiki/Satay

Sausage roll

A **sausage roll** is a type of savoury pastry. In addition to retail outlets they are available from bakeries as a take-away food item. A miniature version is popular as a buffet or party food.

Composition

The basic composition of a sausage roll is generally a sheet or sheets of puff pastry formed into tubes around sausage meat and glazed with egg or milk before being baked. They can be served either

Sausage rolls

hot or cold.

Historically, during the 18th century they were made using shortcrust pastry instead of puff pastry.

Sales

In the UK, bakery chain Greggs sells around 2.5 million sausage rolls per week, which is around 140 million per year. This led to it complaining about the addition of Value Added Tax added by the British Government to hot food takeaways in the 2012 budget.

Source http://en.wikipedia.org/wiki/Sausage_roll

Sevpuri

Sevpuri
Origin
Place of origin India
Details
Main Puri, Sev, potatoes,

ingredient(s) onions, chutneys
Variations Bhelpuri, Dahipuri, Pani Puri, Sev papdi chaat

Sev puri is an Indian snack and a type of chaat. It is a speciality that originates from Mumbai. In Mumbai, sev puri is served by street vendors as well as five star hotels. Recently, supermarkets have started stocking ready-to-eat packets of sev puri and similar snacks like bhelpuri.

Preparation

Although there is no fixed recipe for sev puri, the basic ingredients used widely are the same. Sev puri is essentially made of puri which is loaded with diced potatoes, onions, three types of chutneys: tamarind, chili and garlic and topped with sev. It is seasoned with raw mango, when raw mango is in season or with a hint of lemon and chaat masala.

Variations

Sev puri can be made with a variety of fillings and garnishing ingredients. Some popular variations are *dahi sev batata puri* (sev puri with yogurt and potato), palak sev puri (Sev Puri with spinach) and corn sev puri. Sometimes mint chutney and paneer are also added in its preparation.

Source http://en.wikipedia.org/wiki/Sevpuri

Sfenj

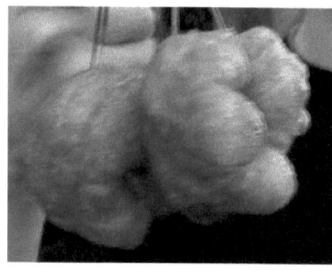

Origin
Place of origin Morocco, Algeria, Tunisia, and Libya
Type Doughnut

Sfenj (from the Arabic word "isfenj" which means sponge) is a Moroccan, Algerian, Tunisian and Libyan doughnut, cooked in oil. *Sfenj* is eaten sprinkled with sugar or soaked in honey.

Source http://en.wikipedia.org/wiki/Sfenj

Shawarma

Shawarma in a pita
Details

Type Meat
Main ingredient(s) Meat: lamb, chicken, turkey, beef

Sandwich: Shawarma meat, pita or wrap bread, chopped or shredded vegetables, pickles and assorted condiments

Shawarma (Arabic: شاورما) is a Levan-

tine Arab meat preparation, where lamb, chicken, turkey, beef, veal, or mixed meats are placed on a spit (commonly a vertical spit in restaurants), and may be grilled for as long as a day. Shavings are cut off the block of meat for serving, and the remainder of the block of meat is kept heated on the rotating spit. Although it can be served in shavings on a plate (generally with accompaniments), *shawarma* also refers to a sandwich or wrap made with *shawarma* meat. *Shawarma* is eaten with *tabbouleh*, *fattoush*, taboon bread, tomato, and cucumber. Toppings include *tahini*, *hummus*, pickled turnips and amba. It is now a fast-food staple worldwide.

Etymology

The Arabic word *shawarma* (Arabic: شاورما *Shāwirmā* Egyptian Arabic: [ʃæˈwermæ], Levantine: [ʃaːˈwɪrma, ʃaːˈwerme], Gulf: [ʃɑːˈwɪrmɐ]...) comes from the Turkish word *çevirme* [tʃeviɾˈme] "turning", and has Shawarma origins in Anatolia, Turkey.

It is similar to the dish called *döner kebab*, "turning kebab", in Turkish, and the Greek *gyros*, "turned", formerly called ντονέρ /doˈner/. A related Armenian dish is *tarna*, literally meaning "to turn".

Preparation

Turkey shawarma in Jerusalem

Shawarma is made by alternately stacking strips of fat and pieces of seasoned meat (beef, lamb or marinated chicken) on a stick. An onion, a tomato, or a halved lemon is sometimes placed at the top of the stack for additional flavoring. The meat is roasted slowly on all sides as the spit rotates in front of, or over, a flame for hours (see rotisserie). Traditionally, a wood fire was used; currently, a gas flame is common. While specialty restaurants might offer two or more meat selections, some establishments have just one skewer.

While cooking, the meat is shaved off the stack with a large knife, an electric knife or a small circular saw, dropping to a circular tray below to be retrieved.

Shawarma is eaten as a fast food, made up into a sandwich wrap with pita bread or rolled up in an Armenian Lavash flatbread together with vegetables and dressing. A variety of vegetables come with the *shawarma* which include: cucumber, onion, tomato, lettuce, eggplant, parsley, pickled turnips, pickled gherkins, pickles, and cabbage. One has the option to get French fries in some countries, including: Jordan, Syria, Lebanon, Israel, Turkey, Egypt, Saudi Arabia, also countries in Europe such as Romania, Germany, Bulgaria and the U.K. Other options include thick cut French fries served inside the lavash to help soak up the sauce and juices keeping them inside the wrap.

Dressings include: tahini (or tahina), Amba sauce (pickled mango with Chilbeh), hummus, or flavored with vinegar and spices such as cardamom, cinnamon, and nutmeg. Chicken shawarma is served with garlic mayonnaise, toum (garlic sauce), pomegranate concentrate, or skhug (a hot chili sauce). Once the shawarma is made, it might be dipped in the fat dripping from the skewer and then briefly seared against the flame.

In Saudi Arabia, goat is as common as beef or lamb. Less common alternatives include fish and sausage. Some shawarma stores use hot dog buns or baguettes, but most have pita and lavash.

Source http://en.wikipedia.org/wiki/Shawarma

Sicilian pizza

The *Pizzòlu* in the province of Siracusa

Origin

Place of origin	Italy
Region or state	Sicily
Type	Pizza

Sicilian pizza is pizza prepared in a manner that originated in Sicily, Italy. In the US, the phrase *Sicilian pizza* is often synonymous with thick-crust or deep-dish pizza.

History of Sicilian pizza

Pizza was a popular dish in western Sicily by the mid-19th century . The version with tomatoes was not available prior to the 17th century . It eventually reached America in a slightly altered form, with thicker crust and a rectangular shape.

Pizza in Sicily

Traditional Sicilian pizza is typically thick crusted and rectangular. It is often topped with onions, anchovies, tomatoes, herbs, and strong cheese such as Toma . Other versions do not include cheese. The Sicilian methods of making pizza are linked to local culture and country traditions, so there are differences in preparing pizza even among the Sicilian regions of Palermo, Catania, Siracusa and Messina.

The *Sfincione* (or *Sfinciuni* in Sicilian language) is a very common variety of pizza that originated in the province of Palermo. Unlike the more familiar Neapolitan pizza, it is typically rectangular, with more dough, sauce and cheese. An authentic recipe often calls for herbs, onion, tomato sauce, strong cheese, and anchovies . The sauce is sometimes placed on top of the toppings to prevent it from soaking into the thick dough.

In the province of Siracusa, especially in Solarino and Sortino, the *Pizzòlu* is a kind of round stuffed pizza.

Sicilian pizza in the US

In the United States, a Sicilian pizza is typically a square pie with dough over an inch thick. It is derived from the *Sfinciuni* and was introduced in the States by the first Italian (Sicilian) immigrants. Thick-crust and deep-dish pizza is often mistakenly called *Sicilian pizza* in the US. Sicilian-style pizza is popular in Italian-American enclaves throughout Boston, Detroit, Portland, Connecticut, New York and New Jersey, and also in Utica, New York, a city whose sizable Italian-American population is predominantly Sicilian. Detroit-style pizza is a direct descendent of Sicilian pizza.

Source http://en.wikipedia.org/wiki/Sicilian_pizza

Smoke's Poutinerie

Industry	Restaurants
Founded	Toronto, Ontario (2008)
Founder(s)	Ryan Smolkin
Headquarters	Toronto, Ontario, Canada
Products	Poutine

Website SmokesPoutinerie.com

Smoke's Poutinerie is a Canadian nation-wide poutine franchise founded by entrepreneur Ryan Smolkin. It is the first poutine-exclusive restaurant in Toronto.

History

Founded in Toronto in 2008, the restaurant is named after owner Ryan Smolkin. Smolkin was inspired by Montreal restaurant La Banquise, which serves many different kinds of poutine. Smolkin frequents La Banquise whenever he visits Montreal.

The restaurant offers over 22 different kinds of poutine and has locations in Toronto, St. Catharines, London, Guelph, Winnipeg, Ottawa, Waterloo, Mont-Tremblant, Fredericton, Halifax, Montreal, and St. John's and with new franchises in the works in Hamilton, Kingston, Edmonton, Vancouver and Whistler.

Source http://en.wikipedia.org/wiki/Smoke's_Poutinerie

Souvlaki

A serving of pork **souvlakia** with fried garlic bread and lemons

Pair of firedogs with zoomorphic finials, 17th century BC, Akrotiri.

Souvlaki grilling at the 2011 Greek Festival in Piscataway, New Jersey

Souvlaki (Greek: σουβλάκι, [suˈvlaki]) plural **souvlakia** is a popular Greek fast food consisting of small pieces of meat and sometimes vegetables grilled on a skewer. It may be served on the skewer for eating out of hand, in a pita sandwich with garnishes and sauces, or on a dinner plate, often with fried potatoes.

The meat usually used in Greece and Cyprus is pork, although chicken and lamb may also be used. In other countries and for tourists, souvlaki may be made with meats such as lamb, beef, chicken and sometimes fish (especially swordfish).

The word *souvlaki* is a diminutive of the Greek σούβλα *souvla* 'skewer', itself borrowed from Latin *subula*.

History

Souvlaki is attested in Greece since antiquity and it was known with the name ὀβελίσκος (*obeliskos*), dim. of ὀβελός (*obelos*), "spit", mentioned amongst others in the works of Aristophanes, Xenophon, Aristotle, etc. A meat and bread recipe which resembles the way pita souvlaki is served today, with pita bread was also attested by Athenaeus in Deipnosophistae and called the plate *kandaulos*. The skewered meat, kebab-like recipe, existed as a favourite in ancient Greece at Archaic times, as the earliest references are attested in Homer. However, excavations held in Akrotiri on the Greek island of Santorini by professor Christos G. Doumas, unearthed firedogs (stone sets of barbecue for skewers; Greek: κρατευταί - *krateutai*) used before the 17th century BCE. In each pair of the supports, the receptions for the spits are found in absolute equivalence, while the line of small openings in the base formed a mechanism to supply the coals with oxygen so that they remained alight during its use.

Kalamaki

Kalamaki (*little reed*) is a synonym for souvlaki proper in Athens, in order to differentiate it from other forms of souvlaki.

For *kalamaki*, the meat is cubed into 1-inch chunks, marinated overnight in lemon juice and olive oil along with Greek herbs and spices such as oregano and on occasion thyme, etc., in a pinch. Then it is skewered on wooden skewers (the "little reeds"), broiled over charcoal, and generously salted and peppered.

The terminology used in Thessaloniki and most parts of northern Greece is different, the word *kalamaki* is derided since the item is called consistently a *souvlaki*; a joke suggests that any Athenian or other southerner visiting Thessaloniki asks for a *kalamaki* will be mockingly given a drinking straw (also called "kalamaki").

Souvlaki-merida

Mérida means *portion*. While souvlaki/kalamaki is eaten plain on hand as a fast food, it is also served as a full plate, served with fried potatoes, vegetables, sauce, and quartered pita bread. Usually it consists of the ingredients of a souvlaki-pita (see below), but laid out on a plate, instead of wrapped together for eating on hand.

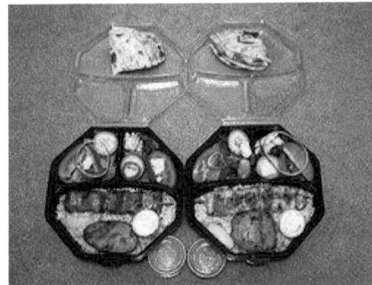

Souvlaki Platters for take-out

Pita

Pita is a form of unleavened flat round bread with a diameter of approximately 15 cm, used to wrap souvlaki or gyros. It comes pre-baked and will additionally be grilled on the meat drippings just before serving, unless the customer requests it not to be.

Souvlaki-pita

Souvlaki sandwich

This course consists of souvlaki meat garnished with sliced tomatoes and onions, sauced with tzatziki, and wrapped in a lightly grilled pita. When chicken is used instead of pork meat, tzatziki and onions are replaced with a special sauce and lettuce to be compatible with its taste; Various other garnishes and sauces are possible, including shredded lettuce, paprika, fried potatoes, ketchup, and mustard, though these are considered heretical by purists. In Athens and southern Greece it is called pita-kalamaki. Any of these components may not be included, at the request of the customer. Hungry customers may occasionally request a two-pita wrapping (*diplopito*) and/or a double meat serving (*dikalamo*).

A difference between southern and northern Greece is that "souvlaki ap'ola" (souvlaki "with everything") typically includes tzatziki sauce in Athens, unlike Thessaloniki.

In Corfu, a special tomato sauce is added to souvlaki, plainly called "red sauce" (κόκκινη σάλτσα).

Gyros-pita

Similar to souvlaki pita. The souvlaki is replaced by gyros (kebab usually made of pork or chicken). This is also nicknamed *souvlaki* in common speech due to its resemblance to the above, and because gyros meat is rotated on a mechanical skewer.

Gyros-merida

Like souvlaki merida, gyros merida is the ingredients of a gyros-pita, served on a plate. Replace kalamaki with gyros. Gyros merida is the only related plate that is never called souvlaki.

Cypriot souvlaki

In Cyprus, souvlaki refers to the small chunks of meat on a skewer, as well as the whole package of it being wrapped up in bread and salad, etc. A large pita is used, and it has a pocket in the middle so it is not wrapped around the meat and salad. This contains lamb, pork or more recently chicken souvlaki and/or sheftalia, with tomatoes and cucumbers and white cabbage mixed within. Lettuce is rarely added, only for tourists. Raw onion and parsley are very popular with souvlakia in Cyprus, as are pickled green chili peppers. Like all grilled meat dishes in Cyprus, souvlakia are always accompanied by fresh lemon halves or quarters, and plain thick yogurt or tzatziki are also popular accompaniments. The meat is cut into slightly larger chunks in Cyprus, and more ingredients are stuffed into the pita. The portion sizes are normal and "reinforced"-enischimeni. The pita in which souvlakia are served is a little thicker than the flat pita available in other countries.

Source http://en.wikipedia.org/wiki/Souvlaki

Spizzico

Spizzico is an Italian franchise quick-service pizza restaurant chain, which belongs to the company Autogrill operating world-wide. There are currently 169 restaurants in Italy, Greece, Switzerland, France and the USA. Typical locations include motorways, airports, railway stations, high streets, shopping malls and trade fairs. Often Spizzico restaurants share the same building with other fast food restaurant chains run by Autogrill. Spizzico's staple are slices of large pizzas (far larger than the regular pizzeria-served or home delivered ones) which are sold in one-eights, -fourths or halves with a variable number of dressings (some fixed, some seasonal, some special), along with pizza slices calzones, fried panzerotti and other fast food fares such as fries, soft drink, salads, and desserts are available. Meals can be eaten in the restaurant or take-away.

Source http://en.wikipedia.org/wiki/Spizzico

Street food

A food stall in Seoul, South Korea. Steamed corn, grilled chestnuts and tteok (white rice cake), dried persimmons, cuttlefish, squid, octopus and filefish.

Sorry, your browser either has JavaScript disabled or does not have any supported player.
You can download the clip or download a player to play the clip in your browser. A video clip of a vendor making churros in Colombia.

Candied fruit for sale in streets of Tianjin, China

Street food is ready-to-eat food or drink sold in a street or other public place, such as a market or fair, by a hawker or vendor, often from a portable stall. While some street foods are regional, many are not, having spread beyond their region of origin. Most street foods are also classed as both finger food and fast food, and are cheaper on average than restaurant meals. According to a 2007 study from the Food and Agriculture Organization, 2.5 billion people eat street food every day.

Today, people may purchase street food for a number of reasons, such as to obtain reasonably priced and flavorful food in a sociable setting, to experience ethnic cuisines and also for nostalgia. Historically, in places such as ancient Rome, street food was purchased because the urban poor did not have kitchens in their homes.

Street food in China: chuanr (roasted meat on skewers) of starfish, seahorse and scorpions.

History

Small fried fish were a street food in ancient Greece, although Theophrastus held the custom of street food in low regard. Evidence of a large number of street food vendors were discovered during the excavation of Pompeii. Street food was widely utilized by poor urban residents of ancient Rome whose tenement homes did not have ovens or hearths, with chickpea soup being one of the common meals, along with bread and grain paste. In ancient China, where street foods generally catered to the poor, wealthy residents would send servants to buy street foods and bring meals back for their masters to eat in their homes.

A traveling Florentine reported in the late 1300s that in Cairo, people carried picnic cloths made of raw hide to spread on the streets and eat their meals of lamb kebabs, rice and fritters that they had purchased from street vendors. In Renaissance Turkey, many crossroads saw vendors selling "fragrant bites of hot meat", including chicken and lamb that had been spit roasted.

Aztec marketplaces had vendors that sold beverages such as *atolli* ("a gruel made from maize dough"), almost 50 types of tamales (with ingredients that ranged from the meat of turkey, rabbit, gopher, frog, and fish to fruits, eggs, and maize flowers), as well as insects and stews. After Spanish colonization of Peru and importation of European food stocks like wheat, sugarcane and livestock, most commoners continued primarily to eat their traditional diets, but did add grilled beef hearts sold by street vendors. Some of Lima's 19th century street vendors such as "Erasmo, the 'negro' sango vendor" and Na Aguedita are still remembered today.

During the American Colonial period, street vendors sold "pepper pot soup" (tripe) "oysters, roasted corn ears, fruit and sweets," with oysters being a low-priced commodity until the 1910s when overfishing caused prices to rise. As of 1707, after previous restrictions that had limited their operating hours, street food vendors had been banned in New York City. Many women of African descent made their living selling street foods in America in the eighteenth and nineteenth centuries; with products ranging from fruit, cakes and nuts in Savannah, to coffee, biscuits, pralines and other sweets in New Orleans. In the 1800s street food vendors in Transylvania sold gingerbread-nuts, cream mixed with corn, and bacon and other meat fried on tops of ceramic vessels with hot coals inside.

French fries probably originated as a street food consisting of fried strips of potato in Paris in the 1840s. Cracker Jack started as one of many street food exhibits at the Columbian Exposition. Street foods in Victorian London included tripe, pea soup, pea pods in butter, whelk, prawns and jellied eels.

Originally brought to Japan by Chinese immigrants about a hundred years ago, ramen began as a street food for laborers and students, but soon became a "national dish" and even acquired regional variations. The street food culture of South East Asia today was heavily influenced by coolie workers imported from China during the late 1800s. In Thailand, although street food did not become popular among native Thai people until the early 1960s when the urban population began to grow rapidly, by the 1970s it had "displaced home-cooking."

Street food around the world

Street food vending is found around the

Street vendor of snack foods in Nepal

world, but has variations within both regions and cultures. For example, Dorling Kindersley describes the street food of Viet Nam as being "fresh and lighter than many of the cuisines in the area" and "draw[ing] heavily on herbs, chile peppers and lime", while street food of Thailand is "fiery" and "pungent with shrimp paste ... and fish sauce" with New York City's signature street food being the hot dog, although the offerings in New York also range from "spicy Middle Eastern falafel or Jamaican jerk chicken to Belgian waffles" In Hawaii, the local street food tradition of "Plate Lunch" (rice, macaroni salad and a portion of meat) was inspired by the *bento* of the Japanese who had been brought to Hawaii as plantation workers.

Cultural and economic aspects

The presence of street food vendors in New York City throughout much of its history, such as these circa 1906, are credited with helping support the city's rapid growth.

Differences in culture, social stratification and history have resulted in different patterns how family street vendor enterprises are traditionally created and run in different areas of the world. For example, few women are street vendors in Bangladesh, but women predominate in the trade in Nigeria and Thailand.

Doreen Fernandez says that Filipino cultural attitudes towards meals is one "cultural factor operating in the street food phenomenon" in the Philippines because eating "food out in the open, in the market or street or field" is "not at odds with the meal indoors or at home" where "there is no special room for dining".

Walking on the street while eating is considered rude in some cultures, such as Japan. In India, Henrike Donner wrote about a "marked distinction between food that could be eaten outside, especially by women," and the food prepared and eaten at home; with some non-Indian food being too "strange" or tied too closely to non-vegetarian preparation methods to be made at home.

In Tanzania's Dar es Salaam region, street food vendors produce economic benefits beyond their families by purchasing local fresh foods which has led to a proliferation of urban gardens and small scale farms. In the United States, street food vendors are credited with supporting New York City's rapid growth by supplying meals for the city's merchants and workers. Proprietors of street food in the United States have had a goal of upward mobility, moving from selling on the street to their own shops. However, in Mexico, an increase in street vendors has been seen as a sign of deteriorating economic conditions in which food vending is the only employment opportunity that unskilled labor who have migrated from rural areas to urban areas are able to find.

In 2002, Coca Cola reported that China, India and Nigeria were some of its fastest growing markets; markets where the company's expansion efforts included training and equipping mobile street vendors to sell its products.

Health and safety

Despite concerns about contamination at street food vendors, the incidence of such is low with multiple studies showing rates comparable to restaurants.

As early as the 14th century, government officials oversaw street food vendor activities.

With the increasing pace of globalization and tourism, the safety of street food has become one of the major concerns of public health, and a focus for governments and scientists to raise public awarenesses. In the United Kingdom, the FSA provides comprehensive guidances of food safety for the vendors, traders and retailers of the street food sector. Other effective ways of enhancing the safety of street foods are through mystery shopping programs, through training and rewarding programs to vendors, through regulatory governing and membership management programs, or through technical testing programs. In 2002 a sampling of 511 street foods in Ghana by the World Health Organization showed that most had microbial counts within the accepted limits, and a different sampling of 15 street foods in Calcutta showed that they were "nutritionally well balanced", providing roughly 200Kcal of energy per rupee of cost.

In the late 1990s the United Nations and other organizations began to recognize that street vendors had been an underutilized method of delivering fortified foods to populations and in 2007, the UN Food and Agriculture Organization recommended considering methods of adding nutrients and supplements to street foods that are commonly consumed by the particular culture.

Source http://en.wikipedia.org/wiki/Street_food

Street food of Mumbai

A street vendor prepares Bhelpuri in Mumbai

Street food of Mumbai is the food sold by hawkers from portable stalls in Mumbai. It is one of the characteristics of the city. The city is known for its distinctive street foods. Although street food is common all over India, street food in Mumbai is noted because people from all economic classes eat on the roadside almost round the clock and it is sometimes felt that the taste of street food is better than restaurants in the city. Many Mumbaikars like a small snack on the road in the evening. People of Mumbai cut across barriers of class, religion, gender and ethnicity are passionate about street food. Street food vendors are credited by some for developing the city's food culture. Street food in Mumbai is relatively inexpensive as compared to restaurants and vendors tend to be clustered around crowded areas such as colleges and railway stations.

Variety

Vada Pav is noted as the most popular street food in Mumbai. Other noted street foods in Mumbai include Panipuri, Bhelpuri, Sevpuri, Dahipuri, Sandwiches, Ragda-pattice, Pav Bhaji, idlis and Dosas, all of which are vegetarian. In terms of non-vegetarian offerings omelette-pav, kebabs and fish are found on Mumbai streets. The amount of variety of street food is attributed to the cosmopolitan culture of the city. In the 1980s Indianised Chinese food was an emerging trend on Mumbai streets.

Kulfi (a type of ice cream) and gola (type of ice cone) are among the desserts and coolants found on Mumbai streets. Apart from snacks, Mumbai has several juice and milkshake bars on the roadside that offer a variety of juices and milkshakes. Fresh Sugarcane juice vendors are synonymous with Mumbai roads and offer a cheap form of refreshment. Tea vendors cycle around the city, selling the beverage hot on the streets. Street vendors normally remain unaffected by general strike calls and do business all year around. Paan, a betel leaf preparation eaten as a mouth freshener post meals in India is also sold at Mumbai's roadside stalls.

Areas and spread

Lanes with a sizable cluster of street food stalls are known as "Khau Galli's" locally. Girgaum Chowpatty beach is noted for its Bhelpuri and kulfi. Street vendors at Nariman Point, one of the city's financial hubs, do brisk business during the lunch hour.

Mumbai's street food has made its way into kitchens of restaurants in the city, including five star hotels. In fact, restaurants in various parts of the world have incorporated Mumbai's street food into their menu cards. Homegrown fast food companies that serve street food in Mumbai have been launched in recent years.

Controversies

Many people, especially from elite classes, avoid eating on the roadside because of hygiene issues. Restaurants and hotels have capitalised on this phenomenon by offering street food to their clientele. As many of the street food vendors are North Indian, street food vendors were targeted during the 2008 attacks on North Indian migrants in Maharashtra. A large number of hawkers trade illegally, without mandatory permits from the local municipality, by bribing officials. Drives to evict hawkers are regularly held, though the hawkers return after a short period of time. Equipment and other goods seized from illegal hawkers are returned by the municipality after the hawker pays a fine.

In 2007, the Supreme Court ruled in a case against illegal hawking by asking the municipality to demarcate 230 areas in the city as legal hawking zones, a number that was later increased to 1700 areas; this is still to be implemented. A news report in 2009 claimed that no hawking licenses had been issued in Mumbai for 20 years and that out of the estimated 2.5 Lakh (250,000) hawkers in the city only about 17,000 had a valid license.

A controversy emerged in 2011, when a panipuri vendor from Thane was filmed urinating into a container that was also used to serve the customers. The event led to a public uproar and a major political drama in the city; Shiv Sena and Maharashtra Navnirman Sena members again attacked North Indians, targeting the Panipuri and Bhelpuri sellers of Mumbai and Thane. The vendor concerned was arrested by the police and taken to court, which fined him and thereafter let him off with a warning. After action against all panipuri vendors across the city by political parties, the vendor in question, who himself was in the business for 15 years, chose to give up the trade altogether and take up a job with a private security agency.

Source http://en.wikipedia.org/wiki/Street_food_of_Mumbai

Taco

Carnitas tacos

Origin

| **Place of origin** | Mexico |

Details

| **Type** | Finger food |
| **Main ingredient(s)** | Tortillas, meat, vegetables, cheese |

Barbacoa tacos.

A **taco** (pron.: /ˈtɑːkoʊ/, pron.: /ˈtækoʊ/) Nahuatl: *tlacopan* [tɬa.ˈko.pan] is a traditional Mexican dish composed of a corn or wheat tortilla folded or rolled around a filling. A taco can be made with a variety of fillings, including beef, pork, chicken, seafood, vegetables and cheese, allowing for great versatility and variety. A taco is generally eaten without utensils and is often accompanied by garnishes such as salsa, avocado or guacamole, cilantro, tomatoes, minced meat, onions and lettuce.

Etymology

According to the Real Academia Española, publisher of *Diccionario de la Lengua Española*, the word *taco* describes a typical Mexican dish of a maize tortilla folded around food ("Tortilla de maíz enrollada con algún alimento dentro, típica de México"). The original sense of the word is of a "plug" or "wad" used to fill a hole ("Pedazo de madera, metal u otra materia, corto y grueso, que se encaja en algún hueco"). The Online Etymological Dictionary defines *taco* as a "tortilla filled with spiced meat" and describes its etymology as derived from Mexican Spanish, "light lunch," literally, "plug, wadding." The sense development from "plug" may have taken place among Mexican silver miners, who used explosive charges in plug form consisting of a paper wrapper and gunpowder filling.

History

The taco predates the arrival of Europeans in Mexico. There is anthropological evidence that the indigenous people living in the lake region of the Valley of Mexico traditionally ate tacos filled with small fish. Writing at the time of the Spanish conquistadors, Bernal Díaz del Castillo documented the first taco feast enjoyed by Europeans, a meal which Hernán Cortés arranged for his captains in Coyoacán. It is not clear why the Spanish used their word, "taco", to describe this indigenous food.

Traditional tacos

Adobada meat for *tacos al pastor*, carved to order.

Grilled shrimp taco.

There are many traditional varieties of tacos:

Tacos de Asador ("spit" or "grill" tacos) may be composed of any of the following: *carne asada tacos*; ***tacos de***

tripita ("tripe tacos"), grilled until crisp; and, *chorizo asado* (traditional Spanish style sausage). Each type is served on two overlapped small tortillas and sometimes garnished with guacamole, salsa, onions, and cilantro. Also prepared on the grill is a sandwiched taco called *mulita* ("little mule") made with meat served between two tortillas and garnished with Oaxaca style cheese. *"Mulita"* is used to describe these types of sandwiched tacos in the Northern States of Mexico, while they are known as Gringa in the Mexican south and are prepared using wheat flour tortillas. Tacos may also be served with salsa.

Tacos de Cabeza or head tacos, in which there is a flat punctured metal plate from which steam emerges to cook the head of the cow. These include: *Cabeza*, a serving of the muscles of the head; *Sesos* ("brains"); *Lengua* ("tongue"); *Cachete* ("cheeks"); *Trompa* ("lips"); and, *Ojo* ("eye"). Tortillas for these tacos are warmed on the same steaming plate for a different consistency. These tacos are typically served in pairs, and also include salsa, onion and cilantro with occasional use of guacamole.

Tacos de Cazo for which a metal bowl filled with lard is typically used as a deep-fryer. Meats for these types of tacos typically include: *Tripa* ("tripe", usually from a pig instead of a cow); *Suadero* (tender beef cuts), *Carnitas* and *Buche* (Literally, *"crop"*, as in *bird's crop*; here, it is fried pig's esophagus.)

Tacos sudados ("sweaty tacos") are made by filling soft tortillas with a spicy meat mixture, then placing them in a basket covered with cloth. The covering keeps the tacos warm and traps steam ("sweat") which softens them.

Tacos Al pastor/De Adobada ("shepherd style") are made of thin pork steaks seasoned with adobo seasoning, then skewered and overlapped on one another on a vertical rotisserie cooked and flame-broiled as it spins.

Tacos dorados (fried tacos, literally, "golden tacos") called *flautas* ("flute", because of the shape), or taquitos, for which the tortillas are filled with pre-cooked shredded chicken, beef or bar-

Tacos de suadero (grey) and chorizo (red).

bacoa, rolled into an elongated cylinder and deep-fried until crisp. They are sometimes cooked in a microwave oven or broiled.

Tacos de pescado ("**fish tacos**") originated in Baja California in Mexico, where they consist of grilled or fried fish, lettuce or cabbage, pico de gallo, and a sour cream or citrus/mayonnaise sauce, all placed on top of a corn or flour tortilla. In the United States, they were first popularized by the Rubio's fast-food chain, and remain most popular in California, Colorado, and Washington. In California, they are often found at street vendors, and a regional variation is to serve them with cabbage and coleslaw dressing on top.

Tacos de camarones ("**shrimp tacos**") also originated in Baja California in Mexico. Grilled or fried shrimp are used, usually with the same accompaniments as fish tacos: lettuce or cabbage, pico de gallo, avocado and a sour cream or citrus/mayonnaise sauce, all placed on top of a corn or flour tortilla.

As an accompaniment to tacos, many taco stands will serve whole or sliced red radishes, lime slices, salt, pickled or grilled chilis (hot peppers), and occasionally cucumber slices, or grilled cambray onions.

United States and Canada

Hard-shell tacos

Beginning from the early part of the twentieth century, various styles of tacos have become popular in the United States and Canada. An early appearance of a description of the taco in the United States in English was in a 1914

Hard-shell taco, made with a prefabricated shell.

cookbook, *California Mexican-Spanish Cookbook*, by Bertha Haffner Ginger. The style that has become most common is the hard-shell, U-shaped version described in a cookbook, *The good life: New Mexican food*, authored by Fabiola Cabeza de Vaca Gilbert and published in Santa Fe, New Mexico in 1949. These have been sold by restaurants and by fast food chains. Even non-Mexican oriented fast food restaurants have sold tacos. Mass production of this type of taco was encouraged by the invention of devices to hold the tortillas in the U-shape as they were deep-fried. A patent for such a device was issued to New York restaurateur Juvenico Maldonado in 1950, based on his patent filing of 1947 (U.S. Patent No. 2,506,305). Such tacos are crisp-fried corn tortillas filled with seasoned ground beef, cheese, lettuce, and sometimes tomato, onion, salsa, sour cream, and avocado or guacamole.

Soft-shell tacos

Traditionally, soft-shelled tacos referred to corn tortillas that were cooked to a softer state than a hard taco - usually by grilling or steaming. More recently the term has come to include flour tortilla based tacos mostly from large manufacturers and restaurant chains. In this context, *soft tacos* are tacos made with wheat flour tortillas and filled with the same ingredients as a hard taco.

Puffy tacos, taco kits, breakfast tacos and tacodillas

Since at least 1978, a variation called the "**puffy taco**" has been popular. *Henry's Puffy Tacos*, opened by Henry

Veggie tacos of U.S.

Lopez in San Antonio, Texas, claims to have invented the variation, in which uncooked corn tortillas (flattened balls of masa dough) are quickly fried in hot oil until they expand and become "puffy". Fillings are similar to hard-shell versions. Restaurants offering this style of taco have since appeared in other Texas cities, as well as in California, where Henry's brother, Arturo Lopez, opened *Arturo's Puffy Taco* in Whittier, not long after Henry's opened. Henry's continues to thrive, managed by the family's second generation.

Kits are available at grocery and convenience stores and usually consist of taco shells (corn tortillas already fried in a U-shape), seasoning mix and taco sauce. Commercial vendors for the home market also market soft taco kits with tortillas instead of taco shells.

The breakfast taco, found in Tex-Mex cuisine, is filled with meat, eggs, or cheese, with other ingredients.

The tacodilla contains melted cheese in between the two folded tortillas, thus resembling a quesadilla.

Indian tacos

Frybread taco

Indian tacos, sometimes known as *Navajo tacos* but served in various parts of the American West and Midwest, are made using frybread instead of tortillas. They are commonly served at pow-wows, festivals, and other gatherings.

Source http://en.wikipedia.org/wiki/Taco

Takoyaki

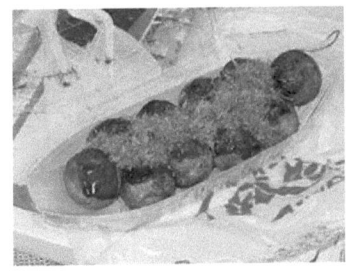

A *boat* of takoyaki

Origin

Place of origin	Japan
Region or state	Japanese-speaking areas

Details

Course	Snack
Main ingredient(s)	batter, octopus, tempura scraps (*tenkasu*), pickled ginger, green onion

Takoyaki (たこ焼き *or* 蛸焼) is a ball-shaped Japanese snack made of a wheat flour-based batter and cooked in a special takoyaki pan. It is typically filled with minced or diced octopus, tempura scraps (*tenkasu*), pickled ginger, and green onion. Takoyaki are brushed with takoyaki sauce, a sauce similar to Worcestershire sauce, and mayonnaise. The takoyaki is then sprinkled with green laver (*aonori*) and shavings of dried bonito (*katsuobushi*). There are many variations to the takoyaki recipe. For example, ponzu i.e. soy sauce with *dashi* and citrus vinegar, goma-dare i.e. sesame-and-vinegar sauce or vinegared dashi.

Takoyaki was first popularized in Osaka, where a street vendor named Tomekichi Endo is credited with its invention in 1935. Takoyaki inspired by Akashiyaki, a small round dumpling from the city of Akashi in Hyōgo Prefecture made of an egg-rich batter and octopus. Takoyaki was initially popular in the Kansai region, but later spread to the Kantō region and other areas of Japan. Takoyaki is associated with *yatai* street food stalls, but there are many well-established takoyaki specialty restaurants, particularly in the Kansai region. Takoyaki is now sold at commercial outlets, such as supermarkets and 24-hour convenience stores.

Yaki is derived from "*yaku*" (焼く) which is one of the cooking methods in Japanese cuisine, meaning "to fry or grill", and can be found in the names of other Japanese cuisine items such as *teppanyaki*, *yakitori*, *teriyaki* and *sukiyaki*.

Cooking takoyaki

Takoyaki served with mayonnaise
Takoyaki served with grated *daikon* and *tsuyu*
A takoyaki yatai in Nishinari-ku, Osaka

Takoyaki pan

A takoyaki pan (たこ焼き器 *takoyaki-ki*) or—much more rarely—*takoyaki-*

nabe (たこ焼き鍋) is typically griddle

Square takoyaki pan with 16 molds

made of cast iron with half-spherical molds. The heavy iron evenly heats the takoyaki, which are turned with a pick during the cooking process to pull the uncooked batter to the base of the rounded cavity. Commercial gas-fueled takoyaki cookers are used at Japanese festivals or by street vendors. For home use, electric versions resemble a hotplate; stovetop versions are also available.

Source http://en.wikipedia.org/wiki/Takoyaki

Tamale

Wrapped and unwrapped *tamales Oaxaqueños* from Oaxaca, Mexico, filled with *mole negro* and chicken

Origin

Place of origin	Mexico
Region or state	Central America

Details

Course	Main course
Serving temperature	Usually hot
Main ingredient(s)	*Masa*, corn husks, banana leaves
Approximate calories per serving	100

A **tamale** (Spanish: *tamal* [taˈmal], from Nahuatl: *tamalli* [taˈmal:i]) — also **tamales** — is a traditional Mesoamerican dish made of masa (a starchy dough, usually corn-based), which is steamed or boiled in a leaf wrapper. The wrapping is discarded before eating. Tamales can be filled with meats, cheeses, fruits, vegetables, chilies or any preparation according to taste, and both the filling and the cooking liquid may be seasoned.

Tamales have been traced back to the Ancient Maya people, who prepared them for feasts as early as the Preclassic period (1200-250 BC). Maya people called their corn tortillas and tamales both *utah* [utah].

Tamales originated in Mesoamerica as early as 8000 to 5000 BC. Aztec and Maya civilizations, as well as the Olmeca and Tolteca before them, used tamales as portable food, often to support their armies, but also for hunters and travelers. Tamale use in the Inca Empire had been reported long before the Spanish visited the New World.

The diversity of native languages in Mesoamerica led to a number of local words for the *tamale*, many of which remain in use.

Aztec tamales

English	Nahuatl	IPA
tamale	tamalli	[taˈmal:i]
fruit tamale	xocotamalli	[ʃokotaˈmal:i]
fish tamale	michpiltamalli	[mitʃpiɬtaˈmal:i]
worm tamale	ocuiltamalli	[okʷiɬtaˈmal:i]

Mayas

In the pre-Columbian era, the Mayas ate tamales.

Maya tamales		First component			
English	Mayan	IPA	English	Mayan	
tamale	uah	[uah]			
maize tamale	uia	[uia]			
iguana tamale	huh uah	[huh uah]	iguana	huh	

Modern Mexico

A batch of Mexican tamales in the *tamalera*

In Mexico, tamales begin with a dough made from nixtamalized corn (hominy), called *masa*, or a *masa* mix, such as Maseca, and lard or vegetable shortening. Tamales are generally wrapped in corn husks or plantain leaves before cooking, depending on the region from which they come. They usually have a sweet or savory filling and are usually steamed until firm.

Tamales are a favorite comfort food in Mexico, eaten as both breakfast and dinner, and often accompanied by hot *atole* or *champurrado* and *arroz con leche* (rice pudding) or maize-based beverages of indigenous origin. Street vendors can be seen serving them from huge, steaming, covered pots (*tamaleras*) or *ollas*.

In Mexico City, the *tamal* is substantial enough to keep a person satisfied until Mexico's traditional late lunch hour.

The most common fillings are pork and chicken, in either red or green *salsa* or *mole*. Another traditional variation is to add pink-colored sugar to the corn mix and fill it with raisins or other dried fruit and make a sweet *tamal de dulce*. Commonly, a few "deaf", or fillingless, tamales (*tamales sordos*), might be served with refried beans and coffee.

The cooking of tamales is traditionally done in batches of tens if not hundreds, and the ratio of filling to dough (and the coarseness of the filling) is a matter of preference.

Instead of corn husks, banana or plantain leaves are used in tropical parts of the country, such as Oaxaca, Chiapas, Veracruz, and the Yucatán Peninsula. These tamales are rather square in shape, often very large— 15 inches (40 cm) or more— and thick; a local name for these in Veracruz is *zacahuil*. Another less-common variation is to use chard or avocado leaves, which can be eaten along with the filling.

Tamales became one of the representatives of Mexican culinary tradition in Europe, being one of the first samples of the culture the Spanish conquistadors took back to Spain as proof of civilization, according to Fray Juan de Zumarraga.

Today, tamales are often eaten during festivities, such as Christmas, the Day of the Dead, Las Posadas, La Candelaria Day (February 2) and Mexican Independence Day.

In the Philippines and Guam, which were governed by Spain as a province of Mexico, different forms of "tamales" exist. Some are made with a dough derived from ground rice and are filled with seasoned chicken or pork with the addition of peanuts and other seasonings such as sugar. In some places, such as the Pampanga and Batangas provinces, the tamales are wrapped in banana leaves, but sweet corn varieties from the Visayas region are wrapped in corn husks similar to the sweet corn tamales of the American Southwest and Mexico. Because of the work involved in the preparation of tamales, they usually only appear during the special holidays or other big celebrations. Various *tamal* recipes have practically disappeared under the pressures of modern life and the ease of fast food. The variety found in Guam, known as *tamales guiso* is made with corn masa and wrapped in corn husks, and as with the Philippine tamales, are clear evidence of the influence of the galleon trade that occurred between the ports of Manila and Acapulco.

Central America

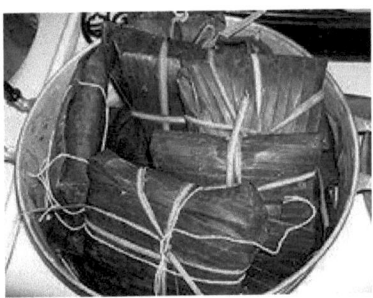

Nicaraguan *nacatamales*

In Belize, El Salvador, Guatemala, Costa Rica, Honduras, Nicaragua, and Panama, they are also wrapped in plantain leaves. The masa is usually made from *maiz* (dent corn in the US, not sweet corn, which is called *elote*). Guatemalan cuisine is known in particular for its hundreds of varieties of tamales; some popular ones include *tamales de gallina* (chicken), *tamales dulces* (sweet), and *tamales de elote* (in Costa Rica, the name can also refer to a type of corn pastry). In Guatemala, a variety of tamales is called *tamales colorados*, which have chicken or pork filling and a tomato-based sauce (*recado*), (hence the *colorado*, which means red). It may also contain olives, red bell pepper, prunes or raisins, capers, and almonds.

The tamale is a staple in Belize, where it is also known by the Spanish name *bollo* or *dukunu*, a green corn tamale. Nicaragua has a large form known as *nacatamales*. In Guatemala, Belize, El Salvador, and Honduras, tamales without filling are served as the bread or starch portion of a meal:
Tamal de elote (made with yellow corn, sometimes with a sweet or dry taste)
Tamal de chipilín (made with chipilín, a green leaf)
Tamal blanco (simple, made with white corn)
During Christmas holidays, tamales made with corn flour are a special treat for Guatemalans and Hondurans. The preparation time of this type of tamale is long, due to the amount of time required to cook down and thicken the flour base.

A *chipilín tamal*

In Panama, where they are considered one of the main national dishes, tamales are fairly large. The most common fillings are chicken, raisins, onions, tomato sauce, and sometimes sweet peas. Pork is also used. Another variation is *tamales de olla*, which are cooked in pots, then served directly onto plates. Tamales are usually served for all special occasions, including weddings and birthday parties, and are always found on the Christmas dinner table.

Tamales in Costa Rica vary according to region and season. Most notable are the varieties from the Central Valley and Guanacaste. One sort of tamales, "tamales mudos" (deaf tamales) are typically served during certain festivities throughout the year. Sweet tamales and corn tamales are popular during Holy Week. Tamales in Costa Rica are typically eaten with Salsa Lizano, a locally prepared Worcester kind of salsa.

South America

Tamales are found in northern Argentina (the provinces of Jujuy, Salta, Catamarca and Tucumán). *Tamales salteños* are made with shredded meat of a boiled lamb or pork head, and corn flour wrapped in *chalas*. *Tamales jujeños* use minced meat and corn and red peppers.

Another version, called a *humita*, is found in Peru, Argentina, Ecuador, and Chile. It can be either savoury or sweet. Sweet ones have raisins, vanilla, oil, and sugar. Salty ones can be filled with cheese (*queso fresco*) or chicken. *Humitas* are cooked in the oven or in the *pachamanca*. They are not tamales by Peruvian and Argentine standards. In Chile, the food known as *humitas* is almost identical to *tamales*.

In Peru and Bolivia the tamales tend to be spicy, large and wrapped in banana leaves. In Lima, common fillings are chicken or pork, usually accompanied by boiled eggs, olives, peanuts or a piece of chili pepper. In other cities, tamales are smaller, wrapped in corn husks and use white instead of yellow corn.

In Brazil, a similar food is called "pamonha", but is not really a tamale and has different origins.

In Venezuela, tamales are called *hallacas*. They are wrapped in plantain leaves and filled with stewed pork, raisins and olives. They are traditionally eaten for Christmas. Also, the Venezuelan *bollos* are similar to tamales, wrapped in corn husks, filled with hot peppers or plain, and eaten as a side dish.

In Colombia, they are wrapped in plantain leaves. The several varieties include the most widely known *tolimense*, as well as *boyacense* and *santandereano*. Like other South American varieties, the most common are very large compared to Mexican tamales — about the size of a softball — and the dough is softer and wetter, with a bright yellow color. A *tamal tolimense* is served for breakfast with hot chocolate, and may contain large pieces of cooked carrot or other vegetables, whole corn kernels, rice, chicken on the bone and/or chunks of pork. Related foods are the *envuelto* and *bollo limpio* which are made of corn, cooked in a corn husk, and resemble a Mexican tamale more closely but have simpler fillings or no filling at all for they are often served to accompany various foods, and the *bollo de yuca* made of yucca flour, also cooked in a corn husk, eaten with butifarra and sour milk (known in the country as *suero costeño*).

Ecuador has a variety of tamales and *humitas*; they can be filled with fresh cheese, pork, chicken or raisins. Ecuadorian tamales are usually wrapped in corn husk or *achira* (canna) leaves.

Caribbean

A *tamal de dulce*, filled with raspberries, raisins and pineapple

In Cuba, before the 1959 Revolution, street vendors sold Mexican-style tamales wrapped in corn husks, usually made without any kind of spicy seasoning. Cuban tamales being identical in form to those made in Mexico City suggests they were brought over to Cuba during the period of intense cultural and musical exchange between Cuba and Mexico, between the 1920s and 1950s.

A well-known Cuban song from the 1950s, "Los Tamalitos de Olga", (a cha-cha-cha sung by Orquesta Aragón) celebrated the delicious tamales sold by a street vendor in Cienfuegos. A peculiarly Cuban invention is the dish known as *tamal en cazuela*, basically consisting of tamale masa with the meat stuffing stirred into the masa, then cooked in a pot on the stove to form a kind of hearty cornmeal porridge.

Corn-husk wrapped tamales are also popular in southeastern Cuba.

Conkies are a corn-based, cookie/tamale-like delicacy popular in the West Indies. The ingredients include corn flour, coconut, sweet potato, and pumpkin, and the dough is steamed in banana leaves. Conkies are thought to have originated in West Africa, where a similar type of kenkey known as *dokompa* is popular in Ghana.

In Barbados, conkies were once associated with the old British colonial celebration of Guy Fawkes Day on November 5. In modern Barbados, they are eaten during Independence Day celebrations on November 30.

In Saint Lucia, it is called *paime*, and is usually associated with *Jounen Kweyol* (Creole Day) which is on the last Sunday of October every year.

In Trinidad and Tobago, it is called a *pastelle* and is associated almost entirely with Christmas. Raisins and capers along with other seasonings are added to the meat filling. The entire thing is wrapped in a banana leaf, bound with twine and steamed. The sweet version is called *paymee*.

In Jamaica, blue drawers, also known as tie leaf or duckunoo, is a similar dish to *tamales de dulce*.

Puerto Ricans prepare a tamale-like food called *pasteles*, which are made with green banana and other starchy meals. Semisweet tamales, wrapped in banana leaves and called *guanimes*, are found in Puerto Rico. *Guanimes* have no meat stuffing, but may have ripe or unripe plantain, cassava, milk, coconut milk, and cinnamon in the sweet corn masa.

United States

Tamales have been eaten in the United States since at least 1893, when they were featured at the World's Columbian Exposition. A tradition of roving tamale sellers was documented in early 20th-century blues music. They are the subject of the well-known 1937 blues/ragtime song "They're Red Hot" by Robert Johnson.

While Mexican-style and other Latin American-style tamales are featured at ethnic restaurants throughout the United

States, there are also some distinctly indigenous styles.

Cherokee tamales, also known as bean bread or "broadswords", were made with hominy (in the case of the Cherokee, the masa was made from corn boiled in water treated with wood ashes instead of lime) and beans, and wrapped in green corn leaves or large tree leaves and boiled, similar to the meatless pre-Columbian bean and masa tamales still prepared in Chiapas, central Mexico, and Guatemala.

In the Mississippi Delta, African Americans developed a spicy tamale made from cornmeal (rather than masa), which is boiled in corn husks. In northern Louisiana, tamales have been made for several centuries. The Spanish established presidio Los Adaes in 1721 in modern-day Robeline, Louisiana. The descendants of these Spanish settlers from central Mexico were the first tamale makers to arrive in the eastern US. Zwolle, Louisiana, has a Tamale Fiesta every year in October.

In Chicago, unique tamales made from machine-extruded cornmeal wrapped in paper are sold at Chicago-style hot dog stands.

Around the beginning of the 20th century, the name "tamale pie" was given to meat pies and casseroles made with a cornmeal crust and typical tamale fillings arranged in layers. Although characterized as Mexican food, these forms are not popular in Mexican American culture in which the individually wrapped style is preferred.

The Indio International Tamale Festival held every December in Indio, California has earned two Guinness World Records: the largest tamale festival (120,000 in attendance, Dec. 2-3, 2000) and the world's largest tamale, [over 1 foot (0.3 m) in diameter and 40 feet (12.2 m) in length], created by Chef John Sedlar. The 2006 Guinness book calls the festival "the world's largest cooking and culinary festival."

Source http://en.wikipedia.org/wiki/Tamale

Tang bao

Origin
Place of origin China
Region or state Jingjiang
Details
Type Baozi
Variations Crab-roe tang bao
Tang bao
Traditional Chinese 湯包
Simplified Chinese 汤包
Literal meaning soup bun

Tang bao is a large, soup-filled baozi from Jingjiang, China. Two forms exist. The first looks similar to normal baozi and the second is steamed in a bamboo steamer. The former is more traditional and is eaten by biting it open to empty its liquid by spoon. The other is more modern and the liquid is first directly drunk with a straw, and the flour skin eaten afterwards. Another form called **Crab-roe tang bao** (蟹黃湯包) exists in Jiangsu.

Source http://en.wikipedia.org/wiki/Tang_bao

Taquito

Beef taquitos with salsa and guacamole
Origin
Alternative name(s) Flauta
Place of origin Mexico; California
Details
Main ingredient(s) Tortillas, beef or chicken

A **taquito** (Spanish pronunciation: [taˈkito], from the Spanish diminutive of taco) or **flauta** (pronounced: [ˈflauta]) is a Mexican food dish consisting of a small rolled-up tortilla and some type of filling, usually beef or chicken. The filled tortilla is crisp-fried. Corn (maize) tortillas are generally used to make taquitos, though flour is sometimes used.

Taquitos as they now exist are claimed to have been invented in at least two places in California, based on family recipes originating in Mexico: in Los

Angeles' Olvera Street, at Cielito Lindo, founded by Aurora Guerrero in 1934 and still serving customers and in San Diego, in 1940, by Ralph Pesqueria, Sr., when customers at his tortilla factory began asking for prepared food items. The tortilla factory became El Indio Restaurant, where taquitos and other Mexican food are still served. There are many varieties of taquitos in different regions. Taquitos most often contain beef, chicken, and sometimes include cheese, pork, potato, or vegetables. They are generally thin and tend to be about 6 inches (15 cm) long. Potatoes are usually involved in the breakfast form of taquitos, which are thick and come with eggs. Taquitos are usually served with a type of salsa and/or guacamole.

In the United States, taquitos are very popular as a frozen food. They are also sold by 7-Eleven and QuikTrip convenience stores in a variety of flavors, as well as established restaurants such as Chico's Tacos. Taco Bell began to sell steak and chicken taquitos in 2006. Taco Bell's versions are wrapped in a flour tortilla and grilled, rather than fried.

Crispy fried taquitos sold in Mexico are often called *tacos dorados* ("golden tacos") or *flautas* ("flutes"). Typical toppings and sides include cabbage, *crema* (Mexican sour cream), guacamole, green chili or red chili salsa and crumbled Mexican cheese such as *queso fresco*.

Source http://en.wikipedia.org/wiki/Taquito

Tokneneng

Fishballs and kwek kwek

Tokneneng, a famous Tempura-like Filipino street food, made by deep-frying orange batter covered hard-boiled eggs.

A popular variation of Tokneneng is **kwek kwek**. The main difference between the two lies in the egg that is used. Tokneneng is traditionally made with chicken or duck eggs, while kwek kwek is made with quail eggs or "itlog ng pugo". Due to their similarities, the two are often confused with some people calling tokneneng "kwek kwek" and vice versa.

Tokneneng is usually served with a spiced vinegar-based dip.

Source http://en.wikipedia.org/wiki/Tokneneng

Turon (food)

One whole *Turrón*.

Turón (Spanish: *turrón de banana*), also known as *lumpiyang saging* (Tagalog, banana lumpia), is a Filipino snack made of thinly sliced bananas (preferably *saba* or Cardaba bananas) and a slice of jackfruit, dusted with brown sugar, rolled in a spring roll wrapper and fried. Other fillings can also be used, including sweet potato, mango, cheddar cheese and coconut.

Turón is a popular street food amongst Filipinos. These are usually sold along streets with banana cue, camote cue, and *maruya*.

In Malabon, the term "turrón" instead refers to a fried, lumpia-wrapper-enveloped dessert filled with sweet mung bean, while *valencia* is used for the banana-filled variety.

Source http://en.wikipedia.org/wiki/Turon_(food)

Vada (food)

Origin	
Place of origin	South India
Region or state	Andhra Pradesh, Kerala, Tamil Nadu, Odisha and Sri Lanka
Details	
Main ingredient(s)	Lentils, potatoes, onions

Masala vadai

Thayir vadai with chili powder, chaat masala, and coriander leaves

Vadai (Kannada: ವಡೆ, Tamil: வடை, Telugu: వడ, Tulu: ವಡೆ, Malayalam: വട, Sinhala: වඩේ"), also known as **wada** or **vade** or **Bara** (pronounced "vah-daa", "vah-dey", or "vah-die"), is a savoury fritter-type snack from South India.

A plateful of Uzhundhu vadai

Description

Vadai can vary in shape and size, but are usually either doughnut- or disc-shaped and are about between 5 and 8 cm across. They are made from dal, lentil, gram flour or potato.

Vadai is a traditional South Indian food known from antiquity. Although they are commonly prepared at home, vadas are as well a typical street food in the Indian Subcontinent and Sri Lanka. They are usually a high calorie morning food, typically about 300 Kcal each, but in street stalls and in railway stations, as well as inside the Indian Railways, they are available as a snack all day.

History

Vadai, pronounced 'Wah-dei', is a traditional food preparation from southern India. They are typically deep-fried in oil and served with savoury accompaniments. It originated in Tamilnadu and since has spread in popularity throughout India and Sri Lanka.

There are two types of *vadai* - *Paruppu vadai* made from *chana dal* (split de-husked black chickpeas), and *Ulundu vadai* made from *urad dal* (de-husked black lentils.) Sliced green chillies, curry leaves and onion are also mixed into the batter, and *ulundu vadai* batter contains rice in addition to these. While *paruppu vadai* is circular and slightly flat, *ulundu vadai* is wheel-shaped with a hole in the middle. Ulundu vadai is bland and usually enjoyed with chutney or sambar.

Sorry, your browser either has JavaScript disabled or does not have any supported player.
You can download the clip or download a player to play the clip in your browser.
Preparation of Vada

Preparation

The general way of preparing vadai is to make a paste or dough with gram flour or mashed or diced potatoes and/or dal lentils. This mixture is subsequently seasoned by mixing with black mustard seeds, onion, curry leaves, which are sometimes previously sauteed, and salt, chilies and/or black pepper grains. Often ginger and baking soda are added to the seasoning. The individual vadas are then shaped and deep-fried. Certain types of vadai are covered in a gram flour batter before frying.

Although battered and deep-fried, the finished product should not be too oily if prepared correctly, since steam build-up within the vadai pushes all oil away from within the vadai.

Serving

Vadai is typically and traditionally served along with a main course such as Dosa, Idli, or Pongal. Nowadays it is also ordered as an À la carte item but is never the main course and is had as a light snack or on the side of another dish and usually not separately as a meal. Vadas are preferably eaten freshly fried, while still hot and crunchy and is served with a variety of dips ranging from Sambar to chutney to curd.

Varieties

The main vadai types are:
Uddina vade (Kannada ಉದ್ದಿನ ವಡೆ), Ullundhu vadai (Tamil: உளுந்து வடை; Malayalam: ഉഴുന്നു വട *Uzhunnu vada*), Medhu vadai, made with Urad dal (black gram) flour. This vadai is shaped like a doughnut, with a hole in the middle (i.e. an approximate torus). It is the most common vada type throughout North and South India.

'Masala Vade' (Kannada) 'Masala Vada' (Telugu) 'Paruppu vadai' (Tamil: பருப்பு வடை; Malayalam: പരിപ്പ് വട). A dal vadai whose main ingredient is toor dal. It is made with the whole lentils and is shaped roughly like a flying saucer. This type of vadai is also called *aamai vadai* (Tamil ஆமை வடை, or "turtle" vadai) in Tamil Nadu.

Other types of vadai are:

Maddur vade (Kannada: ಮದ್ದೂರು ವಡೆ) is a type of onion vadai unique to the state of Karnataka. This is typically larger than other vadai types, flat, crispy (to the point of breaking when flexed) and having no hole in the middle.

Ambode, made from 'split chickpeas without the seed coat' i.e. 'kadale bele' in Kannada.

Mosaru Vade(Kannada:ಮೊಸರು ವಡೆ), Thayir Vadai (Tamil: தயிர் வடை), Hindi Dahi Vada, made by cooking a vadai normally, and then serving the vadai in a mix of yoghurt and spices).

EruLLi bajji (Kannada:'ಈರುಳ್ಳಿ ಬಜ್ಜಿ') (Vengaaya vadai (Tamil:'வெங்காய வடை')(Malayalam:'Uli vada'), made with onion. It is roughly round-shaped, and may or may not have a hole in the middle.

Masala vadai, a softer less crisp vadai.
Rava vadai, vadai made of semolina.

Vada Pav can be found in Mumbai.

Bonda, or Batata vadai, made with potatoes, garlic and spices coated with lentil paste and fried; this form is used in vada pav. In some regions, a Bonda is considered a distinct snack food, and is not held to be a type of vadai.

Sabudana vada is another variety of vadai popular in Maharashtra, made from Pearl Sago.

Thavala vadai, a vadai made with different types of lentils.

Keerai Vadai (Spinach Vadai) is made with spinach-type leaf vegetables along with lentils.

Vada pav, A vadai served in a bun (known as a *pav*) with chutney is known as a vada pav, a common street food in Maharashtra, especially in Bombay.

Keema Vadai, A vadai made from minced meat, typically smaller and more crisp than other vadai types with no hole in the middle.

Bhajani Cha Vada: Vadai made from a flour made from Bajri, Jawar, Wheat, Rice, Channa Dal, Cumin, Coriander Seeds Etc. A speciality of Maharashtra, very nutritious too:

ulunthu vadai

Gallery

Palak Vadai
Uddina Vadai

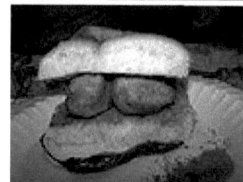

Vada Pav
Bataka Vada.jpg
Batata Vadai

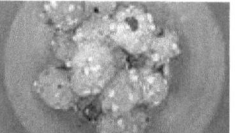

Masala Vadai

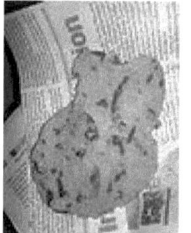

Maddur Vadai

Dahi Vadai

Idli Sambar Vadai
Source http://en.wikipedia.org/wiki/Vada_(food)

Vada pav

Origin	
Place of origin	India
Region or state	Maharashtra
Details	
Type	Snack
Main ingredient(s)	Deep-fried mashed potato patties, chili peppers, ginger

Vada pav (Marathi: वड़ा पाव), sometimes spelled **wada pav** or **Vada Paav**, is a popular vegetarian fast food dish native to the Indian state of Maharashtra. It consists of a *batata vada* sandwiched between 2 slices of a *pav*. The compound word *batata vada* refers in Marathi to a *vada* (fritter) made out of *batata*, the latter referring to a potato. *Pav* refers to unsweetened bread or bun.

Preparation

Vada Pavs

Finely cut green chilies and ginger and a *phodani* (tempering) of mustard seeds, turmeric and salt are added to a mash of boiled potatoes, and after dipping patties of the mash in an herb-seasoned batter of gram flour, the patties are deep-fried.

Vada pav is typically served with a chutney (sauce) which is commonly made out of shredded coconut "meat", tamarind pulp, and garlic.

Variations of the above basic dish include "cheese vada pav" (where slices of cheese are added); there is "schezwan vada pav" (where the pav is layered with schezwan sauce); "samosa pav" (where a samosa is used instead of a vada); and "Jain vada pav" (where vada ingredients do not include onions, garlic and potatoes). Vada pav served in the nearby state of Gujarat is usually fried in butter or edible oil. The pav is first fried in a mixture of butter or oil and dried red chili powder. After that the chutney is applied in the hot fried pav and the vada is placed in between. This is the only difference between vada pav in Gujarat and Maharashtra. In the state of Gujarat, the original un-fried vada pav recipe is referred to as "Bombay vada pav".

This dish was initially started as the most cheapest form of a meal for low income group, but due to its taste, this dish became so popular that many sophisticated hotels also have started dishing out this dish at extra cost. However, this dish is still regarded as a humble dish, and many people have it at breakfast, lunch or even dinner as well.

Private food chains

Frying Vada pav

Private food chains have started selling vada pavs. Jumbo King Foods Pvt. Ltd. is known to be India's largest selling vada pav. Ashok Wada Pav near Kirti College, Dadar is a very famous vendor in Mumbai. The vada pav that this stall serves is piping hot with green chutney & tamarind jaggery chutney. Goli Vada Pav, a chain of 'quick service restaurants', is famous for its vada pav especially the ones with varied stuffings. At one of the numerous Jumbo King outlets across the city, you can eat vada pav in a range of flavors for just 7 rupees (about 14 cents at 50 rupees to the dollar). Jumbo King aims to be the McDonald's of street snacks, and the uniformly wrapped vada pavs are served by plastic-gloved dispensers from gleaming steel fryers, with optional spicy chutney and garlic toppings.

Gajanan Vada Pao centre and Durga in Thane is well known. Joshi Vadevale is one of the popular vada pav chains in Pune, but most famous among the locales is a particular street joint named JJ Garden Vada Pav. Shiv-Vada is also a popular vada pav chain.In the city of wine Nashik, vada pav is very popular in all people basically in the Old Cidco area Jayant Samosa & Wadapav center. In the city of Kalyan, The Ambar Vadapav situated in Karnik Road is famous. Many street corner cart vendors are spread across all small & big cities and towns. Many have developed their own customer following.

Indian Street Food

Batata vada is synonymous with the south Indian Potato Bonda.Vada Pav / Wada Pav is the Indianized burger. Crispy vada sandwiched between soft buns with spicy garlic/ mint/ coriander chutney. It's a hugely popular street food in India and has its origins in the state of Maharashtra.

Source http://en.wikipedia.org/wiki/Vada_pav

Vastedda

Vastedda is the traditional Sicilian bread used to prepare the Pani ca meusa, a sandwich made of cow spleen. It often also includes toppings of caciocavallo and ricotta cheese. It is most common in the city of Palermo.

In Gratteri, nearby Palermo, is diffused a fried version of it called Vastedda fritta. The vastedda fritta is recognized by Italian Ministry of Agricultural, Food and Forestry as a traditional product and is listed into the official list of traditional Italian agricultural and food product.

Sicilian cheese

The term *Vastedda* or *Vastella* in Sicilian indicates also different traditional kinds of cheese like Vastedda della Valle del Belice and Vastedda palermitana both recognized by Italian Ministry of Agricultural, Food and Forestry as a traditional product and listed into the official list of traditional Italian agricultural and food product.

Source http://en.wikipedia.org/wiki/Vastedda

Vietnamese noodles

A bowl of *phở*

Vietnamese cuisine includes many types of noodles. These include:

Noodles by ingredients

Vietnamese noodles are available in either fresh (*tươi*) or dried (*khô*) form. Vietnamese noodles are a popular choice. There are many variations, which include soups and dishes. Spicy beef and noodles is a very popular combination for weddings.

Bánh canh - thick noodles made from a mixture of rice flour and tapioca flour or wheat flour; similar in appearance, but not in substance, to udon
Bánh hủ tiếu
Bánh phở - flat rice noodles; these are available in a wide variety of widths and may be used for either *phở* soup or stir-fried dishes
Bún - thin rice vermicelli noodles
Bún sợi to
  lá- used in Bún lá cá dầm Ninh Hoà

  odles (called *miến*, *bún*
  hin glass noodle made from *dzong* (canna) starch
Mì - wheat flour noodles, which may be either white or yellow
Lá mì
Bánh đa đỏ- red noodles used in Bánh đa cua Hải Phòng - red noodles with crab, a specialty of Hải Phòng
Bánh đa - rice cracker
Banh pho gao lut - brown rice noodles that are like pho noodles but made from wholegrain rice and can be used in a variety of noodle dishes

Noodle dishes

Hot noodle soups

Bánh canh - a soup made with *bánh canh* noodles
Bánh canh cá Nha Trang
Bún bò Huế - signature noodle soup from Huế, consisting of rice vermicelli in a beef broth with beef, lemon grass, and other ingredients
Bún bung - soup made with tomato, Alocasia odora, green papaya, tamarind, green onions and pork.
Bún mắm - vermicelli noodle soup with a heavy shrimp paste broth
Bún ốc - tomato and snail based noodle soup topped with scallions
Bún riêu - rice vermicelli soup with meat, tofu, tomatoes, and congealed boiled pig blood.
Bún riêu cua - with crab
Bún riêu cá - with fish
Bún riêu ốc - with snails
Bún lá cá dầm Ninh Hoà
Bún sứa - noodles with jellyfish
Bún thang - soup made with shredded chicken meat, shredded fried egg, shredded steam pork cake, and various vegetables
Cao lầu - signature noodle dish from Hội An consisting of yellow wheat flour noodles in a small amount of broth, with various meats and herbs.
Hủ tiếu - a soup made with *bánh hủ tiếu* and egg noodles. This dish was brought over by the Teochew immigrants (Hoa people).
Mì Quảng - signature noodle dish from Quảng Nam, yellow wheat flour noodles in a small amount of broth, with various meats and herbs.
Phở - *bánh phở* in a broth made from beef and spices

Dry noodle dishes

Bánh hỏi - extremely thin rice vermicelli woven into intricate bundles and often topped with chopped scallions and meat
Bún đậu mắm tôm - Pressed vermicelli noodles with fried tofu served with shrimp paste
Bún thịt nướng - a cold noodle dish consisting of *bún* with grilled pork
Bún xào - stir-fried *bún*
Hủ tiếu khô - stir-fried *bánh hủ tiếu* with sauce
Hủ tiếu xào - stir-fried *bánh hủ tiếu*
Mì khô (also spelled *mỳ khô*) - stir-fried egg noodles with sauce
Phở xào - stir-fried *bánh phở*

Hot noodle rolls

Bánh cuốn - steamed rice noodle roll, stuffed with minced pork and wood ear mushroom, somewhat similar to a Cantonese dim sum called rice noodle roll, but the rice sheet in *bánh cuốn* is much thinner and more delicate than the rice noodle used for the dim sum.

Cold rice paper rolls

Gỏi cuốn - translated as either "summer roll" or "salad roll"; a cold dish consisting of various ingredients (including *bún*) rolled in moist rice paper

Hot noodle sheets

Bánh ướt - rice noodle sheets, eaten with *nước chấm*, fried shallots and a side of *chả lụa* (Vietnamese pork sausage).
Source http://en.wikipedia.org/wiki/Vietnamese_noodles

Würstelstand

Würstelstand

A **Würstelstand** (literally "little sausage stand") is a traditional Austrian street food retail outlet selling hot dogs, sausages, and side dishes. They are a "ubiquitous sight" in Vienna.

Würstelstands were initially created during the period of the Austro-Hungarian Empire to provide a source of income for incapacitated former soldiers.

Not until the 1960s were the Würstelstands allowed to become stationary. Many of them can be found near transit hubs and around subway stations.

Source http://en.wikipedia.org/wiki/Würstelstand

Yakitori

Yakitori being grilled

Several yakitories in food court areas

Yakitori (焼き鳥, やきとり, ヤキトリ), *grilled chicken*, is commonly a Japanese type of skewered chicken. The term "yakitori" can also refer to skewered food in general. **Kushiyaki** (*skewer grilled*), is a formal term that encompasses both poultry and non-poultry items, skewered and grilled. Both *yakitori* and *kushiyaki* mean the same, so the terms are used interchangeably in Japanese society.

Preparation

The average yakitori is made from several bite-sized pieces of chicken meat, or chicken offal, skewered on a bamboo skewer and grilled, usually over Binchōtan charcoal.

Diners ordering yakitori usually have a choice of having it cooked with salt (shio) or with tare sauce, which is generally made up of mirin, sake, soy sauce and sugar. The sauce is applied to the skewered meat and is grilled until delicately cooked.

momo (もも), chicken thigh
tsukune (つくね), chicken meatballs
(tori)kawa ((とり)かわ) chicken skin, grilled until crispy
tebasaki (手羽先), chicken wing
bonjiri (ぼんじり), chicken tail
shiro (シロ), chicken small intestines
nankotsu (なんこつ), chicken cartilage
hāto / *hatsu* (ハート / ハツ) or kokoro (こころ), chicken heart
rebā (レバー), liver
sunagimo (砂肝), or zuri (ずり) chicken gizzard
toriniku, all white meat on skewer

Common non-poultry dishes

ikada (筏) (lit. raft), Japanese scallion, with two skewers to prevent rotation
gyūtan (牛タン), beef tongue, sliced thinly
atsuage tōfu (厚揚げとうふ), thicker variety of deep-fried tofu
enoki maki (エノキ巻き), enoki mushrooms wrapped in slices of pork
pīman (ピーマン), green bellpepper
asuparabēkon (アスパラベーコン) asparagus wrapped in bacon

butabara (豚ばら), pork belly
ninniku (にんにく) garlic
shishito (獅子唐) Japanese pepper
Examples of yakitori items

Left to right: *Kawa* (chicken skin); *yamaimo*; *shishitō*

Chicken liver

Left to right: Asparagus wrapped in thinly sliced pork; chicken wings

Ginkgo nuts

Left to right: *Tsukune*; *negi* (scallion) and *butabara* (pork belly)

Negima (chicken thigh and scallion)
Source http://en.wikipedia.org/wiki/Yakitori

Yatai (retail)

For a listed company in the Shanghai Stock Exchange, please refer to Yatai Group.

Yatai in the summer festival

A ***yatai*** (屋台) is a small, mobile food stall in Japan typically selling ramen or other food. The name literally means "shop stand."

The stall is set up in the early evening on pedestrian walkways and removed late at night or in the early morning hours before commuters begin to fill the ~ets. Menus are usually limited; ~se cuisine is most common, but ~nd Western cuisine *yatai* are not unknown. Beer, sake and *shōchū* are usually available. A salaryman might relax with colleagues over dinner and drinks at a *yatai* on his way home from work.

Fukuoka is well-known within Japan for having many *yatai*.

A reference to *yatai* in the modern sense is found as early as 1710. The word appears in an Edo-period *sharebon*, a genre of literature revolving around the pleasure quarters. *Yatai* became popular and widespread in the Meiji period (1868 – 1912) and were a two-wheeled pushcart constructed of wood.

Yatai are also set up temporarily for *Matsuri* (Japanese festivals), selling foods for spectators, such as *yakisoba*, *kakigōri*, *takoyaki*, and *okonomiyaki*.
Tempura yatai of Edo period *(Fukagawa Edo Museum)*
Soba yatai of Edo period *(Fukagawa Edo Museum)*
Large *Yatai* in the summer festival *(Himeji Yukata Matsuri)*
Source http://en.wikipedia.org/wiki/

Yatai_(retail)